"It is a high compliment to say that these eight stories from psychoanalytic practice read like fiction. . . . Mystery buffs will appreciate the fine detective work."   —*Boston Globe*

"Swift and insightful . . . a behind-the-scenes look at how psychotherapy works—or doesn't work. . . . Weinberg gives his tales a philosophical as well as a psychological tautness. . . . [He] presents each case as a mystery to be savored, with enough suspense to make an intriguing television series."
                                                                    —*Seattle Times*

"Perceptive, well-written, understanding, fascinating."
                                                                    —*Booklist*

"ATTENTIVE, COMPASSIONATE . . . THESE PEOPLE, AND THEIR PRIVATE MYSTERIES, COME TO MATTER."   —*Publishers Weekly*

"Weinberg's engaged heart and his exemplary display of ethics are a credit to his too-often-maligned profession."
                                                                    —*Tulsa World*

GEORGE WEINBERG, a nationally prominent psychotherapist, is the author of ten previous books, including the bestselling *Self Creation, The Pliant Animal, The Heart of Psychotherapy,* and a previous collection of tales inspired by his practice, *The Taboo Scarf.* He lives and practices in New York City.

nearer to the heart's desire

tales of psychotherapy

GEORGE WEINBERG

A PLUME BOOK

PLUME
Published by the Penguin Group
Penguin Books USA Inc., 375 Hudson Street,
New York, New York 10014, U.S.A.
Penguin Books Ltd, 27 Wrights Lane,
London W8 5TZ, England
Penguin Books Australia Ltd, Ringwood,
Victoria, Australia
Penguin Books Canada Ltd, 10 Alcorn Avenue,
Toronto, Ontario, Canada M4V 3B2
Penguin Books (N.Z.) Ltd, 182–190 Wairau Road,
Auckland 10, New Zealand

Penguin Books Ltd, Registered Offices:
Harmondsworth, Middlesex, England

Published by Plume, an imprint Dutton Signet, a division of Penguin Books USA Inc. This is an
authorized reprint of a hardcover edition published by Grove Press.

First Plume Printing, November, 1993
10 9 8 7 6 5 4 3 2 1

REGISTERED TRADEMARK—MARCA REGISTRADA

Library of Congress Cataloging-in-Publication Data
Weinberg, George H.
     Nearer to the heart's desire : tales of psychotherapy / George
Weinberg.
        p.   cm.
     ISBN 0-452-27090-1
     1. Psychotherapy—Fiction.   I. Title.
PS3573.E3916N43   1993
813'.54—dc20   93-764
                                                                               CIP

Printed in the United States of America

contents

preface

. . .

THE STORIES IN THIS BOOK HAVE,
of course, been altered to protect
the anonymity of my patients. All
names, physical descriptions,
places, times of occurrence, and
identifiable events have been
changed. Obviously my patients
have the right to absolute confidentiality.

Although these stories would be
unrecognizable even to the patients they describe, they still convey the essence of the person's
psychological journey. Identifia-

ble facts are not necessary for this. At the core of an identity is how a person strives, what he or she strives for, and how the person may defeat himself or herself along the way. It is remarkable that no matter how much I have altered externals, these essential ingredients remain.

And besides the deliberate changes that I found it necessary to make, these stories have been changed involuntarily. This is because they have, over time, become part of my own psychic life —in a sense my own mythology. As a result, they bear the mark of my own impressions, added deliberately and often unwittingly. The Spanish poet Garcia Lorca used the term "blood memory" to describe events that have been absorbed and not thought about for a time, and then resurrected. These stories certainly belong in this category.

One more observation will perhaps enrich these stories: it is that what patients do in the therapy hour on a small scale, they also do in their lives on a large scale. It is this fact that gives us license to draw inferences about people from minute events that we see in front of us.

For example, the patient who thinks to ask how we are feeling after we had to cancel because of illness is quite a different person from the one who is simply annoyed because we weren't there. We may expect such a difference to manifest itself elsewhere and to have great repercussions in the person's life. Or, for example, the patient who angrily dismisses us the instant we ask a sensitive question, we should not be surprised to learn, may be the one who walks out on relationships as soon as they become demanding. What takes place in a therapeutic moment, we might say, has the same shape as larger elements of the person's life. Whatever psychological system we hold must account for this.

A recent branch of mathematics called fractal theory studies objects that are the same in miniature as they are on a grand scale. The leaf of a tree, for instance, may look like the whole tree. A tiny fragment of coastline may look like a thousand-mile stretch, so that as one descends in a plane the coastline does not seem different. And it is said that a molecule resembles the universe.

Whatever the future of fractal theory in mathematics, it certainly applies to the psyche, and I have done my best to retain the minute events, the texture of my patients, which in every case afforded important insights into the larger events of their lives.

The title of this book, *Nearer to the Heart's Desire*, was chosen to indicate the variety of dreams that people possess—healthy people as well as those in need. My purpose in practice has been to help people identify their dreams and turn them into realities.

To the best of my ability I have been true to the outcomes of these cases, not all of which were successful. Defeats stay with us therapists, they resonate in our souls whether or not we decide in retrospect that we could have done better. This book is, therefore, more a cross section of cases that held fascination for me than a collection of those in which my results were always the best.

I would like to thank Dianne Rowe for her careful reading of this manuscript at every stage and her multitudinous contributions. Also Margaret Scal, who helped me with the research, my editor at Grove Press, Jim Moser; and his assistant, Susan Tillack.

In addition, thanks are due to those who volunteered ideas along the way: Olivia Katz, M.A.; Bill McBride, who also provided research materials; and a handful of psychotherapists: Drs. David Balderston, Jean Balderston, Henry Katz, Helen McDermott, Cindy Mermin, Louis Ormont, Joan Ormont, and Dr. Hank Schenker.

—George Weinberg
New York City, 1992

Ah, Love! could you and I with Him conspire
To grasp this Sorry Scheme of things entire,
Would not we shatter it to bits—and then
Re-mould it nearer to the heart's desire.

—RUBÁIYÁT OF OMAR KHAYYÁM

the

big

gamble

. . . .

THE DOPPELGÄNGER PERSONALITY
Test consists of asking ourselves a
single question about a person.
Suppose this man or woman met
his double, someone roughly the
same sex and age, with equivalent
accomplishments, and, above all,
with the same character traits.
How would they get along?
Would the two of them click? Or
would they become instantly hos-
tile toward each other, each of
them despising his likeness for

his aggression or jealousy or pretentiousness or false humility?

It's a good sign if they'd be compatible. It means that the person likes himself. But there are many personalities that could never stand the test, and a person's failure to pass always reveals a fault in his or her humanity.

When I applied my Doppelgänger Personality Test to Peter, I was startled. He appeared gentle, calm, conscientious, and under control, but inwardly he was none of these things. In fact, his double standard was so absolute, he was so without real empathy, that if he and his double were locked up in a room, after two hours only one of them would come out alive.

Peter was a graduate student at Columbia University with me, in the program leading toward the Ph.D. in clinical psychology. He was rotund, about five ten, had a black beard and mustache, and dressed more formally than the rest of us. He always did his assignments correctly and on time, and he got near-perfect grades. He was the sort of person who went to Peter, Paul and Mary concerts mainly for the words.

Peter doled out his enthusiasm to the rest of us, as if he had a special book that told him how much each of us was worth. He especially liked good students who were married and quiet. I got top grades but was unmarried and too noisy for his taste. He once criticized me for making a bet on a football game, and I could tell he considered me a fringe character.

He seemed always to be criticizing people in a mood that was more officious than simply declarative. We all feared his lectures and his wry smile. Many of us disliked Peter, but I think I was especially allergic to him. I've always been allergic to sanctimonious people, and regarded them as cannibals at heart.

After Peter became engaged, he would bring his shy bride-to-be to join us in the Horace Mann cafeteria, where he would ostentatiously hold her hand. She seldom spoke. It seemed as if she were waiting for the perfect thing to say. By their presence, the couple seemed to be announcing, "Romance is easy. What's the matter with you?" A few of his professors were invited to his wedding, but, mercifully, we students were not.

Peter's specialty was research, because, as he put it, so far the elements of psychotherapy were "too nebulous." He planned to teach in a university and edit a professional journal to be sure that no unproven datum could waft unseen into the field of psychology and remain there as an impurity.

Peter's phone call to me about four years after graduation inaugurated a series of surprises. After exchanging pleasantries, he criticized an article I'd written. Then he asked me if I could see a patient, whom he would pay for. "My brother. As usual, he's making a mess of his life."

"This is his idea—to see someone?" I asked.

He sounded impatient. "My brother is willing. I told him that's the only way I'd help him. He owes eleven thousand dollars to moneylenders—seventeen thousand with interest. When I called him, he was afraid to go out of his room alone. They'd threatened to kill him."

"How did he get in that deep?" I asked.

"Gambling. He's a compulsive gambler. He almost can't stop. But he's *got* to stop."

"You two are close?" I asked.

"No. As a matter of fact, I hadn't talked to him in almost a year. But I knew he was in trouble."

"Really, how?" I asked, I thought quite reasonably.

"How? He's always in trouble. What's the difference? I just had a sense. I just thought he needed help, that's all. I just guessed. Is that all right?" He sounded flustered and annoyed.

But he quickly caught himself and went on. "So I called him, and he told me he hadn't gone out in two weeks. That very morning some bookies put the note under his door, threatening his life if he didn't pay at least part."

"What's his name?"

"Constantine."

"He's older or younger?"

"Six minutes younger. We're twins. Identical twins. All right?"

"Sure. Have him call me."

He said he would.

I was astonished that Peter had a twin at all, and an identical twin at that. He had a counterpart, with the same brain waves, the same ophthalmological signs, the same nearly everything.

Almost as surprising was the fact that he'd never mentioned his brother. As students, we would all talk about our private lives from time to time, especially when we had personally experienced something related to a topic being discussed in class. I recalled a heated conversation about twins after a student's presentation of research done on the subject. Peter hadn't contributed a word, as we went back and forth.

In that seminar we had been aghast at the similarities uncovered between identical twins, who in many cases had been separated early in life and hadn't even known of each other's existence. In some instances, such twins not only had identical jobs and hobbies and nicknames, they also dressed identically, had married similar partners, and sometimes had even given their children the same names. Did those similarities argue against the power of free will, and reduce the domain of psychology itself? By the end of the class the room boiled with opinions and disagreements, and still Peter hadn't spoken. That was how ashamed of his brother he must have been.

It seemed almost eerie that he'd called Constantine after a year's absence, as if knowing his brother was in desperate straits and needed him. I remembered Dumas's novel *The Corsican Brothers*, about siblings who felt each other's pain. It wasn't so farfetched, apparently. So-called twin telepathy has been observed repeatedly by researchers, though no one understands it. Truly, there are more things in heaven and earth than are dreamt of in our psychology.

I remembered Peter standing up in class and denouncing researchers for what he called "unwarranted assumptions." Peter was like a wasp stinging any of us who imagined we'd found something. "Maybe it was coincidence." "How can you know unless you cross-validate?" He seemed to savor being unconvinced. Could it be that he was more bombarded by the inexplicable than all the rest of us put together? Possibly his hatred of anything mystical, of anything unusual, related to his own experiencing those "messages" that had come to him seemingly by magic.

Of course, I was astonished that Peter had selected me, in view of the contempt I'd imagined he'd harbored toward me. But I also felt excited. I was eager to meet his brother, to see what similarities there were, and maybe even to understand why Peter had refused to acknowledge his existence.

It has been said that with an identical twin, a person is never fully alienated as we other mortals sometimes are. But suppose your twin regards your life as a failure, avoids you for a year at a time. Should it not follow that your sense of alienation is greater than other people's?

Two weeks went by, and then his brother called.

I guess I virtually expected Peter himself to be coming in, because the instant Constantine appeared, I was startled at how different from his brother he looked. Constantine was much thinner, which made him seem taller and better-looking. He was clean-shaven and had dark, darting eyes. Under his leather windbreaker, which he threw on an adjacent chair, he wore faded blue denims and a sweater.

He had the same wavy black hair as his brother, a similar though not identical nose, and the same cleft in the chin. It crossed my mind that they were really about the same height. But the contrast between roundness and bony angularity was great, and then I realized that Peter always wore thick glasses and Constantine had none.

And, I was soon to see, the contrast was psychological, too. Peter embodied soulless sobriety, Constantine seemed never to speak without a dash of humor, a sparkle—he seemed never to come at you straight.

I asked him why his brother had suggested therapy for him.

"I'm not sure. I imagine he feels that I have a very poor lifestyle. I live at night. You're supposed to live in the daytime and sleep at night. Unless you're one of those furry animals that gets on nature television shows, with the big eyes, that sleeps during the day and goes out at night."

"That's it?" I asked.

"And I lost a lot of money betting basketball. Never again. From now on it's only poker."

He stopped abruptly. I felt he was hoping I wouldn't push further in that direction, and obeyed, for the time being.

"Your brother says you aren't in very close contact these days," I said.

Constantine replied, "He's got two kids, and another on the way. He's an assistant professor. I didn't finish high school."

"Still, you think of each other—"

"Think of Peter! Peter's the sort of person you think of the instant you've dropped a tray or broken a glass in the kitchen. You hear him saying, 'Why did you do that?' "

The phrase "stern introject" went through my mind, but I banished it as jargon and adding nothing.

Constantine said with a twinkle, "Actually, if you like my brother, it's a hopeless case."

"What do you mean?"

"Well, it's a joke, my brother's being a psychologist. I mean you could have a pumpkin on your head, and he wouldn't notice. And I don't mean for a minute, I mean for three days."

Then he drummed on the table nervously with his right index finger, resting the heel of his hand on the surface—a gesture just like Peter's. "I might as well tell you," he went on. "My brother doesn't think I should see you."

"What do you mean?"

"Well, he said I needed therapy. But I didn't want him to pick someone like himself. So we went down a list of people he knew. You were at the bottom of his list. When we got to you, he said that you were basically immature. You had a good act but you needed as much help as I did. He said you gambled and maybe you'd be a better bet for my poker game than to help me."

"Really!" I was taken aback.

"Yeah, does it upset you?"

"A little. It's not very complimentary. But you chose me anyhow. Did you call anyone else on the list?"

"No. Just you."

"Why me?"

"I don't know. Maybe you know what my world is like, if you're a degenerate. I mean a part degenerate. Obviously you went through school. So far, at least you don't remind me of my brother."

You don't remind me of Peter either, I thought.

Comparing them, I realized that Constantine's nose had a bump in it, as if it had been broken. Otherwise it would have been exactly like Peter's. The flaw added in Constantine's case to the impression of his having a craggy countenance. Instinctively I painted Peter's dark glasses on his face, and added some pounds, and the similarity leaped onto the page of my imagination. But in their way of addressing life they seemed exact opposites. And even in my mind's eye I couldn't get him into one of Peter's double-breasted suits.

A few moments later he partially recanted about his brother. "I guess I shouldn't put him down. After all, he's a lot better educated than I am, but I guess that's not saying very much. He has respect though, and he's paying for this session. I should make the most of it."

"How can you do that?"

"You tell me."

I asked him to tell me what he wanted most in life that he wasn't getting.

"They got cops with guns inside the banks, that's why I'm not getting it."

"You mean money is what you want most?" I asked him.

"Yeah. It would be a healthy start. I think I could handle the rest. I'd make a few mistakes here and there, but I could stagger along."

"What would you buy with a lot of money?" I asked him.

"Nothing. I'd buy the right to do nothing. Yeah, that's what I'd buy with money."

Later, when he again mentioned having dropped out of high school, I asked him if he felt bad about it.

"Bad about it? I'm only sorry that I stayed a few years after I learned how to read and write. So you gamble. My brother said you play poker."

I told him I used to play a lot, and for high stakes, but that I'd stopped.

"Why did you quit?"

I explained to him that I didn't like the highs and lows of serious gambling, that though I used to love playing poker, I stopped enjoying it.

He acted as if he didn't hear me. "No guts, no glory," he twitted me. "If you're afraid to gamble, you'll never come up with anything big.

"Honestly," he asked me, "wouldn't you like to spend your evenings with big stakes involved? I mean someone could make more in an evening, if they were really lucky, than you could make in a hundred hours of sitting here."

"Constantine, I understand you to a point," I told him. "But it got so repetitious, sitting at a card table. The one thing I dread most on this earth, the one way I don't want to spend my existence, is in repetition. I learned that, believe it or not, playing poker for high stakes."

As I spoke, I had the misgiving that I was lecturing to him, and that I might have sounded like Peter. But he didn't say anything to that effect.

I thought I saw his eyes go blank for an instant, as if I'd touched something very deep inside of him, as if, almost unwittingly, I'd reminded him of some misgiving of his own, some very powerful second thoughts he'd already had. Actually I hadn't imagined that I'd said anything so telling.

He smiled cheerfully, but I didn't believe him. Then, with his left hand, he rubbed his cheek and pushed his hair back, and again, in that instant, I saw Peter standing in front of the class, making that very gesture after a presentation, when he felt rattled by a question from the floor.

Then Constantine was on his feet. "Thank you, doctor," he said sarcastically. "You've been very helpful."

With that he stormed out, and I knew he had no intention of ever seeing me again.

It seemed to me that he had never wanted therapy really, which was why he had chosen me as the one to see. Maybe he'd thought that if I were enough like him, I'd perceive nothing wrong with his life, that I wouldn't compare it with what it might have been —or could be. But instead he had felt reproached, though I hadn't intended to do that.

I had some moments of rebuking myself for saying anything that he could construe as adverse. Suppose I'd just listened—and waited. Waited for what? Waited until he believed in me before philosophizing? No, that sounded too harsh. Still, it was a shame. I liked Constantine, and wished I could have helped him.

Then I thought of Peter, and instantly expected Peter to call up to scold me. Yeah, I think of him when I break a glass—I recalled what Constantine had said. I certainly shared his perception of his brother as stern recorder of our blunders.

About a week later Peter did call, but there was no recrimination, only a request. "Please don't mention that my brother went to see you."

"Certainly not. I promise I won't."

"In fact, don't mention him at all."

"I won't."

"By the way, what would you say his diagnosis is?" Peter asked me.

I evaded the question, as I always do when a relative asks it about someone. Any answer by a professional can too easily become an indelible label. The family ever after sees the person—their child or parent or sibling—as a certifiable whatever.

So I simply mouthed the obvious. "He's doing a lot of gambling and not much else. He's got a lot of charm, though, and he's certainly bright. I wish we could do something."

"Charm!" said Peter in surprise. "I haven't seen that yet."

Even that I took as a criticism of me for seeing what wasn't there.

————

Years went by. I often thought about Constantine and Peter when I read an article about twins. I was fascinated by the similarities that investigators turned up. Time and again twins reared apart, and not even knowing of each other's existence, have made stunningly similar decisions. I pictured Peter reading those articles too, and scoffing at the coincidences.

With one pair of twins after another, even those separated for decades, such coincidences emerged, often numerous, dramatic, and notable. For instance, two girls who had lost touch with each other in early childhood were dressed identically when they met more than twenty years later. Both tinted their graying hair with the same shade of auburn; they liked the same novelists, took their coffee black and cold; they'd both fallen down stairs at fifteen, and both suffered weak ankles. Both met their future husbands (two quiet, hardworking men) at town hall dances when they were sixteen. Both married in their early twenties in big autumn weddings with all the trimmings. Both had an early miscarriage, and then each gave birth to two boys, followed by a girl.

It was obvious that identical twins, being physically similar, would have analogous careers so far as their health was concerned. If one had poor kidneys or a heart murmur, so might the other. In a sense, the sisters who fell down stairs at fifteen were programmed to do so, though even there the exact coincidence of when they fell was surprising.

Similarities in attitude seemed, at least to me, a measure less predictable; I had thought of life experiences and coincidences as very relevant in the formation of attitudes. Still, the genetic contribution to talent is well accepted, and because we tend to like what we're good at, I wasn't completely surprised to read in the twin studies that if one identical twin loved math and was good at it, the other nearly always loved it and excelled too.

However, coincidences of the kind that were uncovered seemed to defy explanation. For instance, it seemed astonishing that a pair of sisters discovered at their first meeting after decades that each had on exactly seven expensive rings and a necklace.

I pictured Peter saying, "Well, both had long, graceful fingers, and both, being very attractive, married wealthy men, who could afford those rings."

"Still, Peter . . ." There I was, playing Constantine's game of seeing Peter as the scourge of imagination. Had I gotten that notion from Constantine? No, I think I'd always pictured Peter that way.

Somewhere along the line, I read an article on "mirror image" twins, who are identical but opposite-sided. If one has a weak right ankle, the other's left ankle is weak; if one has a bad tooth on one side, the other's is on the opposite side. If one of them is right-handed, the other is left-handed. Mirror image twins are identical but reversed.

It flashed into my mind that Constantine and Peter were mirror image twins, *psychologically*. Peter was strict, corrective, literal; Constantine was lax, easygoing, and full of imagination. Peter seemed driven by a need to plan everything in his life, Constantine by a need not to.

Outwardly they were as different as if they had started competing for nourishment from that single yolk sac, which they'd shared when still infinitesimal in size. But could anything in that yolk sac possibly account for the fact that Constantine was so given to metaphor and images when he spoke, while Peter was so literal, so factual and dry, that I couldn't remember his ever using a single image? Surely, even if some differences began back then, something had happened, something profound, that pushed them apart in childhood.

According to my records, it had been five years since Constantine was in my office when he identified himself on the phone and asked to see me. He was surprised that I remembered him.

While we searched for a time we were both available, he commented mysteriously, "I would say it's urgent. But actually it can wait forever. Nothing much is happening."

We scheduled a time.

I deliberately didn't inquire over the phone what was wrong or if he'd had afterthoughts about me. Naturally I was curious. But something told me that whatever else I asked him, I should stay away from the issues of his motivation and his feelings about me. I would leave the so-called transference alone—at least until I felt I had a real grip on what was going on.

It was a frosty Friday. Late afternoon brought one of those Turner skies of mauves and grays. Snowflakes eddied everywhere, and the streets were turning white. The thermometer was dropping, and people were going home from work early.

Constantine burst in, bundled up in an old navy blue wool coat. He needed a shave and looked disheveled. When I asked him in the broadest terms what brought him to my office, he said, "I've been thinking it over for three weeks. Can I sum it up in a sentence?"

"Sure, if you can."

"All right. If I drop dead tomorrow, no one would care."

There was silence.

"That's it," he said.

Another pause, and I asked him how he'd reached that conclusion.

"Actually I was slow. Other people reached it a long time ago."

"Who?"

"My mother. Peter. The poker players. People you don't know and you're better off not knowing."

"What do we do from here?" I asked.

"You tell me, doctor. You're dealing."

I broke the next silence.

"Why do you say Peter wouldn't care?" I asked him.

"Oh, maybe he'd care because I represent him. If I die, his odds of dying go up."

"What do you mean?"

"You know, identical twins and all that. Our life spans are very close. Genes or something. Like those Siamese twins, whatever their names were, the real ones from Siam. One died, and the other knew his time was up. They say he died of fright."

"Well, you and Peter aren't joined at the hip."

"Thank God for that. I mean for his sake. He probably would have died watching what I do with my life. At least he's done something with his. They say we have identical brain waves. But there's something they forgot to measure. There must be."

Then he did a curious thing. He asked me if it was okay for him to talk about a woman he broke up with—Anne.

I told him, "Of course." I wondered what his asking for permission might mean.

"I've connected with a lot of women, but Anne is special. She's beautiful, very elegant. And she's an associate editor, if you know what that means, in a big publishing house. I think she loved me too. Maybe she still does, I don't know. Sex was the best ever.

"But it was ridiculous. She saw a lot of things in me that weren't there. She's young. She's got everything. She deserves a lot better."

I asked him what he meant by "better."

"Someone who's read more than ten books in a lifetime. She signs up authors, I mean famous people. She goes to lunch in fancy restaurants, maybe four times a week—with writers, with millionaires, with politicians, with actors. She was so educated."

I asked him, "Why do you say 'was'? Isn't she still?"

"Yeah. Right. I'm talking about her like she's dead."

"She said she didn't want to see you?" I asked.

"No. I was the one. I couldn't take it anymore."

"What do you mean?"

"I lied to her a lot. She knew I ran a poker game. She thought it was glamorous. But I said it was just until I finished my Ph.D. thesis in psychology. I was going to be a therapist.

"She thought I was someone else. She thought I'd gone to Columbia and had finished my course work. How could I tell her I needed a year and a half before I could even go to college? We were actually talking about living together. She thinks I'm charming, intelligent, kind. I know better."

So he'd borrowed Peter's life—the doctorate at Columbia, his future as a professional psychologist. My life.

"She's beautiful," he repeated. "But she's very naive. She needs protection."

"How did you break up?"

"I kept telling her that I was working on my thesis. Then one day I told her the truth. I told her the whole thing was a scam. I told her that I didn't even finish high school. Poker was the only thing I did. She said she didn't care, you know, that she loved me anyhow. She said she sort of knew, that it was fine. But I knew it wasn't."

"And how did you know that?"

"Come on. Stop kidding me. I saw the blood leave her face. What could she say? She's got style. She was raised that way."

"Well, you tell me, Constantine. What did she say?"

"Some garbage about liking the way I live at night. When I told her this was it, when I said I couldn't put her in this position, she started to cry. I felt terrible. She kept saying she loved me, and that I was so wonderful, and that I was really special. Yeah, I'm special. I'm the only guy who ever ran a card game and worried about the rent. I asked her, 'How could you, a beautiful, educated, classy, classy lady love me?' She said she couldn't explain it, that you can't explain love. I was in her fancy apartment, and I was packing up my stuff.

"On the way out she said I was like the people in those books she liked so much, those Dick Francis books. I think that's when I yelled at her. I told her, 'This is *life*, this isn't a book. I can't give you the things you want. A home, kids, a man you can be proud of.' So I left." He extended his arms, as if to say, "That was it. No more, no less."

As he described going down in the elevator, having resolved never to talk to her again, I thought for an instant that he was going to cry. But he brought his right hand down over his face, and when he removed it, he had regained his composure.

"So that's it," he said. "Do you think there's any hope for me?"

"I do."

He pressed me. "You're a gambler at heart. Once a gambler, always a gambler. What are the odds?"

"On your having a good life?" I asked. "I don't know."

"Well, what do you make the price?" He sounded defiant.

"Look, Constantine, let's not make a price until we have some more facts. It's too early even for the early line." I was just as defiant. "I don't even know the odds that I'll ever see you again."

"Oh, you'll see me, doctor. I like your mind. Maybe because it's like mine."

It was a perverse compliment, but I did feel complimented. I liked Constantine. And indeed, he did remind me of myself, though I had no idea why.

As soon as he'd gone, it was obvious why he'd actually asked permission to talk about Anne. She was sacred to him, and talking about her incurred the risk of blasphemy. Well, at least something was inviolate in his life.

He came in the next week, announcing that he'd won four thousand dollars in a card game the previous month, and he was going to spend that much on therapy.

"That's a big bet on yourself," I commented, and he smiled.

"What do we do next?" he asked.

I asked him about his early life, and as I listened, I found myself constantly on the watch for anything that could help me answer a single question. *What had caused his path and that of Peter, his six-minute-older brother, to so diverge?* I suspected even then that residing in the answer to that question were insights that would prove vital to Constantine's reopening his life.

He'd decided not to tell Peter that he was coming to see me this time. "I showed him that self-help book you wrote, and he said he thinks you're a charlatan. I'm just not in the mood to hear him put you down."

I didn't comment, but I felt relieved at being able to keep my distance from Peter. However, I also felt a twinge of embarrassment when I realized that as a by-product of my therapy with Constantine, I would also be slaking an almost prurient curiosity about what made Peter the person he turned into.

Their mother, who was born in Greece and never lost her accent, was almost forty when they were born; she'd worked as a bookkeeper. Their father, Stavros, born here, was a fur cutter but had a heavy gambling problem. Constantine could remember the two fighting about Stavros going to the track and playing cards, and their eight-year-older sister crying and begging the parents to stop. Constantine knew very early that their mother's income fed them and paid the rent in their dark but adequate three-room apartment in a brownstone overlooking a cemetery in the Bronx.

It was all endurable, except when his mother would turn to the kids and say, "Your father doesn't love you, or he wouldn't do this," while Stavros stood by perplexed. "But, of course, I knew he loved me," said Constantine.

Peter was five pounds at birth, and Constantine almost seven, and in his early years Peter was always sickly. "Mother constantly looked at him to be sure he wouldn't go under."

"How did you feel about that?" I asked Constantine.

"I don't know. It was spooky. Maybe I felt guilty. I don't know why. When I was about fifteen, I read about this guy who had a growth on his arm, like a tumor. When it was removed, the doctors told him it was his twin who got turned into a mummy in the womb and didn't grow. The guy had absorbed a dead twin into his own body. The guy won the fight, you know, in the womb, for oxygen and blood and that kind of thing."

"Really! I'd never heard that."

"Oh yeah. It's common. Identical twins fight right in the womb for comfort. For everything. I guess I won."

"When did you get that idea?"

He shrugged. "I don't know. Maybe I felt bad when I was little because I was strong. I would yell a lot and play sports. Peter would stay home a lot. But we were very close. I would tell him everything. We both used to warn daddy when mother was mad at him. He used to pick us up, one on each arm."

Before seeing Constantine again, I called an internist I knew, who confirmed both the struggle in the womb between identical twins and the occasional discovery of a stillborn, if not at birth, then years later in mummified form in the other twin's body, as Constantine had described. Could one possibly come closer to claiming "original sin" in actuality than to emerge the vanquisher of one's identical twin after a primordial battle in the womb?

Of course, Constantine couldn't possibly have recorded his victory when he was a fetus. Neither the personal values nor the recording apparatus of the mind would have matured so early.

But perhaps his parents, one or both, had an inkling of that reality while he was small, and conveyed it to him. No, even that was simplistic. At most he had felt the misgivings common to a healthy child who has a sickly sibling, and later, when he was a teenager, he used his new information about the battle in the womb to confirm a feeling of wrongness. Whatever took place before birth could be relevant only in that it left some stamp of difference in the start that the two children were given in life.

When Constantine arrived for his next session, his swagger was gone, and his dark, darting eyes suggested fear rather than shrewdness—or maybe a component of both. He spoke readily about his home life, which he remembered as if it were yesterday. Their mother would rise early, make breakfast for them, and rush off to work. Constantine always had a sense of her doing a very important job. "Like running the country."

She got home punctually at six every evening, asked if Stavros was there yet, which he seldom was, and then chatted with the kids while she prepared dinner. Still, she never tired of catering to her husband, asking solicitously if he wanted more chicken or more salad. In her presence Stavros seemed subdued, spiritless, "as if he'd lost a big bet every day." He told his wife whatever he thought she wanted to hear. But she was obviously unimpressed. "We all knew he wasn't working half the time."

"So where was he?"

"Hanging around with the bookies in a restaurant. Maybe going uptown for them, delivering money or collecting some. Small sums. They'd give him a few dollars. Then he'd go to the poolroom and play or bet on a game. He'd stay there until it was dinnertime. Pretty sad, wasn't it?"

I nodded. "It was."

Stavros was very kind to the children, to his daughter, Magdalene, then in her early teens, and to the twins, from as early as Constantine could remember. The philosopher Nietzsche once said of the Greeks of the Golden Age that they dreamed the dream of life most beautifully. Stavros could dream with the best of them. He would regale the kids with stories of the gods and goddesses, for whom all ended well since they were immortal. He would talk to the kids about his heroes, Achilles, Hercules—and especially Ulysses, a mere mortal forced to navigate the high seas in charge of his men until finally he reached his homeland and took his rightful place as king.

There was a strange, unspoken conviction flowing through the household that one day Stavros would resume his rightful place too, would rule with an iron hand over a well-deserved monarchy, that these days of meandering and bluff and loss were but the lengthy ordeals that truly great men must suffer. Constantine and Peter had no doubt during those early years that some day Stavros, Ulysses-like, would guide his crew past the Sirens, between Scylla and Charybdis, and would find their way home and live happily. They saw themselves more as mariners voyaging with him than as family waiting for him to return.

As these stories brightened the evening, mother and the responsible Magdalene could be heard washing the dinner dishes and putting them away. No matter, they too would be included, given prime positions in the kingdom that was to be. Their mother would smile at last, and discard her scowl along with her disbelief in the greatness of her heroic wanderer, Stavros, who had never truly compromised the family, no matter how it had seemed.

Magdalene, by the way, went on to become a medical doctor, married a surgeon, and was raising a family and living in Michigan. "She was always wonderful to me. She still is." She still called Constantine regularly, offered him money, which he never took, and invited him to spend time with her and her family, which he very seldom did. "I can't really leave the game that long."

"Did Peter love your father the way you did?" I asked him a few weeks later.

"Oh yeah." But as he said this, his whole face seemed weighted down, and his eyes went blank, as they had that first day in my office. I made a mental note to return to that question, as he told me more about his early life.

"On Sundays dad would take us both to meet his friends. They were gamblers and bookies, and they'd watch football games at a guy named Harry's house. They used to ask how he could tell us apart. The place was sloppy as hell, beds unmade, stuff all over the floor. We weren't supposed to tell mom we were at Harry's. Just out in the park. So we never told."

Apparently Peter had by then brought his weight up to normal as a result of a special diet. "We resembled each other very closely by the time we were seven. And we had a lot of special signals too.

"I don't remember all of them, but I mean if one of us wanted to leave some place, he would touch an eyebrow, that sort of thing. Like coaches in sports, only we didn't have to talk over our signals.

"Then for our birthday daddy bought us two telegraph sets so we could send the Morse code to each other. He said, 'I know I'm supposed to buy you different gifts, but I learned this code in the army.' Anyhow, we set them up in different rooms and learned the code, you know, dots and dashes. We were great."

In many respects Constantine's childhood was wonderful, with Peter as a comrade. But the chasm between their parents was always there, a space bridged by what all felt to be a very precarious plank. No one mentioned that chasm or the potential drop, but Constantine could remember few joyous moments between his parents, only counterfeited pleasure when they were in company, especially in the homes of their uncles on their mother's side.

Over the months of therapy Constantine often referred to me as a gambler, "even though you don't actually bet money anymore. You don't have to, that's all."

Another time he asked me if I played the stock market, and I told him that I was very conservative but that it wouldn't serve for me to talk about myself further than that.

He was extremely friendly toward me, assuming that I saw the world virtually the way he did but that I had a little more perspective. However, when he disparaged his brother, I was careful never to join in.

He was very receptive to the few interpretations of his behavior that I did venture up to that point. For instance, he had told me that Anne was the only person who ever thought he was kind.

"What led her to that conclusion?" I asked.

"Because there's some old guy, Boris, from Russia. He loves to play poker but he hasn't the first idea of how to play. He's a total dreamer about the game, he can't throw away a bad hand. So, anyhow, Anne saw that I wouldn't let him play in my game, that I wouldn't take his money. And maybe I let him sleep in my place when it was cold from time to time. That's it."

I had commented, "He reminds me of your father."

Constantine had agreed at once. "That's right. My father would have been about his age."

So, as I'd thought, his father was dead. I had inferred that but had been waiting for the subject to come up naturally.

"How old were you when your father died?" I asked him.

"Eleven. I was eleven. Yeah, eleven."

I was startled, of course, at how early it had been. And even if I hadn't known how important that death was to Constantine, his face would have told me. He'd spent a lifetime reviewing the fact of that death, being perplexed by it, and seeking to assimilate it.

"Yeah, Boris does remind me of my father. Maybe that's why I was so good to him."

He was glad to get away from the topic, but his conclusion about himself was simplistic—and unfair to him.

I decided not to let it pass. "Come on, Constantine, you know there's more to it than that."

"What do you mean?" he asked.

"I mean I agree with Anne. I've been watching you, and I agree with Anne. Maybe a lot of people remind you of your father. I don't know. But you do care about people, and that's a lot why you're so unhappy with yourself."

I was surprised to see how shaken he was by what had seemed to me to be a rather obvious assertion of mine. I was sure he found it inescapably true.

He hadn't seen Anne in five months. She had called several times and left messages on his answering machine. But he had girded himself not to call her back. "What's the point?"

His pain surrounding her was great. She had accomplished resurrection of his hope. In her sublime company he had fleetingly reconsidered his whole life, and been forced to survey what he saw as decay and waste. Briefly he had dreamed of a sunlit world with her, but now he could think of her only as a bright light that revealed his faults. In a way I saw myself as continuing the work with him that Anne had begun.

By then I felt sure that there was more inside of him that needed to be expressed. Running counter to the life he had actually chosen, I surmised, was a genuine caring about people—and the impulse to make his presence felt in a wholly new way. Ironically, he was in pain over the growth of the better part of himself.

If I were to succeed in helping Constantine, that pain might have to increase before subsiding. An important part of my therapeutic plan was to surface that "contradiction" between Constantine, the fringe character out to beat the system, and Constantine, who wanted—who needed—to give something real to the world.

However, I decided not to describe that conflict in so many words. Knowing gamblers, and their commitment to cynicism, I feared that if I did, Constantine would sabotage whatever hope might be growing, would hide it from me and from himself. He was too afraid of failure if he threw in this hand and decided to play another.

My sense of kinship with Constantine deepened over the succeeding months, and he became more open with me. He always arrived at sessions on time. He met me with a frolic welcome at the door, and he cheerfully answered my questions.

I felt uncomfortable only when he contrasted me favorably with Peter, whom he would see about once a month when he went over there for dinner. When he disparaged Peter, I continued to desist from joining him. Obviously there was a lot more to that relationship than had surfaced so far. And I realized too that a component of my reaction to Peter was irrational. He was an enemy to the romanticism that I treasured. Still, Peter could remain as pinched, and as pinching, as he wished; he was surely not potent enough to snuff out romanticism in the world.

By then I felt sure that the key to understanding Constantine was to discover what had made him such a polar opposite of his brother. To come upon identical twins, ordinarily so similar, in this case radically different and at odds with each other, meant that something of profound importance must have occurred in their past and shaped both of them.

What had pushed the twins so far apart—in outlook, in psychology, and in appearance? It was certainly my overriding purpose to answer that question.

With no special information I had assumed that they had pulled apart early and been very different as toddlers, with Peter frail and hesitant and Constantine vigorous and devil-may-care.

But then I received some startling new information. It showed that the twins were still very much alike at eight. The real break must have come sometime after their eighth year.

One day Constantine brought in a manila envelope full of family photos. Some were of the boys when they were seven and eight. Not only were the twins dressed the same, they even sat or stood with exactly the same posture. When I asked Constantine about that, he said that they hadn't been posed by the uncle who took the pictures. "That's just the way it happened."

In one shot they were seated on a park bench in sailor suits, their knees together and their hands folded identically on their laps. In another each had a hand over the side of his face, and their forlorn look was identical. They resembled a Michelangelo painting in the Sistine Chapel of a man who has just learned that he is to be eternally damned, except that there were two of them. In another they were smiling identically, standing in front of their sister and parents on a baseball field. Their father was a much bigger man than I'd pictured him, Falstaffian, with cabriole legs. Their mother was a slender, austere-looking woman. The boys were eight in that one.

As I gazed at the photos, I let my mind invent sights and sounds. It was as if I could hear their father laughing sonorously and telling the boys how wonderful they were and how well they had posed, and their mother complimenting them, but more realistically. With each picture I had Constantine identify himself; I admitted frankly that I could never have picked him out.

He was going to show me later pictures, but I stopped him for a time, to assimilate what I'd seen and to ask him a few questions. My first was the most obvious. "How could people tell you apart?"

"Most people couldn't. My uncles used to go crazy. They were afraid to call us anything, I mean to use our names. A lot of people were. They didn't want to insult us or look stupid.

"One day my Uncle Gus noticed that in his house I would never grasp the railing coming downstairs and Peter always did. So Uncle Gus could use that to tell us apart. He mentioned it to us one day. The very next time, we deliberately switched. I held on to the rail, like I was afraid I was going to fall, and Peter didn't grab it. He called me Peter. It worked."

"Whose idea was that?"

"Both of us. We had it at the same time. We didn't even say anything. We just both did our thing."

Some more questions of mine established that what researchers have called twin telepathy was at its height in those years too. It was nothing short of miraculous.

For instance, they could send and receive messages in international code, flawlessly, at thirty words a minute, a speed that excelled that of even most professional telegraphers. "One of us would invent a shortcut, and the other would always know what he meant."

He added, "In those days we could always sense what was going on with each other."

He told me that one day he was playing softball in a vacant lot when he "just knew" that his brother was in trouble. He'd never left a game in progress before. He was always one of those who played until it was dark and the kids couldn't see anymore. But this time he'd just quit and rushed off without explanation. "When I got home, Peter was crying. He had broken a neighbor's window with a model plane. He was afraid the cops were coming to take him away."

When the neighbor finally did ring the bell that night, Constantine took the blame, telling them that it was his plane.

I asked him why he had done that.

He said he had just wanted to. Peter had thanked him every day for weeks after that. "He said he was praying that I would come and tell him what to do."

"You did a lot more than he prayed for," I commented.

"I know," he said flatly.

And then came the second half of the surprise.

He showed me a photo of the twins at twelve, with their graduating elementary school class. In that one, they looked virtually nothing like each other!

When I observed how different they had become, he said, "Yeah. We were barely talking."

It was hard to absorb. I stared at the photo. Constantine looked angular, waggish, unkempt, charming, unpredictable, with his tousled hair and half smile. Like a Dickens kid. Peter looked cherubic, contained, smug, orderly—almost the way he did when I knew him in graduate school. This time I could hear no dialogue— nothing.

Now I was able to construct an interval during which some force had been exerted on the boys, a force that shaped them—and shaped them differently. Whatever it was that drove them apart had occurred in those years between their being eight and twelve. We were closing in on the trail of something very important.

During that interval of manifest change, their father had died. But that alone could hardly explain their disparity. Under ordinary conditions the death of a parent would be more apt to knit the children than separate them. Such an event, likening them in predicament and in prospects, would tend to accent their similarities rather than their differences.

Obviously I would have to look further.

The following week Constantine picked up the story of his early life after that incident in which he had taken the blame for Peter's crime. "Everyone bawled me out, but dad forgave me right away. I knew he would. He told me he'd always be there when I was in trouble. And he always was.

"He told me that I shouldn't do that kind of thing. He said my mother had to pay a lot of money for that window. He said if I ever did it again, I should run.

"Actually we went out a lot after that incident. I think my mother was worried about me. Daddy would take me to the poolroom, without Peter, and he would tell everybody I was his son. I remember those men with their black hats and dark suits. My father was proud of me, and I was proud. I even played a little, sometimes. It was our secret where we went."

I heard myself say, "You really loved your father, didn't you?"

Constantine flashed a look of inexpressible tenderness and said, "Yeah."

He was obviously still thinking about those days, because he added, "I guess I still do. Is anything wrong with that?"

"Not at all," I answered him. "Not at all." He had asked me that tentatively, as if he had truly questioned the legitimacy of loving his father.

I remembered his having asked my permission to talk about Anne. In spite of his cavalier style, there was a taciturn, delicate aspect to Constantine. And now a love of his father that seemed both worshipful and defensive. In that household excessive love of

Stavros might have been frowned upon. I asked him outright if his mother would disparage her husband to the kids.

He told me, "Seldom. Maybe sometimes, when she was very mad at him."

I believed him. And yet, after mulling it over, I could hardly picture her *not* worrying that a child would grow up and be like Stavros. Nor could she have failed to communicate that concern. The fact that Constantine and his father kept concealed from the rest that they spent so many hours together suggests that there must have been some taboo on too close an alliance between them.

In the next session I asked Constantine, "Do you think you might have taken the blame for that broken window so that you could get closer to your father?"

He smiled and asked me why I thought that.

"Well, I know how much you loved to be with him. And you said that whenever you got in trouble, he was there. He was always there, on your side—"

He broke in. "I'll tell you something. It was a lot better to be with him and his crowd than with my mother's family. To answer your question, I don't know. But I think I would have broken *fifty* windows to be with my father. That sounds stupid, doesn't it?"

"Why stupid?"

"Well, you can't run away from your life."

"But you weren't thinking that way then," I reminded him.

So they were outcasts together, minor miscreants, fringe characters who found consolation in each other. And whether or not Constantine actually took the blame to get closer to his father, to become an acceptable comrade of that fine dreamer who lived at the edge, it seemed certain that he would have done almost anything back then to be with the man.

Because Anne had meant so much to him, he saw his unworthiness of her as epitomizing his failure in life. He said, "Even though I know she was too honest to lie to me on purpose, I still can't believe that she didn't hold my life against me. Nothing could have been real with her."

At one point Constantine met a woman on a bus, and they slept together a few times. "But she lost interest when she saw that I didn't have a real job, and you can't blame her."

I suggested to him, "You really see women as practical, as totally practical, and men as romantics, don't you?"

I explained that he didn't even listen to a woman's words if she said she loved him as he was. And I reminded him, "But you yourself said that your mother loved your father. You said she always loved him, which is why she never married again, even after he died. And he sure didn't bring home the money."

Constantine looked at me, puzzled. He asked, "Do you really think Anne wasn't just being polite?"

I told him I didn't know. But why would she lie?

That stopped him.

He brought her up only once after that. "She was fascinated by poker. I taught her how to play. I gave her the key to the game."

"What's that, in your opinion?" I asked him.

"You know. It's never being proprietary about a hand. No matter how good it looked once, if it's no good now, throw it away. You're not stuck with it. You can only lose a lot more. But you know that."

I told him I did.

Then came a clash with Peter, which was painful to both of them but which opened the floodgates to release information that proved invaluable.

Constantine had begun asking Peter questions about his childhood, in order to fill in some blanks. To his amazement, however, he found that his brother remembered very much less than he did. He found Peter polite but distant. Undaunted, he kept plying Peter with questions, until slowly Peter's courtesy gave way to curtness and obvious annoyance.

After a few weeks of this, Peter snapped at him, "What is it with you and all this childhood stuff? The photos and everything. Are you planning a second childhood? You're having trouble growing up as it is."

Constantine reported to me, "I told him I was trying to put the pieces together, that's all."

The next time they saw each other, Peter responded to a question in a way calculated to discourage Constantine once and for all.

"I really don't know that much about daddy," he said. "And, frankly, I don't care that much. Let's face it, he was a jerk."

Although Peter's remark stung, Constantine didn't say anything. Instead he asked incredulously, "But didn't you go over your childhood in your therapy?"

Peter told him that he'd gone to a behavioral therapist. "And we don't believe that going back over the past is necessary. It's a waste of time." He went on to disparage their father brutally and told Constantine to leave the past alone.

In defending himself and his father, Constantine mentioned me, citing me as an expert who didn't necessarily think Stavros was so bad.

"Him!" exclaimed Peter, and the sluices broke.

As Constantine recalled it, "He totally lost control when I said I'd gone back to see you. The next thing I knew, he was shouting, 'I told you that guy is a waste of time. Why didn't you pick someone more capable?'

"I couldn't stand it anymore. We walked into the other room, and I told him he was a fucking idiot, that he put everybody down. I said, 'You don't have half the brain to judge daddy or my doctor.'

"I don't know what he said next, but I shoved him into the wall. Somehow we calmed down. I hate myself for even mentioning you. And my father. I'm sorry. I'm really sorry."

"Sorry about what?" I asked him.

"I don't know. I betrayed you, didn't I?"

"Betrayed me. How?"

"Well, he's a very important person in your field, isn't he? You don't need enemies."

The session ended with Constantine full of self-recrimination, not for losing his temper with Peter, but for what inexplicably felt to him like betrayal of me. The theme of disloyalty, of breaking the faith, had always seemed very strong in Constantine, which was one reason I liked him. But after that hour, in which he would not forgive himself for talking about me, I realized that more lay behind his standard of loyalty than I had fathomed.

In our next session I asked him how his father had died.

"Emphysema. He could hardly breathe at the end. It was terrible. He used to lie down a lot; I'd go in and hang out with him. By then he couldn't work. He said to me one night, 'I'm not a bum anymore. This is what I always wanted—not to be a bum.' I said, 'Daddy, you were never a bum.' They didn't have the medicines they have now."

"Were you with him when he died?"

"No. He died in his sleep. We knew he didn't have much time. He had so much trouble breathing. I used to hold my breath. You know, I just realized, I still hold my breath sometimes, on purpose. I look at a clock and see how long I can hold it. Like a minute, or something like that. Do you think it's connected with my father?"

"Possibly. Go on."

"Anyhow, maybe the doctor told my mother it was near the end. Magdalene says they always do. My mother was very good to him at the end. She really broke up after he died. They were very close, you know, in spite of the arguments. Peter and I caused the worst one."

"What do you mean?"

"I mean we really broke him. I couldn't believe what Peter did —and what I did. And I was his buddy. What I did was worse."

"What was that?" I asked unbelievingly.

"It's funny," Constantine said to me. "You and I, our minds run on the same track. I was thinking about it just last night, how I haven't changed. And how Peter hasn't changed either. And now you're asking me."

I had no idea what I was asking him, but I told him to tell me what he and Peter had done.

"Dad was always promising not to gamble, to get a steady job. He had a hack license, you know. But he went on betting—by then it was mostly the horses—and losing. I knew he was gambling. I would hear him talking to his friends.

"One morning, when no one else was there, he gestured to me to come into their bedroom. I tiptoed in. He closed the door behind us and whispered, 'Come here.'

"I knew it was something big, even before he opened that big brown bureau drawer; I can still remember it. It was full of ten-dollar bills in stacks, with rubber bands around them. He asked me to count it. It was four thousand dollars. He won it on a long shot. He was going to pay off some debts and then buy us all presents, and give the rest to mom.

"I was incredibly nervous. I mean I was ten years old, it was a lot of money to see in front of you. I begged him not to gamble any of it, and he promised he wouldn't."

"Did he?"

"No. Will you please let me finish the story."

"Sorry."

"He made me promise not to tell anybody. He wanted to tell mom himself. I promised, of course. But I did tell someone. I betrayed him. I told Peter. My brother swore he wouldn't tell mom.

"Anyhow, that night there was a terrible fight. My mother and dad were screaming at each other, mostly in Greek, but I knew what they were saying. Peter had told my mother, and she went in and looked at the money.

"It was a terrible night. My father put his coat on once and walked to the door. I thought she was kicking him out. But he was going on his own. She would beg him to come back. He was coughing even then. They were both crying. She wanted control of the money, and he finally gave it to her. She actually paid off a couple of men who came by—hoods that he owed money to."

"Was a lot left?"

"I don't know. Some. Anyhow, I couldn't look at him after that. And I couldn't look at Peter. But my father forgave us. That was the way he was. He'd forgive a rattlesnake if it bit him. It was downhill after that. Then he died.

"After he died, I went into complete despair. Everybody was

really worried about me, for about three months. Then, when I pulled out of it, I gave everybody a hard time. I was terrible. I set a lot of fires. I did lousy in school.

"I always did after that. I was bad news. Peter suddenly started to do great. Oh yeah, I should tell you. One day Peter and I had a big meeting. I never forgave him for what he did, and he knew it. We agreed not to do any more code or count on each other in any way. I told him, 'After this, I owe you nothing, and you owe me nothing, okay?'—that was the deal.

"It didn't really stick. He was always correcting me. He was always telling mom, or telling me he was worried about me. Oh yes, I sent Peter a message in code, 'This is your last message, you bastard.' And he sent me one, 'If I'm a bastard, you're a bastard.' And that was it."

So they had lined up on opposite sides when their father fell out of grace. And they had doubtless done this not once but over and over.

Later I realized that Constantine's recently mentioning me to Peter, and then hearing me attacked, must have been a replay in miniature of that incident in which he had betrayed his father. Their battle over me was a replay of those earlier clashes. No wonder he had so exaggerated his "disloyalty" toward me, to the point that he could hardly forgive himself.

Finally I could surmise the origin of their differences. I had taken too narrow a view. I had understood Constantine as pursuing his father in order to spend as much time with him as possible. That was true, as far as it went. But the decisive impetus was not simply his urge to be liked by Stavros. It was rather his impulse *to be like* Stavros, to resemble him. And when Stavros died, he converted that urge into an absolute mission to *embody* his beloved father.

He had undergone a period of great grief, of desolation and mourning. Then, slowly, he had recovered by personifying the man he had loved so much, by *becoming* Stavros as soon and as fully as he could. In that way, Constantine found himself not nearly so alone. True, the original Stavros was gone. But years later there was still a fellow getting into trouble, upsetting their mother, criticized by Peter—a "fringe character" to use Constantine's own words, a peripheral person, a dreamer.

I had long regarded Constantine as loyal. But only after that insight did I realize to what extent he had kept the faith with his father, and how much it had cost him.

I thought again about the twins' agreement to go their separate ways. By that time Peter was implementing his own unspoken resolution. He would learn from what he had seen. Whatever Stavros did, he would not do.

I could imagine Peter, terrified as he beheld Stavros in the stages of his decline, resolving to avoid such a downslide himself. He would never gamble, he would not be a dreamer. He would become a responsible, literal adult. He would flee into maturity, as it were, as quickly as possible—anything to secure his place and not be sent whistling through the winds. And thus Peter's whole life was spent fighting his father's fate, that of being deprived of dignity, of argument, of respect.

For the first time ever, I felt sorry for Peter. Not that I accepted his high-mindedness or his ferocity as critic. But those same fierce clashes in the home that had shattered Constantine must have horrified him as much—or perhaps *more*, since he was a more fearful child than his twin. The only difference was that unlike Constantine, Peter was petrified by a fiat of the will, he had turned himself to stone.

Thus the twins had responded to the same meteor strike, or rather the same series of them, by rushing in exactly opposite directions away from the crater. Such is the nature of personality that having once started moving in their diametrically opposite directions, they continued on their individual courses. Under the force of their opposite momentums, they continued to differentiate, and became, by adulthood, in the psychological sense, true mirror image twins.

Finally, after nine months of doing therapy with Constantine, I had my answer to the riddle of the twins' disparity. I understood why they were so different, and why they disliked each other so much. And most important, I grasped the guiding fiction of Constantine's life.

By reproducing his father's outlook as his own, he had taken on all his father's restrictions. He had bartered away self-approval. He had renounced the sense of belonging that one can attain only by being generous toward others. His father had never been able to give his family what they'd wanted, and Constantine had felt similarly unworthy with Anne. His imitation of Stavros had cost him far more than he imagined.

The sweeping principle of my future work with him would be to help him see this, and to differentiate himself from his father at last.

However, it wouldn't do for me simply to make a speech about what I had discovered. For Constantine to make use of the information, he would have to assemble the facts for himself and draw his conclusions at his own speed.

I made sure to have him talk about Stavros at least a little in every session. Time and again, when something he said about his father applied equally well to Constantine himself, I underscored that fact. For instance, when Constantine lamented that his father didn't use his talent, I observed that people were saying the same thing about him.

Another time Constantine commented sympathetically about his father, "He hated himself. He knew he was letting us down. He even offered to leave. He said he wasn't worthy of our family."

I replied, "Walking out would have been the easy way. That's what you did with Anne."

Though I let some opportunities for comparison pass, I seized many others. After a few months it started to sound to both of us as if Constantine's *father*, and not his brother, were the real identical twin.

Perhaps because I was as warm in referring to Stavros as I was in talking to Constantine himself, he felt free to look at other facets of his father. His portrayal of Stavros became an interesting ad-mixture of love and the recognition of the pathetic. He described his father as a "terrible loser," but in the same breath he rallied to his defense by contrasting Stavros with himself. "At least he spent his life with real people. I didn't even do that."

I asked Constantine what he meant by that.

"The other night, it was five in the morning, and the players had just left. The sun was coming up. I looked at that green felt table with the two decks of cards and the chips scattered all over it, and the coffee cups everywhere. And you know what it looked like to me? Like a submarine that's never coming up. I threw a chair across the room. And I thought: That's my life. That was my father's life."

Suddenly he was glowering at me. He went on. "I'm a pretty good card player. Maybe that's all I know. But I read you for thinking something. All right. Go ahead, what's your theory?"

I admitted that I had a theory. He had caught me, discovered what professional poker players call a "tell," an involuntary give-away, by some tone or gesture, of the cards they have in their hand.

I felt undone for an instant, embarrassed at my transparency. But then I realized his reading me made no difference. It only meant that he was pushing me to tell him what I understood. It meant he was ready.

I told him in general terms what I thought—my theory that he was doing a complex imitation of Stavros, to his own detriment. "You're like him because you love him. We imitate people we love, we want to be like them. And you've done a pretty good imitation, Constantine. I'd give it a nine and a half."

"Why not a ten?" he asked, as I imagined he would.

"Because you're still alive, and your whole life is in front of you. You can change. He can't anymore. You don't have to end up the way he did."

He didn't fully embrace my explanation, but he didn't debate it either.

That was our first shared view of his motivation. From there I could enlarge the aperture of his memory and understanding. I could help him study not simply how he had copied his father but *why*. He would see that his motive had been more than to win his father over—it had been for him to become Stavros himself.

He could see this best in what he had done after his father died. At that stage Constantine's motive could not have been simply to persuade his father to spend time with him. As a result, the deeper motive, that of his wanting to become his father, stood out prominently in some cases.

For instance, after Stavros had died, and the boys had forsworn each other, one thing they did was quit dressing identically; it was one of the many ways in which they deliberately stopped doing what researchers call "twinning." Constantine remembered arranging to dress exactly the way his father used to, wearing colored shirts with the top button open, and black shoes instead of sneakers.

Also, he had suddenly refused to wear glasses—no one knew back then why he was so adamant, but now he knew: his father hadn't worn them. So what if Constantine did worse in school? His father had been no student, and so failure there was for Constantine more a plus than a minus.

He also recalled a recurrent fantasy he'd had as a boy. He had daydreamed of being taken for his father someday, in the poolroom, and maybe ultimately by some of his father's cronies.

Through all this, Constantine was able to see that he had truly sought to *reincarnate* Stavros. And the more conscious he became of that guiding purpose of his, the surer it grew that, even without my prompting, he would reconsider it.

Soon afterward I realized that Constantine had been able to create such an unusually strong bond with his father in part because he was an identical twin. He had developed his "capacity for oneness" with his brother as what child development experts call "an incubator trait": from earliest days they each virtually knew what their twin felt and wanted. Then, even after he broke with Peter, he retained that highly developed capacity for fellow-feeling, and applied it to his father. He told me there were times when only he knew how much his father was suffering and needed him. Thus, curiously, his very twinning had played a part in strengthening the commitment he still felt to Stavros, and to his way of life.

I felt slightly daunted by this discovery of what seemed almost a supernatural force solidifying Constantine's bond to his father. It crossed my mind that such a bond was rare, and how flattering it would have been to Stavros to know that his son cared for him so deeply.

Only then did it occur to me to ask myself how *Stavros himself* would have felt had he known what Constantine actually did with his life. Stavros would undoubtedly have been miserable if he'd had any idea that, due to his influence, his son fared no better than he did.

I had the strange illusion that Stavros was talking to me from the grave, beseeching me not to let his son follow in his footsteps.

Now that I knew this, I could hardly wait to broach the subject.

I got my chance in the very next session. Constantine was bragging about his poker prowess, almost high on the fact that he'd played brilliantly and won some hands that other people would have lost.

I asked him point-blank: "How do you think your father would feel if he could come back and see what you did with your life—I mean what you're doing these days?"

He stopped talking abruptly. It was as if I'd ambushed him.

But he answered honestly. "He would have *hated* it. Don't you think so?"

He knew that what he said was so. But he needed to hear me say it too, to spell out the reason, so I did. "He would have hated it because he loved you so much. He gave up on himself, but he never gave up on you. He certainly didn't want you to throw your life away—in his image," I said.

He clenched his right hand, but then opened it, as if realizing that he couldn't just punch his way out of this one.

"I understand," he said quietly. "It's lucky he's not here."

Maybe I was too tough, but I refused to let go. "All right," I said. "But suppose he did come back. What would you tell him?"

His face clouded with sadness. We both thought for a while. He just shrugged. What could he tell his father?

Finally I suggested, "Maybe you should tell him to come back in ten years, and he'd be proud of you."

"What do you mean?"

"Well, if you didn't quit on yourself, and you did something good, then he couldn't think he messed you up, could he?"

"That's an idea," he said.

After that we found one instance after another in which Constantine's copying his father was the very thing his father would have wanted least for him to do. For example, Constantine had willingly quit high school before graduating, in part because Stavros had himself never given school a try. Nothing was more evident now than that Stavros would have loved his son to become a college graduate. Constantine even speculated that he'd gotten himself beaten up and his nose broken because his father got beaten up by moneylenders more than once.

No single instance could be proved, but after a while it became as obvious to Constantine as to me that his father's dream was for him to succeed, and not to fail.

Finally he was free. Only real success would satisfy him and his father. And Constantine was at last in a position to decide what success really meant—in his own terms.

He began looking for a job. Although he didn't find one right away, he busied himself with some long-contemplated painting and repairs of his apartment, for which the landlord had promised to pay him. Constantine enjoyed the work and liked making the money in a way that didn't mean he was simply taking it from someone else. He realized that he had always been interested in design, and for a few weeks he contemplated studying that specialty. But then he felt it would require more general education than he could endure, and he became somewhat depressed again.

Luckily the landlord rang his bell one day to ask if he would do some plastering and building in a few vacant apartments to increase their value. Constantine jumped at the chance and got very interested in the financial aspects of the work involved. Although he wasn't yet ready to quit gambling, he finally accepted my suggestion that he force himself to get up by ten thirty and go outdoors unfailingly every day. I wanted him to heighten his sense that there was a real world and that he could play a real part in it.

His break came in the form of a suggestion by his landlord that he apply for a job in a real estate agency that handled half a dozen buildings the landlord owned. The landlord virtually told him that he could have the job if he wanted it. One of the features of the job was that Constantine could express his outgoing nature. He would be going to different buildings and dealing with people. But though he was a natural in this respect, Constantine still felt hopelessly unready.

At about that time I came upon a quote that I knew I had to read to him. It was from Samuel Johnson, commenting on the great writer Jonathan Swift, who had wasted an immense amount of time when young. In middle age Swift had embarked on a prodigious study program whose success, Johnson wrote, should inspire anyone who has "lost one half of his life in idleness not to throw the other half away in despair."

Constantine was marvelously moved by that quote. And it wasn't merely the content. I came to see that he loved references to souls of the past. Such references, and especially actual quotes, gave him a curious sense of belonging—he was not the only one who had lived and been lonely and struggled as he was doing now. I resolved to talk about past figures more often. Because he took such solace in their company, perhaps those of the past could help me exhort him into the future.

He took the real estate job but, he told me, only as his first step into the world.

Meanwhile, he did some reading that I recommended. He especially enjoyed biographies. At times I had the illusion that he was a little boy gulping down tales of heroism, like those his father told him about Ulysses and Hector and Agamemnon, and once I even caught myself wishing that Stavros were alive and there in the room with us. Had I assimilated that idea from Constantine himself? I wondered afterward but could never know for sure.

The daytime, bearing so many people hustling to appointments, so full of bright-eyed children and adults watching over them, was almost too brilliant for Constantine's eyes at first. But he stuck to his daytime life, and to the job.

One day, on a whim, he called Anne. She was genial but reserved.

"She's going with someone. I can tell," he said flatly.

"Possibly," I replied.

During the heavy silence that followed, I consoled myself by thinking that even if Anne were only an idealization, she had lit the way, and I realized that sparks, even of false hope, illuminate every successful life. I wondered, How much had her brightness been Constantine's creation?

He rallied, enough to say, "I'm going to my sister's for a few days. Maybe I'll call Anne when I get back. Do you think it's over?"

I could feel Constantine peering into my eyes, as if I knew what his chances were.

"I really don't know," I told him.

However, he kept surveying my face, using a trick of the master draw poker player, to keep watching one's opponent after a pot is over for some telltale sign he might have concealed while the hand was in progress.

"You won't read me," I said. "Because I don't know. I don't see any more cards than you do." Then I got tough. "You better stop studying other people so much and just play your own hand the best you can."

When he returned from his sister's, he told me that Anne had left several messages on his answering machine. She hadn't known he was out of town.

He didn't know if he would call her back. He said, "If she's with someone, what does she need to hear from me for?"

I asked him, "Why do you think she called you?"

He just nodded, as if he saw where I was going. He was warning me not to push him, not even to strive for clarity about how he stood with her. I knew it was a warning based on fear, and those are the sternest ones.

However, I had one more statement to make. "So you're not really much of a gambler, after all."

He asked me what I was talking about.

"Anne was ready to gamble on you, a lot more than you're ready to gamble on her."

In our next session Constantine told me that he'd finally called her. He said, "Someone from her office was there when I spoke to her on the phone. That's why she wouldn't talk. We're going to get together on Saturday."

They started seeing each other again, resuming where they had left off. They admitted having missed each other a great deal, and their relationship deepened.

Before long Constantine became increasingly involved with his real estate job, and we cut our sessions down to about once a month.

Then one day about six months later he came in very agitated. The previous weekend he and Anne had talked about living together, and about marriage. He felt panic at the prospect.

He told me, "I want to, we're practically living together already. But I'm scared about making it so official. It's hard for me to see myself as anybody's husband—especially someone as great as Anne. But I don't want to lose her."

I asked him, "Do you want to spend your life with her? That's the question."

"Absolutely."

"So what's the big difference if you get married officially?"

"I don't know. The commitment. It's a new idea to me."

I remarked, perhaps mysteriously, that there was nothing new about it. I told him, "Constantine, you've always been committed."

"What do you mean?"

"To your father, for example."

"You mean to be like him and be the opposite of Peter."

"Yes. You were committed not to come through for people because your father didn't. You wouldn't take more from life than he got. But let's not forget—"

"Forget what?"

"That he would want you to have the best. Better than he ever had it. You're not betraying him if you fall in love. Don't worry, your father will always be on board. You won't forget him. And even if you get married, it doesn't mean that you and Peter will be identical."

"Identical twins," he said ironically.

Soon after that Constantine and Anne made arrangements to live together, and it was Constantine who suggested that they get married, which they did.

I saw him only a few times after that. They were both working hard, and money was tight, but they were happy with each other.

About five years after Constantine's last visit to my office, I met him on the street with Anne, and he introduced me to her. An attractive woman, with striking auburn hair and lively blue eyes, she said politely, "I've heard a lot about you."

So sensitive are those meetings with people we've heard about from our patients, however, that I declined to say I'd heard a lot about her too. Even such a light comment could raise questions and sound more loaded than I wanted it to. So I said something trite, and we continued on our way.

I would have welcomed hearing about their lives, about how Constantine was doing at work and whether they had children, and how they were getting along. But, obviously, to ask anything at that stage would have been intrusive. Few outside the profession can possibly sympathize with that sense of being abruptly cut off that we therapists suffer when our work is done. And my account of Constantine's life is necessarily truncated too.

Over the many years since I last saw Constantine, research on twins has suggested some secondary reasons for why he grew up so different from his brother. Their household allowed the twins to evolve more separately than is often the case. For instance, four pairs of identical twins in ten have "twin names," like Peter and Paul, which these boys did not. Constant contrasts between "good twin" and "bad twin," which tend to convert individuality into a sense of being part of a matched pair, were absent in this family.

And studies show that identical twins are so regularly treated as a unit throughout their childhood that they receive far less love and attention from their mothers than other children do. Indeed, on those rare occasions when one twin dies, bereavement tends to be short, as if the loss could be solaced by the presence of the remaining twin. To the credit of Constantine's parents, they paid close attention to all their children, and did not impart to either of the twins a sense of being replaceable.

Constantine and Peter may also have profited by being boys. Research has shown that boy twins are much less likely to be treated as a unit than girl twins are. For instance, forty percent of identical twin boys are put into different classes in their early school years, as Constantine and Peter were. On the other hand, only one in eight pairs of identical girl twins are so separated and thus given the chance to develop as individuals. Like any bias, sexism tends to linger especially in those crannies least discussed and illuminated by public interest.

Perhaps because Constantine and Peter were treated less as a matched pair than most identical twins are, they became exceptions to the rule that identical twins tend to be slower at learning language skills than other children are. Both were verbal when quite young and remained so.

It seems to me that Constantine retraced his steps and returned toward Peter far more than Peter did toward him. Socially this might seem like a good thing, since Peter had a successful life in many respects and Constantine did not. But Peter could obviously have profited a great deal from loosening up and allowing his intuition to run his life more, as Constantine did and as their father had done.

I never saw Peter again either, but, curiously, my work with Constantine softened my attitude toward him. I understood what made him the person he became, and could feel some sympathy. After all, had I not, like Peter, gone into the field of psychology to make sense out of chaos, and perhaps even to find things out about my own life? Once or twice, when I thought about Constantine, I imagined Peter's reevaluating what his brother and I had accomplished together and his deciding that I wasn't as incompetent as he had thought.

As we all know, individual differences are a good thing. One measure of parents is how differently their children develop. Paradoxically, however, the most radical difference between the boys was a mark of their not having developed independently. That they seemed like such opposites attested to the fact that each had been in flight from the other's identity, which each perhaps sensed was a real possibility for himself. Constantine's fighting any impulse he might have had to be conventional mirrored Peter's fear of becoming a derelict. In each case the twin's fear of becoming like his brother had limited his freedom.

smiling through

. . .

LOUIE, A NEIGHBORHOOD POLICE-
man near my office, would sometimes be
waylaid by elderly people demanding
that he do something to stop a voice that
was driving them crazy. There were interludes when Louie had three or four such
folk harassing him.

"One poor old lady thought for sure
it was a communist plot," he told me.
"She insisted that if I went to her apartment, I'd hear the damn thing too. She'd
literally try to pull me up there. So one
day I went. Naturally, I didn't hear a
thing.

"But that didn't matter. Three days later, she was after me again. She was desperate I should get the voice out of her apartment. She'd grab at my uniform every time she saw me in the street.

"Finally, I told her to cover her walls with silver foil, every bit of them. That way the voice couldn't get in.

"When I saw her the next week, she thanked me, and gave me some homemade cookies. I explained to her that this kind of voice can get through steel and brick, but it can't get through silver paper."

Louie told me that the method worked with more than one person, though not with all. I had no reason to doubt him.

The nightclub host lowered the mike to suit his diminutive size. "Our next performer is a very, very funny lady," he promised, and went on with his ill-formed introduction. "She was a smash hit on a cruise ship that just got back. Next week she starts a gig at the Hungry Eye. But we're lucky to have her with us tonight. Let's welcome Jessica Hanlon."

We clapped enthusiastically as she came out onstage. She was about five eight, and chunky in a boxy sequin jacket and black silk slacks. She was comedy before she spoke: her strong jawline and brow made her look masculine, and she was gawky in a way that was liberating.

The crowd, mostly in their twenties and early thirties, applauded, and then waited.

"Some women want to get married real bad," she started. "Like this woman who sees a guy and says, 'Where have you been? I haven't seen you in a long time.' The guy says, 'I was in jail for ten years. I hacked my wife to pieces and they caught me.' 'Oh, great!' she says. 'So you're single again!' "

That got a big laugh.

She jutted her jaw forward and paused before filling us in, "That woman was me."

Another laugh.

"My father wanted me to get married so bad. He suggested the Boston strangler.

"I would have married him too. But I found out he's a phony. He's not really from Boston. He commutes."

While the audience laughed at that one, she fiddled awkwardly with her abundant brown hair.

In the real world such gleeful laughter would have been hard to explain—Jessica's jokes weren't *that* funny. But many in the audience were aspiring comics themselves, together with their claques of supporters. General merriment was required or you wouldn't get laughs when your turn came.

Afterward Jessica came over to our table, all smiles, her sequins glittering in the candlelight.

She sat down next to the young man with us, a fellow comic whose parents had brought me and others to see his act; he had been on earlier. We all complimented her.

She told us a few more jokes, as if we hadn't heard enough. Then she whispered to me, "I hear you're a shrink."

I nodded.

"I need a shrink. No, I really do," she said, as if realizing that everything she said would at first be taken as a joke. "Have you got a card?"

I didn't, but she wrote down my name and number.

About two weeks later Jessica called for an appointment.

She breezed in, commenting, "Nice office you've got here. Maybe you'd like a partner." It was as if she were continuing her routine.

She sat down on my couch and looked around the office, and then at me. Then she said, "This is the funniest thing of all time. I'm hearing voices."

"Voices?"

"Yeah. I hear people talking in my head. Sometimes for a few seconds, sometimes for a whole minute. What does it mean when you hear voices?"

I told her that it could mean any of a lot of things, that I'd have to ask her more questions.

I began by inquiring what the voices were saying.

"Sometimes it's not actually a voice. It's just a buzzing. Sometimes it's definitely a voice, but I can very seldom make out any real words. It's a man talking, though, that I can tell you. And it's always the same man."

"Well, what words can you make out?"

Jessica moved her hands restlessly, and I became aware of two big jangly bracelets on her right hand. "Sometimes the guy tells me numbers. Like forty-seven and sixty-five. And the other day he said something to me as clear as day." She hesitated.

"Go ahead," I said.

"He said . . ." She smiled, as if disbelievingly. "He said—are you ready for this?"

"I am."

"He said, 'Get a ton done with your stun gun.'"

I smiled too, and then was sorry I did.

"What does a stun gun make you think of?" I asked her.

"Nothing. Absolutely nothing. It doesn't mean anything to me."

"And what about the ton? Does that make you think of anything?" I asked.

"Nothing," she repeated. "It made no sense to me. But it's always the same man talking, though. That I'm sure of."

"Have you any idea who the man is?" I asked.

"No," she said.

"Does he say anything else?"

"What do you mean?"

"I mean does he ever tell you to do anything?"

"You mean like kill someone?" she asked.

"I wasn't thinking of that. I just mean to act in any way."

"No. Except he once told me to have a good day, that's about it. That he definitely said."

"When was the last time you heard this man?" I asked her.

"It was Sunday. When he said the thing about the stun gun. I was having lunch at my mother's place, with my sister, Marie, and her husband, Philip. I also have a brother, David, he's two years younger. He lives in Philadelphia."

Then half to herself, "I really thought the guy was gone forever. But he came back. He was louder than ever on Sunday. He was so loud that I turned around. For a minute, I thought my brother-in-law said something to me, but he was in the other room. I asked my mother and sister if they heard anything, and they didn't. I dropped the subject fast.

"I went to the bathroom, to be alone, to try to get away from the damn thing. I turned on the faucet. But the guy *raised his voice* and kept talking to me.

"I got scared and I told everybody I had to go. When I got outside, it was even worse. I ran to the subway and down the steps. A train was pulling in. I was so glad for the noise level, you just couldn't believe it.

"I jumped on the train and grabbed a seat. Then I let myself listen. There was no more voice. It was gone.

"I knew it would go. Once those subway doors close, I know I'm all right. That happened before, also at my mother's house. The guy doesn't follow me into the subway for some reason. Do I sound crazy?"

"I'm not thinking of it that way, Jessica," I assured her.

"Well, it's pretty upsetting," she said, trying to smile.

"I know it is," I said.

I could see that she was trying not to look distraught.

"I can live with it if I know what it is," she went on. "I just want to know what it is. Have you ever dealt with a case like this before?"

"We don't yet know exactly what it is, Jessica," I told her. "But we'll figure it out."

She told me that she'd heard the voice about a dozen times over the past six months, always in the early evening. She hadn't told anyone about it. Most of the time she was at her mother's house when she heard it, but once she had been at a party with friends.

"Do you feel very sleepy when you hear this man?" I asked her.

"What do you mean?"

I explained to her that sometimes people get illusions in drowsy states, such as just before going to sleep. We imagine we see something, or hear something, a doorbell or some other noise, maybe even a voice that isn't there.

She replied instantly. "No, I know what you mean. I've had that happen, you mean did I half dream that voice? I've had that happen, no. I thought that myself at first, but no. I was wide awake, unfortunately."

"Do you take any drugs?"

"No, I don't. Should I?" I was glad to see her sense of humor still with her.

"You don't smoke grass?"

"No. I said no."

"Did you ever have a time, I mean when you took mescaline or anything like that? Think back."

"I don't have to think back. The answer is no. I didn't, and I didn't blow my mind."

I believed her, and besides, though certain drugs, like mescaline and LSD, can have lasting effects, even when they do, visual hallucinations are much more common than auditory ones.

"What about uppers?" I asked her. "I mean maybe to go onstage, to be up at the end of the day, like Dexedrine?"

"You mean uppers can make you hear voices?"

"They can't make you. But if you're really exhausted and you don't know it—you could be in one of those drowsy states, when you're practically dreaming on your feet."

"You mean even if I took Dexedrine years ago?" She looked very frightened. "I did a few times. Maybe three years ago was the last time. You mean maybe I blew my mind?"

"No. No, I didn't mean that," I assured her. "If you're not taking the stuff now, that's all I'm asking about. Obviously, it isn't good for you, but I think we can rule it out."

She nodded.

Suddenly my mood darkened, and I didn't want it to show. I felt very sorry for her. The easy elimination of these possibilities made the unmentioned ones more likely, and some of them were less pleasant. Psychosis, or even the beginning of a deteriorating mental state, was becoming a real possibility. Even more worrisome was an organic condition: a brain tumor, a lesion, or a hemorrhage. If it was organic, we would not have much time.

I felt at a loss for words. I knew that I would have to recommend that she go immediately for diagnostic tests of the brain, and that this would terrify her.

It seemed important for us to spend the rest of the session on her life apart from her condition—on Jessica the person trying to fulfill her dreams in the world. She deserved no less. We would talk about anything other than her auditory hallucination.

Besides, if the real cause was psychological, as I fervently hoped, our tracking down its origin and removing the source would take time, and require my knowing a tremendous amount more about her.

She told me a little about her childhood. Even as a little girl she had wanted to be an entertainer. She would do routines for her family, and later for other kids. In recent years, since she'd become a stand-up comic, she had worked hard on her act.

Like many comics, she looked at virtually everything that happened to her as a possible source of humorous material, and often when she spoke, I got the impression that she was trying out lines on me to see how I would react.

I could see how such an approach could bleach the colors out of otherwise diverse experiences, but that was something to consider at a much later time, if ever. Meanwhile, I was delighted to hear Jessica quip and joke as she told me about herself. She would need all the humor she could muster in the near future.

"What's your dream in life?" I asked her at one point.

"To get on Carson. No, to host Carson, no—to stay on there, so that I'm on there all day; whenever you turn on your set there I am."

"What would that give you?" I asked.

"Fame. Everyone would remember me. No, they wouldn't have to remember me, they would see me every day."

She laughed delightedly at her own conception, and I did too. It was a lot of fun.

At the door she asked me if I thought I could stop the voices.

"We'll deal with them," I told her. "But we have to go systematically. We have to rule out every possibility, until we get to the cause. And once we find it, we'll deal with it. Can you come back tomorrow, and we'll talk more?"

"Of course," she said. She looked comforted, but I knew that she really wasn't. My very asking to see her again so soon must have frightened her, but there was no other way.

After she'd gone, I realized that my mentioning the ruling out of causes must have sounded dire. It had been my initial faltering effort to prepare her for the inevitable brain scans that would have to be done. I knew how hard she would take that prospect. But at least the verdict would come fast.

Only later did I fully understand how terrified Jessica was. It occurred to me that she was a person who presented every facet of her life to the world. Her comedy seemed coextensive with her life, with exposing her own foibles especially. Yet she hadn't told anyone about the voice—not a soul over the six months that it had been talking to her.

I was glad that she had such a good sense of humor. I hoped it wouldn't desert her.

The next morning I made arrangements for a neurologist at Columbia Presbyterian Hospital to see her. When I told him the symptom, he confirmed the need to hurry, and we scheduled Jessica right away with the radiology department for the usual brain mappings.

I winced as I anticipated telling Jessica. I would have to bring it up early in the session so she'd have plenty of time to tell me how she felt about the idea.

Jessica came in wearing a pullover shirt with a loud print, one of her many "joke outfits"; the whole top was cut like the head of a lion, the mane composed of bits of feathers fluttering down, and brass buttons. She started the session by telling me a joke. I laughed. She had heard it on the cruise ship, where she'd done a two-week stint of five shows a week. "The pay is great, and you can try out new material. Nothing that will shake up the passengers, though."

"You mean you can't mention the *Titanic*," I said dryly.

"So you do have a sense of humor. I was wondering. That's good," she said.

Jessica had gone out twice on cruise excursions, and she hadn't heard the voice either time. On her second trip, only the previous month, she'd actually felt that as the ship went out, she was escaping the voice.

"I was relaxed, I guess. I had this weird sense that the farther I got from home, the safer I was." By "home" she meant the Bronx apartment she had grown up in. She had moved out only a few years previously to get her own place, which was in Manhattan.

About ten minutes into the session I told her that I wanted her to go to a neurologist, and then to a radiologist, who would take pictures of her brain.

She blanched. "Why do they want to look at my brain? They won't find anything," she said.

"I'm sure they won't," I told her.

"You mean you don't think I have a brain either," she said, trying to be light.

"I mean I don't think there's anything wrong with your brain," I said firmly.

She was leaning forward, with her hands cupped on her kneecaps, as we talked.

"You think it's a brain tumor, don't you?" she asked me flatly.

"No, I don't," I said. I held my position. She needed me to.

"Then why do they want photographs of my brain? Am I that photogenic? Maybe I need an eight-by-ten glossy."

"We have to be thorough—" I started to say, when she interrupted me.

"Do you send all your patients to these guys?" she asked.

"Some," I said, wishing I could say more.

"Like who?" she inquired.

"Well, if a person has a severe migraine, for instance—"

"I'll have to think about it," she said, taking a deep breath.

"That's not a good idea. It's simply got to be done, Jessica," I said.

She ran her hands through her hair, playing with it angrily. She said, "I don't want to die."

"Jessica, you're not going to die."

"Never?" She smiled tauntingly. "My father just died. Why not me?"

"Did he?" I asked. "Very recently?"

"Seven months ago."

"You and he were close?" I asked her.

"Very," she said. "He was my best audience." Jessica told me that she had been his favorite. He had run an old-fashioned candy store, where all the family members worked when they had time. Jessica had delighted her father by doing imitations of people—of movie actors, of customers, even sometimes of him. He'd had several heart attacks before dying of one, in his sleep. She missed him terribly. "I often dream about him," she said.

I asked her what went on in those dreams.

"Oh, I'm just walking with him, or he's telling me jokes, or saying that some joke of mine was good."

The dreams were halcyon interludes, but they made waking up worse, with the slow realization that her father was gone, that she would never see him again, never regale him with an anecdote or lighten his day.

Her very conjuring up her father in talking about him to me was a balm to her. She leaned back and moved her hands as she did when she was relaxed, in that gawky, humorous way. And she even smiled, as she must have when her father was alive and with her. For the moment she had accomplished the impossible, turned back the clock.

But I was keenly aware of the present. I knew that I had to convince her to go for the tests at once.

She surprised me by asking, "What's a hallucination?"

"It's when you see or touch or hear something that isn't there," I told her.

"You mean a sound?"

"That's one possible kind."

"How loud does it have to be?"

"It could be a buzz, or a whisper, or very loud. It could be vague, or it might be words that are very clear."

"I see." She stopped. She apparently thought better of pursuing the inquiry. I was more than glad, I wouldn't have known what else to say.

I went forward. "I set up an appointment for tomorrow with a Dr. Carpey, a neurologist, for three o'clock," I said. "Here's the address."

She took the card from me.

"Do you think I'm going to die?" she asked.

"I told you no." I was still staunch.

"I'm scared," she confessed at last.

I waited, and when the silence seemed to produce more tension than it relieved, I broke it. "Can you get someone to go to these doctors with you?" I asked.

"My sister Marie would."

"I think you should ask her," I said. "It's good to have company."

By her face I knew that her humor had returned, even before she spoke. "Maybe I'll meet a doctor and marry him," she said. "Then I can diet forever and my life will be complete."

She promised to call me after the testing, though we wouldn't know the results for several days. The neurologist would collate the findings and then notify her; he would let me know at the same time.

I felt satisfied that I'd done what I had to do. Yet she left my office that April evening very much poorer in hope than she had been before her session with me.

Naturally I thought about her that evening and the next day, always with the same pointless wondering: What will they find? I edged on succumbing to the very fault that physicians are sometimes accused of, that of regarding the patient as merely an illness, or a possible one, rather than as a human being. However, at other moments I was with her in spirit, as she sat with friends in the club or went to bed alone, in the pangs of terror.

I was thus hardly aware of something else that troubled me. She had extolled her father, and indeed her whole family, as if they were the perfect, encouraging unit. That had surprised me. It had felt discrepant with what I had anticipated. I had no idea why, but I'd imagined her as at odds with at least certain of her family members, and with her father in particular. This seeming contradiction evoked a vague unrest in me, but at the time it was eclipsed by my larger concern.

Dr. Carpey called after seeing her and said that the EEG showed nothing. "But I'm very suspicious," he said. "There was no unusual spiking, but she does hear a rhythmic thumping sometimes right before the voices."

I hadn't known that, and asked him what it could mean.

"It could mean she's hearing an artery in the medial temporal lobe. Does she ever pass out?"

"I don't think so," I told him.

"She didn't remember when I asked her," Dr. Carpey said. "I was just wondering. You know, these people sometimes remember things one time and can't remember them the next."

I hadn't realized that.

His phrase, "these people," sounded ominous. But after we hung up, I told myself to stop guessing. Radiology, with its newfound ability to make computerized maps of every section of the brain, would soon yield its answers.

But a few days later radiology too showed absolutely nothing.

"Nothing?" I asked Dr. Carpey, who had the report.

"Nothing. Tomography didn't give us a thing."

"That's something," I muttered mostly to myself.

"Do you want to see the NMR results?" he asked, as if I had doubted him.

"No. Of course not."

"Well, it's in your ballpark now," he said, sounding piqued. "But we do want to see her in six months."

"Of course. She knows?" I asked.

"My nurse called," Dr. Carpey said, "but couldn't reach her."

"Thanks."

When we hung up, I tried Jessica, but she wasn't there.

That night I called her at the club.

"Should I tell her this is an admirer?" asked the MC in his familiar raspy voice.

"Just give her the name, please."

When I told Jessica there was absolutely no abnormality, there was silence, and I imagined her in shock. But she bounced back. "So everybody's wrong who says I'm abnormal."

"All the pictures, all the tests were absolutely okay," I said.

Only after this call did Dr. Carpey's words sink in. It really was in my ballpark now.

I had no doubt that Jessica would hear the voice again, and I knew I had to keep pressing her to try to identify whose voice it was, or at the very least to tell me what it was saying.

She started the next session with a joke, as she had begun all our meetings. Then when I asked her about the testing, she said it had been boring. "Like sex with Bruce, it's over before you know it."

"Who's Bruce?"

"Oh, just some guy I used to go out with. You've got the picture already."

A little later, when I asked her if she had ever passed out, she replied, "Passed out? Only when I'm making love, and that hasn't been too often lately."

"Do you really?" I asked seriously.

"No," she said. "It's supposed to be a funny. You're really not a very good audience."

I had her fill me in more on her early years. She talked about her father as lovingly as she had the first time, but this time I had the distinct feeling that she was putting me on. I studied her every word, as if some secret truth about him were being imparted to me in a way I hadn't yet identified. But I could find no justification for what I felt. There was no hint of disappointment with him, or even of complaint.

I told her that he sounded wonderful, and then asked her point-blank what his limitations as a father were.

"He was perfect," she snapped back, with no trace of humor.

Then suddenly I realized why those tributes to her father had sounded hollow. Her comedy routine! Onstage she had portrayed him as not giving a damn about her. Minutes earlier she had told me that after his second heart attack, he would call her into his room and clasp her hand, and say, "I only want you to be happy." Now, as the leitmotif for these words, I could hear her onstage, saying, "My father wanted me to marry the Boston strangler . . ." She had left nightly audiences convinced that he was a self-willed, contemptuous man.

I had no idea what to do with this contradiction. Or whether it was really a contradiction at all. If art can't embellish, what can? And shouldn't stand-up comics have the right to entertain us by creating characters and elaborating upon real ones? Nor had I ever actually thought of a comic's husband or wife or boss or mother-in-law as the actual person being portrayed in a gag. I decided simply to purge my own view of Jessica of anything I'd learned about her through her act.

However, I soon realized that this wasn't so easily done. More than with anyone I'd met, Jessica's life and art seemed inextricable.

Jessica used humor continuously with me, and presumably with everyone. And not just humor: her *comedy routine!* Time and again I realized right after taking seriously something she'd said that she had said it only to try out a line for her act. She was constantly practicing lines with me to see how they would go over onstage. She was using me as much to rehearse her evening routines as to find out about herself.

As a result, it was hard to know when she was serious—she

would say almost anything, true or untrue, for the sake of its effect. It turned out, for instance, that Bruce, the boyfriend she had lampooned to me and had made the butt of humor in her act, was an actor she was in love with who had dumped her. She'd found out that he was sleeping with other women during their romance, and he had walked out.

Jessica's jokes about her father, her portrayal of him as a brutal maniac, had a twofold purpose. It was good comedy; anything for a laugh. And I further saw that as with her joking about the brain scan, she used comedy to weather painful experiences. Laughter helped her endure the loss of her father.

Similarly her depiction of Bruce and their relationship, her making light of the whole thing, was an attempt to surmount the defeat, while wringing some funny lines out of the experience.

And even her humor about the voice, which terrified her—quite obviously that too had been an attempt to siphon off some of its horror.

Over the next few weeks she joked about it more. "No, I haven't heard the guy lately, but next time I wish he'd tell me a couple of good gags. I could use some fresh material."

I felt sure that the prospect of its returning scared her more than she let on.

And I felt just as sure that it would return—there was no reason for it not to.

I came to see why, though Jessica had many acquaintances, she had few friends and no intimate ones. Jessica was a near embodiment of what some psychoanalysts call the defense mechanism of "smiling through." By constantly manufacturing good cheer and substituting it for her true underlying feelings, she could keep smiling. But such a front made real communication impossible.

I saw that it must have been hard for a friend to get taken seriously—Jessica was so afraid to take herself seriously. A lover would go crazy in a week. I could see that Jessica had only occasional access to her own emotions; it took guesswork on my part to know what she was feeling. She constantly balked at my efforts to get to know her by saying things merely because they were funny.

Naturally my primary concern was to identify the voice, whose it was and what it meant—and, ultimately, why it came to her. However, it was vital for me to approach Jessica in the warmest, fullest way I could. As when working with any patient with an encapsulated problem, such as stuttering or overeating or any obsession, I would approach the person rather than the problem. I would endeavor to improve Jessica's love of life, her efficiency, and her sense of personal security.

Conceivably the complaint would turn out to be a symptom and disappear, and even if not, I could learn about it this way. Of course, I would also keep inquiring about "the voice," but I would not devote myself to it alone. That would be reducing Jessica to the status of a nonentity with a very unusual affliction.

Because Jessica's defense mechanism of smiling through was camouflaging the rest of her personality, I began studying how she used that device. Technically psychoanalysts call it a "resistance," which Jessica was using to avoid having to face what she really thought and felt.

My method, I determined, would be to bring this resistance of Jessica's to her attention. She had every right to distort for the sake of humor when she was onstage. However, I had every right, and indeed the obligation, to reveal to her exactly how she distorted reality.

To help Jessica appreciate how often she resorted to the false but funny, I decided to take everything she said at face value. I would stay serious so as not to let us both get sidetracked. Perhaps she would see on her own that she was as much in the grip of her own humor as she was deliberately employing it. No one could ever know her, and she could never know herself, until she could learn to go forward without it—at least for brief intervals of time.

I began the next time I saw her. She came in with new makeup on. Her eyes were framed in a shade of blue-green that made her look pop-eyed. She told me an anecdote about getting her face done at Bloomingdale's. It was funny. But I resisted it.

"You don't think it's a good story?" she asked, sounding a trifle hurt.

"It's not bad," I said flatly, adhering to my program.

Later she commented deadpan about Bruce, whom she had seen the previous weekend in the street. "He's pretty bad-looking, but the trouble is he's broke."

"I thought he was good-looking," I said, as if I'd taken her seriously.

She frowned, and explained that she was kidding.

I just nodded.

After a few more sessions of my not looking amused, Jessica charged me with being angry at her.

When I asked her why she thought so, she told me she didn't know, but accused me of being unresponsive. She scratched her forehead with her long red artificial nails.

During the ensuing discussion I maintained that I was very involved with her, but I wasn't there to be entertained. I said I wanted to know what she really felt.

However, she only worked harder at getting me to laugh.

One evening it was pouring. Thunder boomed, and it was dark outside, with that unusual light that sometimes accompanies brief summer storms.

In my office, after seeing a flash of lightning, Jessica said archly in an accent like Bela Lugosi's, "Tonight I'm going to bring a dead person back to life."

"Really," I said believingly.

"Yeah, *you*," she snapped.

"I guess you did that with your father," I replied. "You said you made him laugh at the end of the day."

Her mood changed. "He said he always looked to me for a fix. I was his fix."

She said her whole family enjoyed her humor.

"Was that a way you convinced yourself that they loved you, I mean by getting them to laugh?" I asked her.

She told me it was.

A week or so later she informed me that she'd added a line to her newest routine. After going onstage in one of her zany outfits and getting an instant laugh and applause, she announced to the audience: "My shrink says I get people to laugh with me so they won't laugh at me."

"So I see now I'm part of your act too," I said.

She shrugged her padded shoulders. "Did you mind my saying that about you?" she asked nervously.

"Why should I mind?" I said. "You can make up what you want. I'm only interested in what you really feel."

To my astonishment, Jessica said, "You know, I'm furious with you, even though you're an all-right guy."

I didn't respond. I just nodded to show that I heard her and it was okay.

I speculated about why Jessica felt as she did. It occurred to me that I was the first person in a long time to accept her, indeed to *prefer* her, without her humor—her devices. In effect, I had conveyed to her, "Jessica, you're good enough yourself. You don't have to prove your worth by bringing goodies to every session. You're fine without them."

I didn't say any of that to her, but I harbored it as a hypothesis. I was starting to feel that we were headed in the right direction.

Two months went by without Jessica hearing any voices. I actually considered the possibility that they were gone. I certainly didn't say that to her, though. I still had no inkling of what the voices meant or where they came from. But the fact that she hadn't heard them, I imagined, might help explain her affection for me. I had slain the dragon. My presence in her life had frightened them away.

Then came a session in which Jessica and I discussed a major decision she had to make. She had been offered several gigs on cruise ships; it was sure work and paid better than the local clubs, which were still hit-and-miss. However, for a comic who wanted a big career in nightclubs and on TV, working cruise ships was an inferior choice. There were no agents on ships, and without visibility an entertainer could soon be forgotten. Jessica told me, "I don't want to be a man without a country."

As important, she would be the only comic on those cruises. That was a major drawback because, as Jessica told me, working comics should spend long hours together, trying out routines and giving one another ideas. In the city she would meet a few times a week with a little group of entertainers, and she said they were wonderful for one another. They would laugh together for hours as they sat in a cafeteria that was open all night.

"Can they turn off the humor when they want to?" I asked.

She seemed taken aback by my question. "Sure," she said flatly.

Looking serious, she resolved to stay in the city for the long-run advantages. I took this as a vote for herself and the cultivation of her own skills.

That session she looked directly at me more than she ever had. Almost involuntarily she thanked me on the way out. At long last she was starting to differentiate her act from real experience.

But the next time she came in looking morose. She had heard the voice again, louder than ever, though she still couldn't make out what it was saying. She seemed shaken. And now she said she knew who it belonged to.

"It's my father's voice."

"How do you know?"

"I know his voice. Don't try to comfort me. I know my father's voice." She sighed deeply.

Then she said, "I'm sorry. I don't mean to be nasty. But it's driving me crazy."

I asked her what her father might want, why he would speak to her. She didn't know.

"Maybe he thinks I'm going to die."

"Why do you think that?"

"Oh, it's just a thought that came into my mind."

I pressed her, but she couldn't say any more about it.

After she'd gone, I censured myself for not having previously considered that it might be her father. People often imagine the voice, or even the sight, of a loved one who has recently died. Most of us know we're imagining the thing, but understandably Jessica, who so ran the paints of life and imagination together and whose father was so important to her, might be confused.

So hers could be what psychologists call a "deprivation hallucination." Especially in the absence of other explanations, I resolved I would pursue this avenue.

But why, I wondered even then, would a voice come to someone so confusedly, so seemingly pointlessly? If it had any psychological or personal function, would it not say something, beyond declaring itself as her father's voice? I had written down the only words that Jessica could make out, those few numbers and the line about the stun gun, and none of them had ever made sense to her.

I could see during the next month that Jessica was changing—for the worse. She had less to say; she stopped even trying to entertain me. I had the feeling that she might be engaging in lengthy dialogues with the voice, though when I asked her, she said no. "He talks to me sometimes, but I have no idea what he's saying. 'Have a good day' is all I can make out."

Once she looked at me plaintively and said, "He's trying to get through. I know you don't believe it, but he's trying."

I never let a session pass without asking her opinion about why her father would talk to her. She didn't know.

I asked her, "Are you doing anything he would object to?"

"Plenty," she answered.

"What, for instance?" I asked. But she didn't say anything. Again I saw that Mona Lisa smile. I couldn't make sense out of it. Was she deliberately withholding an answer because she didn't trust me? Or was she slipping away as one might on a ship brought out to sea by the tide, so that I was seeming more distant and unreal to her?

I kept beseeching her to tell me what her father was saying, but she couldn't. She did volunteer, "I know he's talking only to me."

"How do you know that, Jessica?"

She smiled, but she seemed confused.

I had wanted to think of the voice as less than a true hallucination. Examples of bereavement fantasies, often quite vivid, came to me—experiences of patients in my own practice. Involuntarily, I sought as precedents people who were grounded and otherwise quite lucid who reported such experiences. I recalled a moving poem by Heinrich Heine, whose "Old love came in weeping/From Death's immense domain." And had not Shakespeare given the expression "in my mind's eye" to Hamlet to describe Hamlet's experience of his father's coming back to him from the grave? I told myself that such experiences were not in themselves proof of insanity.

But I could not so console myself. Jessica's grip on reality was slipping. Sitting a few feet from me in my office, she was supernally far away.

She heard the voice again, this time accompanied by music, and it made no sense to her except that her father was happy.

"I'm not imagining it. Do you think I am?" she asked, and I could tell that she wasn't actually asking but was testing me to see if I was truly on her side and trustworthy.

"I believe you," I said, not sure what I believed, except that the voice itself was a symptom of a generalized collapse of order, of meaning, as when a city is set on fire and chaos reigns.

By that time Jessica refused to talk about her nightclub act, asserting only, "You don't want to hear about that."

She started coming late, then very late. I protested that we needed all the time we could get, but she hardly heard me. She had given up on me, and I didn't blame her. I wondered if I had done the right thing in surfacing her use of humor. By assisting her to see that mechanism, and to see herself employing it, had I removed the membrane between sanity and insanity? Had I involuntarily brought on the collapse I now was witnessing?

I began to think that my approach had been premature. I should have waited before touching Jessica's comic aspect, which disguised her fey ideas, clothing them as inventions designed to entertain. By making her starkly aware of her ready use of humor, and self-conscious about it, I had robbed her of her disguise both for the public and for herself. I hated myself.

And suppose the voice was, in actuality, telling Jessica to do something, among its instructions might well be one not to inform anyone of her mission. Patients in mental hospitals have on occasion concealed their messages, maintaining that they no longer hear a voice and so have earned their release. In some cases it has been discovered too late that their missions involved suicide or murder. I didn't suspect violence here, but I wondered if indeed the voice was telling Jessica more than she let on. And if this were not the case, were there "command hallucinations" in store for Jessica, perhaps soon?

I pleaded with her in one session, "If the voice tells you to do anything, please call me and let's talk about it."

She said she would.

By then she was hearing the voice more often. "I'm starting to forget things," she said. "And when he doesn't talk to me, I don't like that either. I'm half waiting for him. He's driving me crazy."

She told me that she had taken a new job on a cruise ship and would be leaving in about two weeks. Then she added, "I won't be seeing you before that. I'll be busy working on my routine and getting ready."

I could feel myself being phased out, perhaps deservedly, but I hated the idea of losing and I didn't want her to disappear. I asked her why she had changed her mind about that kind of work. She gave me reasons—the pay was good, she could rehearse new material, the summer was dead in New York anyhow—but I knew the real reason, and brought it up.

"It's to get away from the voice, isn't it?" I asked her.

She nodded her head yes.

"Do you think you really will?" I asked her.

"Of course I will."

Although I was sure she was wrong, I had no intention of confronting her. I even had an eerie sense that any refutation of mine might open her up to the voice at sea. Reflecting upon that motive later, I concluded that it wasn't as bizarre as it seemed. Jessica in her present state was remarkably suggestible.

At first I questioned whether such suggestibility was a trait of psychosis. We are taught to think of emotional disturbance as insulated, and of the sufferer as almost hermetically sealed off against what other people say. But then I realized that the "waxy flexibility" for which catatonic patients are so well known, which results in their holding for hours any physical posture that one places them in, is, after all, a flexibility of the mind. My possible impact on Jessica was somewhat analogous: nearly anything I might say could leave an imprint more durable than I had intended.

I was glad that she had her nightclub routines to occupy her, and her knot of fellow performers, who continued to meet regularly and who apparently welcomed her. That week they had exchanged clever lines on how to cope with hecklers in the audience, and afterward Jessica had tried out a few on the voice to discourage it, but in vain.

Jessica turned down my request to see her once more before the cruise, but she agreed to stay in touch on the phone. She said she would come in to my office after returning.

Before leaving that day, she extended her hand. I took it, though even then I recognized the finality in that gesture of hers. Jessica had no intention of seeing me again, ever. I had failed her. The voice had won.

I pleaded with her one final time: "If the voice does tell you to do something, don't just do it. Please call me and let me know. Make your own judgment."

Then she left.

The next day I thought of Jean-Paul Sartre's line "If a voice speaks to me, it is I who must decide if it is that of an angel."

Over my adult life that line has burst into my mind as often as Jessica's voice burst into hers; it seemed especially applicable now.

Jessica didn't keep her promise to call me. I hadn't expected her to. I called her a few days before her cruise ship was to leave and was glad that she seemed pleased to hear from me. I think she still liked me, though I had failed her. She promised to stay in touch, and I wished her the best. There seemed nothing more for either of us to say.

While Jessica was gone, I talked with a few colleagues about the case. But beyond their agreeing that since medical tests had uncovered nothing the cause must be psychogenic, they could offer no useful insights. I found myself going down the list of possible causes of auditory hallucinations, sometimes involuntarily, but nothing new came to me either.

Toward the end of September, when I realized that Jessica had been back for a few weeks, I felt bad that she hadn't contacted me. I called her. Her answering machine promised a return call as soon as she got the message. But a few days later I still hadn't heard from her.

I tried again, and when again she didn't call me back, I considered that she might be avoiding me. However, as the days went by, I had the worse worry that something really bad had happened. I tried her at several night spots where I knew she had entertained. Those who answered had no idea where she was either, and didn't care.

Finally someone did know. It was that MC with the raspy voice who had introduced Jessica to the audience the night I'd seen her act. "Oh, Jessie! She's not working clubs anymore. She works only cruises."

Instantly I recalled her phrase "a man without a country." Could it be that she truly didn't hear the voice on those cruises and in desperate resignation had settled for the life of an eternal wanderer to escape the voice? Nothing else seemed as likely. I consoled myself with the thought that at least she had kept her apartment.

I left a last message on her home tape, entreating her to call me back when she returned, just to let me know how things were going.

About a month later she called and told me quite simply, "Things are the same. I guess I'm just different from other people, that's all." She was being polite, rather than burden me with the anguish that she was suffering.

"Okay, let's just stay in touch," I said, more in hope of a miracle than because I expected any insight.

The miracle, if it was one, came wholly unexpectedly, about four months later.

Early one morning I was reading the newspaper over coffee in a local restaurant, when a conversation sprang up around me.

Some of the breakfast regulars were trying to remember the various wives that Charlie Chaplin had divorced. Among the participants in the discussion were Burt, a businessman, in his usual rumpled black suit; Marcie, an authoritative woman who looked like a young Margaret Thatcher; and another woman, a tensile jogger with a crew cut, whose name I didn't know.

Then they started talking about those terrific old movie musicals and wondering why Hollywood doesn't make them anymore.

I heard Burt say, "They used to have great stars. What happened to them?"

They all contributed names—Joan Davis, Dennis Morgan, Evelyn Keyes, and others from out of the past.

I was back in the sports section when I heard them discussing a film whose name they couldn't remember.

"The lead was a really good-looking guy. I think his name was Michael O'Shea," one of them said.

"Yeah, and that Brazilian singer, what was her name? She started hearing voices in that picture, right? She thought she was a radio, didn't she?" said someone.

"What do you mean, she thought she was a radio?" I asked before I knew it.

"The star of this picture. She thinks she's a radio. Nobody knows what it is at first. But then it turns out she's got some metal in her tooth, and she starts picking up all kinds of radio stations."

"What was the name of the movie?" I asked, as if my life hung in the balance.

"Carmen Miranda," said Burt. "Yeah, she was great. You remember that song about the bananas—"

" 'Chiquita Bacana,' " someone said.

I implored them to tell me anything more they could about the film. But that was all they could remember—Carmen Miranda and Michael O'Shea were in it, and Carmen Miranda heard voices.

"Do you think that could really happen?" one of them asked.

My mind was spinning as I tried to process the information. Could this conceivably have happened to Jessica? For reasons I couldn't yet put my finger on, it seemed more than a mere possibility that it had.

Logically, I realized, the odds were very much against Jessica's having a "dental radio." Since I had never heard of the phenomenon, it had to be extremely rare. In fact, it might even have been the screenwriter's fantasy. At the time I couldn't explain the exhilaration I felt. I experienced a sense of discovery, as if I knew more than I had a right to know.

Only later that day, after I'd had time to think it through, did I see why I had been so excited. I had sensed a lot of other evidence clicking into place that I was beginning to identify. Jessica had seemed especially subject to hearing the voice when she was in a particular neighborhood, the one near her mother's home. She had reported being out of its reach when she went down into the subway. And surely I had been most influenced by the fact that she could apparently escape the messages by going on cruise ships, at sea she would be utterly out of the range of ordinary radio transmission.

It was Burt who had asked me if that kind of thing could really happen, and he was asking me again.

I told him I didn't know. But without saying so, I resolved to find out.

My first step would be to try to track down the film script. Conceivably, if the story was based on a real-life incident, the script would offer some clue about how to find out about that incident. It might even mention the case itself. It could narrow my search through the medical and dental literature.

The next afternoon I went to a local theater bookshop. After a quick survey of Carmen Miranda's credits, the owner found the name of the film; it was called *Something for the Boys* and indeed costarred Michael O'Shea. The original writers were Dorothy and Herbert Fields, the owner told me. But the film had been released way back in 1944, and he had no idea how I could get hold of the shooting script, or any other script for that matter.

My next stop was the Lincoln Center Library, to which students of the performing arts flock from all over the country. After an hour's research I found that the film was based on a play of the same name by the same writers. It had starred Ethel Merman and had been on Broadway a year before the movie came out. The librarian had no difficulty locating the script for me.

In the play, Blossom, the heroine, worked on an assembly line as part of the war effort. One day she said there was too much noise and asked her friends to turn off their radio. They said they didn't have a radio, and after the usual movie confusion, her friend Twitch figured out what was happening.

Twitch decided that since Blossom was hearing music, as well as ads from a chop suey palace, she had somehow turned into a radio. "I tell you, my noisy friend, you are the equivalent of a receiving set," Twitch explained to her.

Somehow the characters pinpointed the exact cause. Small flakes of a metal called carborundum, used on the assembly line and virtually as hard as a diamond, had lodged in Blossom's mouth. The particles had induced a current to flow, and the miniature radio thus created by accident was broadcasting the sounds to Blossom.

However, the script gave no clue to an actual case on which this might be based. And one thing suggested that the authors had not taken their story from reality. They had not seen the horror of the experience, or at least had not conveyed it. What proved fun in Hollywood's version was certainly no fun for Jessica.

As I proceeded in my inquiries, I sometimes felt a bit other-worldly myself. I began talking to some dentists and oral surgeons. The first few could tell me nothing, but then one, considerably older than the others, said he had heard of such a case. He generously arranged permission for me to do research at the New York University Dental Library. However, I didn't have the slightest idea of how to look for the phenomenon—under what headings, in what categories.

Slowly I located more dental experts who said that they had also heard of such occurrences. But they were so completely unable to document their memories that I suspected they'd only seen the play or film, or had spoken to someone who had.

Five months had gone by since I'd talked with Jessica, and I worried that she might be getting worse. If the voice was a symptom of psychotic disturbance, she could be deteriorating. Worse delusions might be slowly eclipsing her judgment. And even if Jessica was an essentially stable person, and merely victimized by an unexplained natural phenomenon, she would surely break down before long. Few of us are so intact that we can hear a capricious voice talking to us over a lifetime without going at least half mad.

I thought about Jessica in perpetual flight on those cruises. I wanted to call her, but as yet I had nothing to offer beyond a statement of concern. Technically she wasn't my patient anymore; it had been her choice to end therapy, and it didn't seem fair for me to chase after her unless I had at least the hope of something tangible to present to her.

Soon after that I spoke with Dr. Hank Schenker, a psychotherapist with an engineering background and a broad range of interests. He gave me some insight into how the radio phenomenon could occur. "Certain substances—carborundum is one—can produce a diode action," he explained, "that is, an electric current that flows only one way. That's just about all you'd need to receive broadcast signals."

He explained that bone conduction in the head might translate the message. In fact, Dr. Schenker told me, the so-called cat's whisker radios built in the twenties relied on little more than a galena crystal, which would work like carborundum. The gist of it was, Dr. Schenker assured me, that Dorothy and Herbert Fields weren't simply imagining the possibility of such a phenomenon.

A few days later Dr. Schenker called me with an afterthought. My patient's hearing those pulsing sounds—that too was consistent with the radio hypothesis, he said. That throbbing noise might be music heard very indistinctly. Bass sounds carry far better than treble ones. We've nearly all had the experience of hearing only the pounding beat of music coming from a radio or TV on another floor of a building. He suggested that perhaps my patient's experience was akin to that.

I was almost there, but in another sense I was nowhere, I thought to myself.

I still hoped I could give Jessica something real, but for that I would need more evidence. Then it occurred to me that I ought to go to a professional researcher.

David Shulman, a noted researcher, was the person I called. He took on the assignment, promising nothing. But his reputation and the fact that *The Oxford English Dictionary* turned to him so often were promise enough. On the phone he asked me if the reviews of the play had mentioned whether it was based on a real incident. I felt like a fool. I had never even looked up the reviews.

A few days later Shulman read me the original *New York Times* review over the phone, and it did indeed report that the play was based on real occurrences. Shulman said that besides looking through dental and medical abstracts, he planned to consult a specialist in dental materials and at least one expert on early radio broadcasting.

In his research Shulman learned that carborundum was once used in drill bits for just the same reason that it had been used in factories, because it was both hard and abrasive. The specialist in dental materials told him that the wearing away of a denture, resulting in metallic contact, could produce what amounted to a radio receiver.

Now we had established that a radio could be formed by accident in the mouth. But for a month Shulman met with no more success than I had in his attempt to dig up a documented case of such a radio having been created.

Then one morning Shulman called and said he had something interesting to show me. I met him for coffee, and he handed me an article that appeared in the October 1933 issue of *Scientific American* under the heading "Metals in Teeth May Generate Electricity."

I read it in fascination. It included the following passages:

It is well known that when teeth are repaired or replaced with different kinds of metals, electricity may be generated in the mouth. . . . Cases in which this electricity causes pain and sores in the mouth were recently reported to the American Medical Association by Everett S. Lain. . . .

Human saliva is a good electrolyte, Dr. Lain has found from repeated experiments. Thus every mouth in which there are plates, bridges, crowns or fillings of dissimilar metals may become a complete *galvanic battery*.

It was a tantalizing article, mentioning the existence of documented cases, though, admittedly, it still didn't give me names, dates, or details.

However, better evidence was coming soon.

A few weeks later Shulman called me excitedly and read me a piece that had appeared in the *New York Times* in January 1934. It was a bull's-eye!

HIS EARS A RECEIVING SET, UKRAINIAN SEEKS RELIEF

RIO DE JANEIRO. News comes from Paranha that a Ukrainian, long resident of that State, has applied to the medical authorities of Curityba for advice and relief. His complaint is rather unique. He asserts that his ears, radio-like, register broadcast sounds; in fact, he is a walking antenna.

In these hard times, when many citizens would like to own,

but cannot afford to buy a radio, it is held that this Ukrainian should feel highly elated in owning an irremovable receiving-set. On the contrary, however, he wishes to be rid of this gift or to be at least provided with means of shutting it off. He asserts it is injuring his health, because the noises keep him awake at all hours of the night.

Finally I had an actual story of a normal person who was physically picking up radio broadcasts by a strange accident. True, I still lacked plenty of details. I wasn't even sure that the teeth were at fault in the Brazilian case, though I suspected they were.

Then for the first time I felt queasy about everything I'd been doing, doubtless because my having to act on the information was coming closer as a reality. How should I proceed with the knowledge?

I pictured myself calling Jessica. "Jessica, please go to a dentist so he can look for a radio in your mouth."

If ever an experience would feel uncanny to her, it would be that of hearing me say this.

Of course, I could approach her more diplomatically. "How are you today? I have a theory . . ."

But no matter how I imagined telling Jessica, I felt absurd. I realized that it was harder for me to broach the issue of getting her teeth checked than it had been to ask her to go for the brain scans. Frightening to Jessica as the prospect of brain scans had been, at least that request had a plausibility that she could grasp. But this one seemed utterly out of left field.

Jessica might, understandably, consider me weird, or worse yet, she might not know what to think. What could be more upsetting to someone already confused about the real and the unreal than a phone call from a therapist that itself sounded bizarre?

I felt caught between reluctance to call Jessica and a sense of obligation to call her. I likened myself to one of those Board of Health workers in old movies who discover that someone has come into contact with a deadly virus and doesn't know it.

I was still considering how to proceed when my final piece of evidence arrived.

I had lunch with a former mentor of mine, a psychiatrist I'd known for many years. I told him about my patient who reported a voice, and my radio hypothesis, and instead of being taken aback, he said he'd heard of such things.

The psychiatrist told me that when he had been a first-year resident at Pilgrim State Hospital, he had heard a story that itself had been making the rounds for years. Apparently, two men had been admitted to Pilgrim within weeks of each other, both hearing voices. The two, who did not know each other, worked as metal grinders in local factories, and both were released when it was discovered that metallic substances had lodged in their teeth, producing the radio effect. However, my friend could supply absolutely no documentation of the story beyond his own memory.

It seemed now that I really had to call Jessica. I could imagine her literally being driven mad by the voice. The gain in helping her would be immense; compared with it, my embarrassment and the inconvenience to her if I intruded into her life and we failed seemed trivial. With such an imbalance, I realized I had to try, no matter how outlandish what I had to say might seem.

I called Jessica, expecting to get her answering machine, as I usually did. I was relieved when she herself answered on the third ring.

As before, she seemed glad to hear from me, perhaps partly because I had kept her secret and never condemned her for the voice. We chatted about her comedy routines and how she was faring generally.

"Do you still hear the voice from time to time?" I asked, and realized instantly how preposterous I seemed trying to sound off-handed about it.

She told me she still did, and when I commented, "I wonder why you never hear it on those cruises," she repeated her explanation, that out there she was utterly relaxed and under no stress.

Then she asked me if I believed in God.

I didn't answer but wondered if she'd begun to think it was God talking to her. If so, it might not be long before she got specific orders and followed them—that thought scared me.

I told her I had called because I'd had an idea. I invited her to come in for twenty minutes, adding that I wouldn't charge her for the time. It seemed only fair to present such a farfetched thesis in person, and I also wanted her there so that I could try to prevail on her if she dismissed my suggestion at first.

Jessica seemed very willing to come in, and we set a time.

That week I called Dr. Gayle Grenadier, who was then Chief of Staff of Oral Surgery at St. Luke's-Roosevelt Hospital. She was one of those I had consulted early on in the case. And now I hoped that she would agree to see Jessica and look for the radio, if Jessica was willing to let her.

I thought that Dr. Grenadier, a young woman, might seem less frightening to Jessica than a man would. And besides, as well as being an expert in her own profession, Dr. Grenadier knew a great deal about electricity. I was delighted when she consented to so offbeat an assignment as searching for a possible radio and removing it. I trusted Dr. Grenadier completely, and since I doubted that Jessica would try twice, I wanted to make sure that she saw the best person I knew.

I put one of Dr. Grenadier's cards into my wallet to have it ready for Jessica.

Jessica came in on the dot, and I thought it best to dispense with small talk. She knew that I had something very particular to say to her, and my starting out with chitchat would only make it seem ominous.

I told her I had an idea about what might be causing the voice. "By the way," I asked, "have you had a lot of dental work done, especially in recent years?"

"Oh, you heard my dental routine," she said, and beamed.

I told her I hadn't.

"Oh!" She looked disappointed. "Yes, I did. I guess my teeth are not my strong point."

"You mean you have a comedy routine about dentists that you based on your own experiences?" I asked her.

"Four minutes. That's a long time, but I'm cutting it. I go to a dentist, and he starts asking me about my molars, and I tell him, 'Doc, I'll tell you the truth. To me, my mouth is a mystery.' We go on from there. Everything he does, he asks me a stupid question. Even when he's got instruments in my mouth. I'm afraid if I don't know the answers, he's just going to pull my teeth out."

She was practically onstage, doing her routine, when I broke in.

I said, "So you had a lot of work done? Anyhow, it's possible that a tooth has something to do with the voice—"

"You mean my teeth are talking to me?"

I laughed at her joke and had an instant misgiving. But then I asked myself, "Why not? She *is* funny, and I'm not trying to surface a resistance anymore."

Then I told her the story about the two patients who went into Pilgrim State Hospital until they found the source of the voice.

Now it was Jessica's turn to laugh. "You do some pretty good material, yourself, doc. I knew I always liked you for a reason."

I assured her that though it sounded weird, such things apparently happened. She only half believed me when I told her about the play and the movie based on it. But when I showed her the clipping about the Ukrainian who wanted to get rid of his radio, her eyebrows rose.

I told her that no one could be absolutely sure about any one of these cases, but with so many quite independent instances, I absolutely believed that the thing did occur sometimes.

"You mean maybe I'm not crazy?" she asked.

"I never thought you were," I assured her.

When I asked her if she had ever felt pain that the dentists couldn't understand, she said that she had, but then observed that I sounded like the dentist in her comedy routine. She deepened her voice in mimicry of her dentist as she said, " 'I want you to *name* the *pain!* ' "

I could imagine that it was a very funny routine and told her so.

"Funny to you, maybe. Not to me," she said, sounding hurt.

"Jessica, I didn't mean to laugh—"

"No, that's just a line in my routine. I say it to the audience. It gets a laugh."

"I have another article to show you," I told her, and took out the one about Professor Lain, who talked about the possibility of accidental galvanic batteries in the mouth causing pain.

Jessica read it fast and then said with mock seriousness, "I'm always suspicious when a guy named Lain talks about pain."

Jessica had kept things light so far, and I was very pleased. It seemed quite natural for me to say, "Jessica, we've got to check it out."

"I know," she said. She brought up the idea of going back to her old dentist, but demurred.

She seemed pleased when I told her that I had made arrangements for her to see Dr. Grenadier if she wanted to, that I knew her to be at the very top of the field of oral surgery. "She doesn't think the whole idea is so farfetched," I told Jessica.

I offered to call Dr. Grenadier myself with Jessica in my office, but she told me she would prefer to call.

When Jessica was gone, I realized that I hadn't needed to use any of the various approaches that I'd rehearsed—apologizing for breaking in on her life, admitting that this solution was truly not within my field and, technically, none of my business, or emphasizing the need to try everything we could possibly think of.

I wondered how often she was actually hearing the voice these days. Something she had said on the phone suggested that it was weekly or even more often. But I couldn't recall exactly what it was.

A few days later Dr. Grenadier called and reported that Jessica had made an appointment to see her.

I had moments of feeling almost certain that we'd really located the origin of the voice. Of course, even if Dr. Grenadier found what seemed to be a diode in Jessica's mouth and removed it, we wouldn't know right away whether it was the basis of a radio that had been producing what Jessica heard.

But if after that Jessica heard nothing for a month, we could be pretty sure. And if she still didn't hear anything after two months, we could start celebrating. Jessica hadn't been free of those intrusions of sound for more than a few weeks during the last half year.

The day of her appointment with Dr. Grenadier came and went. I had half expected Jessica to call me, but she didn't.

The next day I called Dr. Grenadier. She was in surgery but got back to me an hour later. "Your patient had an enormous amount of metal in a partial denture put in two years ago," she told me. "And there was a gold crown on the abutment tooth. That could easily have done it."

She explained that an abutment tooth is the one a bridge is attached to. She told me, "I didn't measure voltage, but I wouldn't be surprised if there was a lot of current flowing one way up there."

She said that she had taken the gold crown off the abutment tooth, had put in a temporary plastic one, and had sent Jessica to a dentist for a porcelain crown.

"No more radio?" I asked.

"If that was the radio, it's gone," was all Dr. Grenadier would volunteer.

We agreed to watch the case together.

After Jessica went to the dentist and got the final crown replacement, she called me. It had been nearly a week, and so far she hadn't heard the voice. She felt good about that, but it was hardly indicative. She'd gone much longer stretches without hearing it.

As lightly as I could, I suggested that we stay in touch, and she said okay. She promised to call me on the Friday of the following week.

I did a fast calculation to myself. If she still hadn't heard the voice by then, it would be thirteen days.

When Jessica did call that Friday and said things were still quiet, that she still hadn't heard the voice, I began to feel like a genius.

When I went out for coffee one morning later that week, the breakfast regulars at the local diner suddenly looked better to me than they ever had. I had the curious feeling that I ought to pay attention to their conversation; though it might sound trivial, it had yielded one gem and might contain others. I listened to their speculations about how much money Michael Jackson made per concert, as if I half expected to glean something potentially useful. As I said good-bye to them, I mused that this morning I hadn't learned anything, but who could tell about the future?

I was starting to feel increasingly confident of our proof that Jessica's voice had been a dental radio and nothing more. As I savored my success, I went back over the case in my mind. I had worked in several mental hospitals, and even in my office I had treated many patients who had heard voices. Some of these had been drug users, others were psychotic, and still others had neurological problems of one kind or another. But never in all my practice had I gone looking for some cause that was, strictly speaking, neither psychological nor medical. So what had led me to consider Jessica a special case and to welcome the offbeat explanation that I had pursued?

With medical causes eliminated by the battery of brain scans and other tests that Jessica had undergone, drug use or psychosis would, ordinarily, have had an absolute claim. But in spite of Jessica's constant playing with reality, she had seemed honest, and I believed her assurances that she didn't use drugs.

And why had I decided that the voice was not a psychotic symptom? The main reason was that in general when a psychotic person hears an imaginary voice, the voice is distinct. A voice created by a psychotic person has some function in the person's psyche. Typically it represents a particular impulse or fear and *formulates it in words*. The voice would, for example, tell the person to punish himself, or avenge himself, or do something or not do something. The fact that Jessica's voice had spoken to her indistinctly, while not ruling out psychosis, had made it very unlikely. Moreover, Jessica had no other discernible symptoms of psychosis—at least none that I could see. She came across as a person without either mood disorder or gross confusion, and more than capable of running her life.

At the same time, all her descriptions of the sounds she'd heard had a curious familiarity. It was that familiarity, which I had subsensibly registered, that had led me to feel that I was hearing something relevant and important when the breakfast regulars talked about the radio in the film. It was a familiarity based on a number of facts that I must have observed.

As I thought about it, I went over some of those facts. I had already realized the significance of Jessica's hearing the voice in a certain neighborhood, the one her mother lived in, which was doubtless in a good position to pick up a certain signal; and of her losing the signal when she went underground to the subway or left the neighborhood; and, of course, of her not hearing anything out at sea.

And now as I thought about it more, I could fit other details into the explanation. The only words that had come through intelligibly were numbers, that weird line about the stun gun and the phrase "Have a good day."

It occurred to me that those numbers might have been weather forecasts—they were apt for the time of year when Jessica heard them. The advice to have a good day could easily have been a radio announcer signing off. As for the line about the stun gun, perhaps those were words in some rock song that I'd never heard. Or maybe they even came from an ad—all I could think of was an ad for some kind of garden spray or roach killer.

Perhaps if I'd had nothing else on earth to do, I would have contacted all the local radio stations to find out where their signal carried. I would have inquired if they'd been running an ad or playing a popular song that contained the words "stun gun" at around the time that Jessica heard those words. Sherlock Holmes might have done that utilizing the footwork of the whole of Scotland Yard, but such detective work would have been full-time employment, and I could hardly do it. Anyhow, it scarcely mattered now. A few more weeks, certainly another month or two without a voice, and the dental hypothesis would be proved.

Jessica kept in touch with me, and when five weeks had elapsed without her hearing a sound, I was almost sure we had removed the voice. Grandiosely I credited not just myself but my army of experts with curing her of her radio. I wondered how many other people who suffered inexplicable pain or heard sounds were also responding to accidental batteries. Of course, I had been lucky. With absolutely nothing in the recent literature, others were unlikely to stumble upon the solution. I resolved that after another month—no, two or three, to make sure—I would write up the phenomenon in a professional journal.

I spoke to Jessica on the day that marked exactly eight weeks since the receptor had been dismantled. She was feeling exuberant. She had gone to her mother's house, stayed overnight—and heard nothing. "No sign of a signal," was the way she put it.

"You told me you would get rid of the voices, and I always believed you," Jessica said. "I know I didn't act as if I did, but I always did. I believed in you completely. I never had any doubt."

Not knowing what to say, I just thanked her.

She surprised me by adding, "I'm sorry. I shouldn't have kidded around as much as I did. But I put my complete faith in you. You were all I had."

Now I really felt on the spot. Right after we hung up, I busied myself in something, out of an unexamined desire not to think about the call. However, that evening and the next day, I could sense something luminous in the dark that kept beckoning me. It was that last call, which kept glowing in my mind, and finally I paid it attention.

I realized that Jessica's absolute faith in me made me very uncomfortable. Even her certainty that the voice was gone troubled me, though I believed it was too. Now if it came back, it would be truly devastating to her. I hated to think of myself as having been her last hope, but, apparently, I was.

Then I remembered her word "faith," and I saw what had so upset me. Suppose there were no dental radio at all and never had been one. If Jessica, having unconsciously created the voice, had believed strongly enough that she was removing it, perhaps she did in fact banish it. If that were the case, her faith in me had been critical. But this meant that I had unknowingly provided her with a ritual and nothing more. It seemed increasingly possible as I remembered how highly suggestible Jessica was.

I thought about the widespread employment of similar rituals—of faith cures, of licensed physicians giving placebos to patients all over the world. Resort to such practices predates history itself perhaps by a million years, and the primordial impulse to employ them seems immanent in the human brain. Perhaps in helping Jessica banish the voice, I had done no more than play the role of sage, of "ritual knower" in any of the prehistoric tribes. With this thought in mind, I mused, I would be more appropriate reporting my cure of Jessica to some folklorist, perhaps sending it for inclusion in an updated version of Sir James Frazer's *The Golden Bough*, than writing it up for a modern scientific journal.

And suddenly it crossed my mind why if there were other cures of this kind, they too had not been reported. How could an expert prove what he had done, or even know for sure that he had removed a dental radio? One would have to put such a radio back in and remove it a number of times to ascertain that it was the cause, and all that without telling the person.

Another month went by, and another—and still Jessica heard nothing. I found it hard to accept that we would never know if we had removed a real radio or not. From Jessica's standpoint, it might not matter, so long as she never heard the voice again. But if there had been no radio, then the stun gun, the advice to have a good day, those mysterious numbers, all had been Jessica's creations, and she had removed them with a stroke, the way one annihilates a world of dreams by the single act of waking up.

I also hated to think that all those who I imagined had contributed their expertise to Jessica's cure might in reality have played no part in it at all. The breakfast regulars, my colleague with the engineering background, my researcher, the oral surgeon—it was hard to accept that the contributions of all those people had been irrelevant.

I spoke to Jessica after six more months, and there was still no sign of the voice. By then she was convinced that it was gone forever, and so was I.

Only then did it occur to me that even if the voice were imaginary and we had banished it by ritual, my various experts had each contributed to the cure. Without the breakfast regulars, I would never have had the idea, and had it not been for my diligent researcher I would not have put it into practice. And whether the oral surgeon removed a real radio or not, her expertise and the confidence she inspired in Jessica proved the turning point in the case.

My realization that, either way, these people all contributed to Jessica's cure made it easier for me to accept the possibility that there never was a real radio. I believe there was, but though I met Jessica in the street five years later and the voice was still gone, it remains impossible to know.

It was sometime after that, perhaps a year before this writing, that Louie the policeman told me his story about recommending silver foil to elderly people who complained of hearing voices. Louie told me that his method succeeded with more than one person, and I had no reason to doubt him.

the

promised

land

ELINOR HAD BECOME A STRANGER
to optimism in the last six months,
which surprised her because she'd
always been a cheerful person. She
had chosen operating room nursing because she could buoy the
spirits of the most downcast patient facing surgery. Her friends,
who had always enjoyed her, were
all astonished at the change that
had taken place in her recently.
Obviously her relationship with
Larry, a fledgling surgeon, wasn't

doing what it was supposed to do. I had seen her for four months, and when she spoke about him, it was always tonelessly. She never smiled when she mentioned him.

Elinor was barely twenty-two, Larry was ten years older, with family money as well as a steadily increasing income of his own. He was the only man she had ever slept with; that had been twice in his New York co-op apartment and one night in the family home in East Hampton.

"What was it like?" I asked her.

"I don't know. I guess I'm very inhibited. He kept calling me young and saying I have a beautiful body. It embarrassed me. He said I looked young even for my age. I asked him, 'How do you know?' He just smiled. He said I have beautiful, long greyhound legs. I felt funny. He said I'd get over it."

Larry was a hard-muscled, well-dressed type who jogged four miles before breakfast every day. He watched his calories, and though Elinor was quite thin, he wanted her to do the same. And she tried to. But in his absence, feeling depressed, she would get ice-cream sandwiches out of the hospital vending machine.

Elinor was a pale young woman with a pretty face; she was elegantly tall but sabotaged her appearance by poor posture. Her hair was cut short, "So I don't have to fuss with it and can put a scrub cap on easily."

Though she wasn't happy with Larry, she had no thought of turning him away either. He was important to her, but not simply because he was a successful doctor who could upgrade her social status by marrying her. She was impressed by his accomplishments and worldliness, but if he hadn't initially kept after her for dates, she would never have gone out with him.

Nor was it clear why he wanted her, unless her very indifference whetted his appetite. She never telephoned him, and she showed no hint of jealousy when he was busy for a week and didn't call. In what seemed to me an attempt by him to provoke a reaction, he once said that he would consider marrying her if she got more mature. Far from showing elation, she didn't even ask him what he meant. When he got angry with her for not replying, she said simply, "I'm sorry. I guess I should have."

With me too she could best be described as obedient. She was respectful, never disagreed or raised her voice, thanked me after every session. Such compliance is invisible for a time, since the patient is ostensibly doing what the therapist wants. But before long I began to feel that I was with someone virtually under post-hypnotic suggestion. And though Larry was often bombastic and condescending, I could understand some of his frustration. She was a mirror who, far from reflecting back to him the picture of himself that he wanted to see, swallowed the reflection and showed him no picture of himself at all.

As I learned about her childhood, I came to understand more about her presentation of herself as so compliant and low-key. She had assumed it as a shield in a volatile and abusive home. Her parents, both second-generation Welsh, felt constantly in danger in New York City. While her father was working days in a hardware store, her mother kept enlarging the catalogue of her fears by succumbing to one after another. For instance, Elinor's mother was afraid of crossing the street near her apartment building because the cars came off the highway too fast and also because the pollution from the buses might kill her. She was terrified of the superintendent of their building, an Oriental she imbued with magical powers.

Both parents foresaw instant ruination if someone lost a credit card or filled out a wrong number on a form. Her mother loved to tell the story of how Elinor once almost devoured six aspirins, and the story of how a ladder had fallen onto Elinor's bed minutes after the little girl had gotten up to go to the bathroom.

With Elinor's father doing all the financial providing, her mother eventually reduced her range of activities to going shopping in the neighborhood, returning home, and staying there. The family had only one or two friends, and after her mother imagined that one of her father's fellow employees flirted with her, they stopped having people over.

Elinor could recall a childhood full of seemingly hairbreadth escapes and near misses. Almost daily, troubled shrieks from another room would bring her father running to see what had gone wrong in her mother's life this time. Her mother might be screaming because a book had fallen down or the cat was prowling too near a vase. Or Elinor herself was doing something amiss.

Elinor, an only child, got scolded for virtually every kind of personal preference. She was told to turn off classical music, not to pray for too much, not to read too much, and to appreciate Joe McCarthy for protecting the world from left-wingers. If the little girl's mind went too far in any direction, to her parents she was a communist.

The worst part was that at her mother's request, or if her mother seemed distraught and her father concluded it was Elinor's doing, he would take Elinor aside and spank her. Not surprisingly, Elinor felt stupid growing up, and had terrible nightmares. And sometimes in the middle of the night her father would wallop her even for those.

Her period of rebellion must have been short, if there was any at all. She soon hit on the low-profile, seemingly docile style, and it served her well. She became a favorite of the teachers at her religious school and was silent in the home. She never had friends over, boys or girls, though she was encouraged to seek out the company of one little girl, Etta, who I concluded was either utterly broken in spirit or was playing Elinor's game of seeming so, by following every rule and always looking respectful.

All the while, however, Elinor had fantasies of escape. At six and seven she would envision the magic land of Tiff Tiff, where the inhabitants loved one another and played together and considered her very smart. In Tiff Tiff she was a leader, renowned for her kindness toward even the least important citizen. She would imagine herself giving them lectures on how to behave, while they listened reverently.

Once, walking down the street, she was delivering such a lecture and to her embarrassment was overheard by a classmate. She was careful never again to refer to Tiff Tiff aloud. The land of Tiff Tiff was her personal secret, and her face reddened when she finally told me about it. Tiff Tiff reminded me of the wondrous nation that the Pied Piper promised the children in his music, which only children could understand, and that they thought he was leading them to.

How would she reach that land? *When* was clear; she would reach it "someday"—and that sufficed. But when I asked her *how*, she smiled and said she didn't know.

"Would you go there with someone else or alone?" I asked her.

Her expression was one of innocent surprise. "I guess I'd go there with someone," she said.

She smiled serenely. She could hardly believe we were talking matter-of-factly about what had been a figment, an airy nothing and yet a very important motif of hers for a lifetime. Even in talking about it, in taking her seriously, I was in her territory, and our being there together seemed to make it more real for her, to make her pilgrimage someday more plausible.

"So how do you get to Tiff Tiff on earth?" I asked her.

"It's funny to hear you use that word," she said.

I persisted. "Would it be with Larry?" I asked.

"Maybe, but I would never tell Larry about that. I think Larry's right. I have a lot of growing up to do. Do you think we could have a good life together?" she asked me.

When I didn't answer, she went on. "What bothers me is that Larry is everything that I really want. He knows so much and he's so sure of himself, and he's so successful. He's so respected. I should be happier. I don't deserve him."

Larry, indeed, had the cosmopolitan manner and the wherewithal to improve her life tangibly. He could bring her across the ocean of style to live among the rich and educated. With him she could escape her parents forever. She knew this, and so did her parents. She had brought Larry to their home once, at Christmas, and they were overwhelmed by his charm and his attainments. They stammered, not knowing what to say to him, and that day they addressed her as if she were a highly accomplished stranger who had deigned to visit them along with him. Though Larry didn't flaunt his status, he was subtly condescending toward them, as in his fulsome "Thank you so much for your superb dinner." And they marveled at his Mercedes parked outside. But Elinor seemed not to savor any of this triumph of her having found a better world. In fact, in the next session she told me that she had felt sorry for them.

That night she dreamed that she and a young man were on

shipboard, under the rule of some horrible old sea captain. She begged the young man to jump overboard with her. At first he wouldn't, but she persuaded him to, and, hand in hand, they leaped into the billowing waves together and were happy.

I asked her if the young man was Larry, and she snapped at me, "Definitely not."

Later I thought about the dream. It was an escape fantasy, but not one of being rescued. But that was as far as I got with it.

Her nurse friends would sometimes talk about being saved from their hard labor by marrying a physician or some other prestigious person. But Elinor never joined in. When they said to her that she was lucky to have Larry so interested in her, she told me that she never answered, and I imagined that she looked sad. She showed absolutely no desire to live up to Larry's standards or improve in the ways he suggested.

In fact, I began to see that Elinor was deliberately denying Larry his satisfactions by not putting forth as he wanted. She was always on time for sessions with me, and she said she was never late with friends, but she often remarked that she had arrived late for an appointment with Larry. Her emotional unresponsiveness to him went beyond indifference. I came to see it as defiance, as if she were imparting the message "Don't think that you can get more out of me than I want to give. And that's next to nothing in your case."

Interestingly, it was at moments when Larry was trying to be the most reassuring that Elinor felt saddest.

One afternoon the two of them went to see a videotaped demonstration of a new instrument by a world-renowned surgeon, a Dr. Garrick. The hospital video-screening amphitheater was packed with surgeons and nurses from Larry and Elinor's hospital as well as others. Ostensibly people were there to learn about the new clamp that Dr. Garrick had just invented. But actually they were more excited about watching his famous surgical technique than seeing the new device.

With animation and obvious absorption in the subject, Elinor told me about the tape. "Dr. Garrick was removing a tumor from the large intestine," she said.

"When the film started, the mayo stand was already over the patient and the sterile drape was laid down. I looked at the tray, and there were mostly the basic instruments there—you know, knives, forceps, hemostats, retractors, and needle holders. And I saw the Garrick clamp, which had a strange curve."

Elinor went on to say that it was incredible how quickly Dr. Garrick's hands moved, and how deftly. And his scrub nurse handed him what he needed without his having to ask for it. Elinor heard the surgeons seated around her whispering about Dr. Garrick's speed and sureness, and of course about the use of the special clamp. But Elinor herself was most taken by his extraordinary relationship with his scrub nurse—it seemed so effortless and trusting, without a word being said. The scrub nurse too was a genius, Elinor thought.

In the last few minutes of the film, Dr. Garrick addressed the audience from his office. He had removed the special mask he used to cover his beard; he had silver hair, a long bony nose, and steel-rimmed spectacles. By his manner she could see that he was obviously not a gentle soul. He virtually told the listeners that anyone who doesn't use this clamp is crazy.

Afterward Larry asked her what she had thought. "He sure is wonderful," Elinor told him. "And so is the scrub nurse. I don't know if I could ever be that good—really top-notch like that."

Larry assured her that she could be the best at whatever she went after. He told her that they could have a wonderful life together, at which point she could hardly hold back tears.

In my office she couldn't imagine why she had gotten so upset. Was it that she didn't love him? She wouldn't say that. Yet, as they got closer, she told me, she was crying more often than ever.

Although Larry's occasional condescending behavior bothered me at times, it didn't seem to bother her. Besides, who can become a young surgeon, revered in society, saving lives, always in demand, without some swollen sense of one's own importance? Larry would doubtless settle down. And it did seem that he loved her. If Elinor truly didn't love him, her sorrow would make more sense, her increased depression as they bonded more. But things weren't that simple. I began to sense that there was an extra twist. Something unseen was at work.

With me too there had to be more. She had descended to an even steadier, lower-key course than when she started. In our second and third month she had shown no elation, no despair; she had made no new discoveries. More than once I thought of her as comporting herself as in the operating room—gloves on, never touching anything, simply doing what others, more experienced, expected her to do. Her personal signature was the lack of a signature.

This economy of presentation left me no handle to lift whatever it was that I had to lift.

To my dismay I began to see also that her relationship with me, like that with Larry, was depressing her. She was *afraid* of me. And, just as if she had done with her parents, she was coping with me by going through motions but never revealing anything special or singular about herself. It was as if she were saying to me, as she did to Larry, "I've given you all I choose to. The rest is up to you. Don't think you can get more out of me."

I encouraged her to confide in me.

"Elinor, is there anything important to you, or even not so important, that you have decided not to tell me?"

She assured me no.

Another time, I asked her how she thought I would react if she disclosed having done something her father might disapprove of.

"Oh, I know you wouldn't care."

"How do you know?"

"You've heard everything already in your profession."

When I realized that I was waiting for the collapse of a wall that she had built to withstand the onslaughts of a bull-necked army man five times her weight who would beat her regularly, I told myself that this could be a long siege.

Then it crossed my mind that I still had some untried

leverage—her very compliance might work for me, and for *her* in the long run.

"Elinor, you've been coming here for four months now," I told her. "Is it all right if I give you some assignments?"

"Of course," she said at once. Her alternative was to say that it wasn't, and she was too compliant for that.

"What I want you to do this weekend is go through your life and think of something that you have been withholding from me up to now, that you've decided not to tell me."

She looked suddenly apprehensive. At the time, I felt a little rotten about pulling what seemed like a dirty trick on her.

She agreed, and I let it go.

After she'd gone, I realized that I'd felt bad because I'd seen her blush. It occurred to me that this assignment had brought her to full awareness of something that she had consciously and deliberately been withholding from me from our very first session.

Then I tried to tell myself that I hadn't really used undue force, but had simply confronted her with a paradox much like those that so delighted the ancient Greek philosophers. But I still felt bad. However, for the first time in a while I was very much looking forward to our next session.

Whatever I had anticipated, Elinor certainly didn't come crashing in with any big revelation. She wafted in, in her nurse's outfit, looking depressed. If she'd even thought about my assignment, she didn't let on. I'd given more thought to it than she had—or so it seemed.

She began the session with a diatribe, one commonly brought in by patients, against New York City—the shoving, the squalor, and the rotten way people treat one another. When I asked her what had prompted it, she said that nothing particular had happened, she was just sick of the city. She seemed to be feeling hopeless, and possibly angry with me for not helping her. Or else why choose this particular time to let off steam against a city essentially unchanged? Did she feel that we were making as little progress as New York?

She told me, "I'd like to get out of this city."

"Where would you go?" I asked her.

"I don't know. People around here think I'm sick."

"Who?"

She mentioned Marie and Jennifer, two nurses she worked with, who constantly talked about their dates and who encouraged her to go ahead with Larry.

I asked her, "Why do they think you're sick? Did they say so?"

"No, but they see."

That day a famous plastic surgeon had visited the hospital. Jennifer had told the others that he was from Boston, and showed them an article in the current issue of *People* magazine with his picture. He had done face-lifts on some very famous actresses and newscasters.

Then Marie announced that she'd had a nose job in college, and soon a group of nurses were talking about what kind of plastic surgery they'd like to have done someday. It was a fun conversation until Elinor's turn came. She mentioned that she wanted a small bump taken off her nose. Marie declared, "That would be easy. You'd be as good as new. No one would ever suspect. Anyone can have anything these days."

Even as Elinor repeated those words to me, her pale, drawn face contorted with emotion. A moment later she was crying.

"Why? What did that mean to you?" I asked, aghast.

She was wiping her face when I asked again, "Do you know why you're crying?"

She said yes, and nodded.

Then, to my surprise, she said, "But I don't want to talk about it. I can't. I mustn't."

I felt it would be wrong to push her. We had proceeded a giant step. At last she had admitted that she was deliberately withholding something from me.

Before the session was over, I told her, "Look, Elinor, I'm not pressing you to talk to me. But think to yourself about why you don't want to talk about this. Try to figure out why."

Her answer was quick and definite. "I don't have to think about it. I know why."

I was glad that my instinct had told me to go easy. Only after Elinor was gone did I realize how staunch she had been. Any step of pursuit by me would have driven her ten steps away. In her mind I was the burly inquisitor who would make her pay in pain for whatever I found out concerning her secret. I was her father, who had mocked her and often struck her for whatever about her displeased him.

How could I help her appreciate that I would not humble her or disgrace her? She would need to reconsider that eternal interlude of growing up as her parents' prisoner. If I could prevail upon her to describe those childhood iniquities—to tell me, in as much detail as she could recall, how her parents abused her emotionally—if I could return with her to revisit that dungeon, then after a time she might see the difference between them and me. And after seeing that difference, if only she would confide in me more, confide in me *anything*, she would convince herself that the difference between her father and me was real.

She was very amenable to answering my questions about events that occurred while she was growing up. Apparently her parents screened her girlfriends not only for their own virtue, but to be sure that their parents weren't Jews or blacks or communists.

When Elinor was twelve and her breasts started growing quickly, her father made sure that her blouses hid them. At about that time, when a neighbor told her mother that she looked fifteen, the comment reached her father. He immediately took away from her all the makeup that she was experimenting with, and he lectured her about the embarrassment that her appearance was causing the family—as if her maturation were itself an evil act. Shortly after the Vietnam War began, her father almost broke her arm for saying that she wasn't sure she would join up if she were a boy. Both her parents despised a certain teacher of Elinor's for opposing the war. But though they warned her to avoid that teacher, Elinor sustained a friendship with her, and her parents never found out.

Often after she would tell me about another such iniquity, I would comment that it wasn't surprising that she didn't trust me. "Still," I would add, "we lose a lot by your not seeing the difference between them and me."

Not until weeks later did I mention, casually, that the one way she hadn't cooperated with me was by not doing the assignment.

"What assignment?" she asked.

Had she forgotten?

"You were going to think of something you'd been refusing to tell me," I reminded her.

"Oh, I did think of something," she said. "It was easy."

I waited.

"I did what you asked. You asked me to think of something, but you didn't say that I had to tell you what it was. *That* I won't do," she said. For the first time that I could remember, she smiled. It was a very pretty smile that wreathed her face, and though it was a smile of opposition, I enjoyed it.

I didn't chastise her for her secrecy over the weeks that followed. She had the right to remain silent on any issue, but I had the right to observe to her that she was doing so.

"You're pretty good at putting up a barbed-wire fence to keep people out, aren't you?" I commented once, and she nodded that she was.

Of as much concern to me as the secret was the fact that in opting not to disclose it she was surely reinforcing in her own mind her perception of me as untrustworthy, perhaps even malevolent, in the image of her father. She was reinfecting herself with a fear of me that had no basis in fact. She would have to start trusting me in order to melt that fear.

When she referred to "Walter" for the first time, it was so smoothly as to give me no inkling of his gigantic importance in her life.

She was talking about her father, who, though in his fifties, bragged to his fellow workers that he was physically stronger than any of them. During a lunch break, in an unprovoked attempt to show off, he lifted a huge crate of canned goods but dropped it on his foot, breaking two toes. "Walter used to say he was as graceful as a bear on a skateboard," she said, smiling broadly.

I smiled too, and then asked, "Who's Walter?"

"Oh, a friend," she responded at once.

Two weeks later Walter came up again. This time also it was connected with her parents. Her mother would spit desperate lectures at her when she caught Elinor eating bread or anything she considered fattening.

"You must be crazy. Men don't even look at women who are fat. These are your best years, don't waste them. You won't be attractive by the time you're thirty-five."

One night her mother was doing her usual women's magazine exercises. She had insisted that Elinor join her, and when Elinor refused, her mother had violently insulted her, predicting that she was going to fall apart in a couple of years and no one would ever want her.

Elinor had left their apartment and gone to see Walter, nearly collapsing in misery. She reported, "I didn't know what to do. Then Walter told me, 'What do you care what she says? She's falling further behind in her *Family Circle* exercises every week.'"

Elinor had treasured that comment and thought of it often since. When she repeated it to me, she grinned, and I think I did too.

That she and Walter had known each other quite well was obvious. And both times she had mentioned him, it had been with a twinkle.

I didn't follow up that time. But a few weeks afterward I brought up Walter myself. "You've mentioned your friend Walter a few times," I observed. "He sounds like a lot of fun. How come you never see him anymore?"

"A lot of fun? I wouldn't say that."

That was all she would say. But I thought I saw melancholy in her eyes, which then narrowed toward me, as if she were calling me a fool.

Later I felt the force of her expulsion of me from the topic of

Walter. It was as if she had said, "Who are you to talk about him?"
For the first time I got the idea that Walter was inside that special
territory I was not to enter. I was angry with myself for what now
seemed like my glib and clumsy comment about him, and I could
only hope that she would mention him again so that I could show
more deference.

When after a few weeks she didn't bring him up, I did. "That
fellow Walter sounds like someone you were really close to. How
come you don't see him these days?"

She told me that Walter was teaching in Cleveland. They had
said goodbye about six months ago and hadn't spoken since, though
she had sent him a birthday card.

Meanwhile, nothing much changed with Larry. They would have
a few lunches together during the week and go out once over the
weekend. She went to bed with him when he forced the issue, but
there was no pleasure in it for her.

She reported that he was getting exasperated, and added, "I wish
I could make him happy. But I can't."

"Why do you want to make him happy?" I asked, perhaps sounding a trifle adversarial.

She seemed surprised by the question. After a moment she said,
"Well, he's really a very dear person. I mean, I think he wants to
marry me and take care of me, but I don't know why."

"I'm starting to wonder myself," I said, and she burst out laughing.

"I know. I'm not really very good to him."

"Do you love him?"

"Maybe. In a way."

But, obviously, something radical was missing in that relationship
from her point of view. I framed a question for myself, as I sometimes do, as a kind of alert to my unconscious—If you can think
of an answer, let me know. The question was, "Why does the
relationship feel so wrong to Elinor?"

However, all I could think of were indictments of her childhood.
Accurate as they might be, they didn't explain Elinor's conscious

refusal to embrace the knight who had come to rescue her from the chaos of those early days.

At about noon one day, one of the sequence of ambulances that came to the back of the hospital deposited two attendants bearing a young man on a stretcher. Elinor quivered as she told me, "He was a curly-haired Spanish man, about twenty-four. He was dead when they brought him in. The lips were drawn back from his teeth. It looked like he was grinning, except some blood was still oozing from his mouth in little bubbles. His throat had been slashed. You could see where the knife went through the arteries. His eyes looked surprised. I was so shaken by the blood."

"Why the blood?" I asked her. "You must see that all the time."

"I know. This sounds funny. But it's one thing when you expect it. But this boy. His shirt was all red. And his shoes. It's just so terrible to see blood on someone's shoes, I don't know why. There's something about blood on the shoes that gets me.

"Larry was there. He was on his lunch break. He just watched, and then he saw me and came over. I was in shock, I must have been.

"I told Larry, 'It's hard to imagine he was once alive.' Once? That morning. It could have been a million years ago. Larry said it was more recent than that. He was explaining how you could tell he'd been dead less than an hour. The stomach gases were still rumbling. I was terribly shaken. The boy was so thin, with black curly hair. He looked like Walter. I started to think about Walter.

"Larry could see how upset I was. He asked me to go for a walk with him, and we sat down on a park bench. All I could think about was Walter. Larry was really very nice. He told me he had bought me a necklace and he wanted to give it to me. I told him that I didn't want it. Then he said something, I don't remember, about our being lovers, and I told him I didn't want to sleep with him anymore, that I couldn't."

She looked into my eyes, perhaps to see if there was disapproval in them.

"Anyhow," she said, "Larry was very hurt, and I felt bad, so I said I didn't mean it, that okay we were lovers. And he said it would be great someday. But I don't know. All I could think about was Walter."

"Do you want to tell me a little about Walter?" I asked.

She nodded and then said yes.

But I didn't pursue it then. She had gone through more than enough that day, and to press her for any further disclosure felt tantamount to rape. I knew she would tell me soon.

About a week later I brought him up, gingerly.

"Walter?" she said, having surely expected me to ask about him. "Walter Burton is a very close friend. I mean we *were* very close. We used to talk every day. He was the only one I could say everything to."

They had met when Elinor was in nursing school and both were eighteen. One night before a very hard test, she'd decided that she'd do better going out to study, and went to the local coffee shop for a hot chocolate. The place was jammed, mostly with students, and the only seat open was one opposite Walter at a table for two in the corner.

She soon became so engrossed in her notes that she reached over and picked up one of Walter's books by mistake. Realizing what she had done, she smiled in embarrassment and handed the book back to him. He absolved her by smiling warmly and observing that the two books did look similar in size and color. She laughed nervously and mentioned that she wished she could read his novel instead of her text; it would be more interesting.

He asked her if she was from the nurses' residence, and she told him she was. They chatted for a few more minutes and then both resumed reading.

After that, they would meet, but only in that coffee shop and always "by accident," at the same time, about ten at night.

She told me, "Walter was very serious and talked mostly about novels he was reading and great writers. He has beautiful dark curly hair. He's very frail. He talks very quietly, but his eyes are very strong. He's going to write a great book himself someday, I'm sure of it."

After six months they still hadn't even exchanged phone numbers. "I didn't ask, and he didn't ask." Over all that time, Walter never repeated anything a single friend of his had said or even mentioned one. "I assumed he was very shy," she said.

"He hardly spoke about himself, except to say that he was going to City College. For some reason, though, I told him everything about myself, particularly about my parents. I guess I had to tell someone, and Walter would always listen with such interest. He didn't comment much, but he had a way of looking at me that seemed so sympathetic. I knew he understood how much pain I was in with them.

"The only thing he said about his folks was that his father had died when he was fourteen."

"Did you hope that he would ask you out?" I inquired.

"Not really. Not at first. I don't think so. It was wonderful just knowing he'd be there. I didn't think I was falling in love with him until he didn't show up for four nights in a row, and I went into a panic. I thought I might never see him again. I couldn't believe how upset I was."

"What happened?"

"He just had a virus, that's all. He'd been in his room. He came back to the coffee shop a few nights later."

"You told your friends about him?"

"No. Never." She seemed shocked at the suggestion.

One Saturday evening in the coffee shop, she and Walter were looking at the newspaper together and saw photos of some polar bear cubs at the Bronx Zoo.

"I was oohing and aahing about them, and Walter asked me if I wanted to go with him to see them the next day. I was surprised at the suggestion, but I said yes. Later he said he too was surprised he had asked me.

"It was funny to be out with him in the daylight. But we had a wonderful time. He's so gentle and considerate."

But for many more months after that they continued to meet only in the cafeteria and "by accident."

As time went by, Walter revealed more snippets of his life. His mother had gone off with another man, taking Walter's two younger sisters with her. They had left Walter with his alcoholic father in a transient hotel. That was when Walter had started to do all his reading.

After Walter's father died, the boy returned to live with his mother for a few years, and there too he continued his regimen of reading for long hours every day. He had always planned to get a doctorate someday, and he wanted to teach.

For two years, while Elinor was in nursing school and Walter was getting his bachelor's degree, they kept seeing each other. Mostly they spent time in that coffee shop and in a few other restaurants, or going for walks or sitting in the park. That was it. She never went to his room and he never visited her.

"He had this dream to teach underprivileged kids. That was his mission—to go teach in some inner-city school, to give kids a chance who didn't know how to read.

"We finally took each other's phone numbers, just so we wouldn't hang around places if the other one wasn't able to come," she said.

Then Walter got word of a job in Cleveland, and one evening he told her that he'd be leaving New York right after graduation. That was to be only three months away. He described the job to her. They both felt bad that they might not see each other anymore, and they kept talking well into the night.

That evening Walter told her about his childhood, and went into more detail about how his father had died. It was in a terrible fire.

Elinor said, "Walter told me that his father had left a lit cigarette on a pillow, and the whole place was full of smoke, you couldn't even tell where the flames were. Walter's eyes filled with tears, and that made me cry too. He had never shown any emotion like that before."

Elinor said, "I remember that evening with him so well. I asked Walter, 'Where were you during the fire?' and he said, 'Oh, I was there.' I asked him, 'Were you all right?' and he said, 'Yeah, I made it.' I could see he was fighting tears, and I wanted to touch him but he didn't want me to. He pushed me away. He didn't like feeling sorry for himself."

She seemed relieved to have told me this about Walter. I wondered why she'd been so incredibly secretive about him. She was as protective of him as a wolverine of its young. And why weren't they still in contact? It had to be more than mere timidity on either side. Something had happened that banished him from her life, though surely not from her memory.

When she was gone, I recalled her telling me about Tiff Tiff, that magic land she had conjured up for herself in childhood, whose inhabitants loved one another. Her venturing to tell me about that Utopia had been a precursor; she had commented with amazement that she couldn't believe she was really talking about it. Her mentioning Walter now seemed like a second revelation, which followed, logically and psychologically, from the disclosing of Tiff Tiff.

She hardly mentioned Walter over the next few weeks, but I could see that her saying as much as she did about him had changed things between her and me.

One evening, as I looked at her in her tweed skirt with a blazer and light gray blouse, I realized that she was actually dressing up more for her weekly sessions with me, as if she had chosen to honor our work together. Her very mentioning him had been for her a dangerous sortie into enemy territory, and she had returned to her fortress without incident. Perhaps I was not truly the enemy.

I surmised that she'd elevated me because she realized that I believed in her, and not simply in her future but in her present— and in her *past*. She saw that I perceived her as having been worthwhile during that early period of life when her parents had held her up to ridicule.

Trusting me more, she revealed to me what an enormous fulfillment it was for her to be an operating room nurse. She loved talking to patients before and after their surgery, she would tell them what to expect and comfort them when they were afraid. Often, Elinor informed me, the patient who has put up the best front to the family, allaying their fears, is the one who becomes the most terrified when they leave the room minutes before surgery is about to begin.

Elinor told me, "When I can get that person to smile again and look at the bright side of things, it's wonderful."

The morning of a surgery, as she would scrub down and then put on her sterile gown over her greens, she would always be eager to get started. "And when I'm there, right up at the field under the bright lights, working with the surgeon, it's just great," she said.

She wanted to be the best, and when she had doubts, Larry was always there to assure her that someday she would be. However, he had never actually seen her work. When on occasion Elinor pointed that out, he told her he didn't have to, she was so obviously talented.

The relationship with Larry continued to hobble along. Once during a session I thought of a line from a song of Bob Dylan's: "He not busy being born is busy dying." On paper Larry was almost perfect—sociable, successful, respected, a surgeon in a society that reveres doctors. He seemed the ideal man to rescue Elinor from her history, to bring her to the promised land, if that was what she wanted. However, apparently she didn't. I sometimes wondered why she never felt even tempted to escape with him.

As I came to realize how fond she and Walter were of each other, I began to wonder why, over all that time, their relationship had remained nonsexual. So far as I knew, she and Walter had never even kissed.

When I finally posed the question to her, she shrieked at me with a ferocity that seemed to come from nowhere. "Not all love has to be *fucking*, all right?"

No sooner did I feel hurtled backward than she softened, as if realizing that whatever was bothering her was not my fault. "I'm sorry," she said. "You weren't wrong to ask me. But there are some things I just can't tell you about Walter, some things I can never tell you."

She seemed upset with herself and instinctively put the back of her hand over her lips, as if she'd said something wrong and gotten into trouble. It was a little girl's gesture. Then she looked at me, as if trying to read my expression.

I assured her that I didn't mind her telling me off if she felt like it. "I'd a hundred times rather you did that than kept something to yourself and didn't trust me," I said.

The subject was dropped.

The next time I saw her I asked her if she had ever shouted at her father.

She responded, "Only once, when he threw out a collection of photos I had."

That time her father had actually said he was sorry, but Elinor was still inconsolable for days over her loss.

"I guess he destroyed a lot of things that were precious to you," I said, and added, "However, I'm not him. Whatever you tell me I accept as a sacred trust, whether you believe that or not."

A few weeks later she came in wearing an Indian silver and turquoise bracelet, which she said Walter had given her for her birthday. Then she showed me two photos of Walter, in a dark turtleneck sweater. He had a long, narrow face and intense eyes.

Feeling on trial with my response, I searched for something neutral to say, and observed that he looked like a poet.

"He is. He's very poetic," she said proudly.

I thanked her for showing me the photos, knowing that it had taken great trust on her part, though as yet I had no inkling why it did.

I was starting to sense that her ultimate leap of trust was coming soon—that she would, before long, disclose the full story of what had happened with Walter.

It was critical that she do this, and not just for the sake of revealing the facts, whatever they were, and lightening her burden of carrying them alone. She would have to trust other people in order to convince herself that we *merited* trust, that at least some of us were truly loyal and on her side.

I had by then come to see Elinor as a victim not just of her parents' cruelty, but of the play-safe defense she had put into practice to avert trouble. While she was growing up, her very secrecy, which she maintained everywhere, had made it impossible for her to recognize the many people who would never have violated her. She could hardly feel at home in the world, or see friends as they truly were.

Only by her confiding in someone, and by that person—me, in this case—proving worthy of her trust, could she discover what was possible. And so I had come to perceive her every act of trust in me as an axe blow against the wall she had built around herself and which so secluded her.

In those weeks, while she was telling me more, I could virtually feel her impulse to trust me still further.

The psychologist Wilhelm Wundt, one of many to write about the unconscious before Freud, postulated that lurking truths have a force of their own, propelling them toward the surface. At times I sensed that Elinor was eyeing me, measuring how much to tell me, as if her secret with Walter were thrusting itself toward the surface. But even then a sense of honor on her part, which I did not yet understand, held her back.

The evening when she finally did tell me everything had an appropriateness that was almost eerie.

At twilight I took a brief walk in the park before Elinor was due to arrive. As sometimes happens at that time of day, the city seemed strangely empty. It was in its refractory period, when people were mostly at home, recovering from their day's dealings and not yet quite ready to rush out again to the restaurants and bars and theaters.

It was a ghostly evening, with red clouds holding still in the sky

like streaks in a metamorphic rock. Such a night induces the sense
that nothing trivial can possibly happen, that only star-crossed
events can occur. At least, that was how I felt.

I was hardly surprised when Elinor began the session by telling
me that she had assisted at an operation at which the patient had
died.

"A little bald man. He was riddled with cancer. The last thing
he told me was that he knew he'd pull through," she said. "He was
lucky he didn't make it. Maybe Dr. Jaffe helped him out."

"The surgeon, you mean?" I asked.

"No. The anesthesiologist, she's a wonderful person. I guess I'll
never know. It's good the man was religious, if he really was."

"He had a family there?" I asked.

"No one. His wife had died. His sons were alive, but they didn't
come. Maybe they were busy. I don't know where they were. He
was alone. That's what life is, I guess."

"What do you mean?"

"All alone. All alone."

"Your life, you mean?" I asked.

She nodded.

"You're feeling lonely?" I asked naively.

"Of course I am. How can you ask?"

"Is it that you miss Walter?" I suggested, and I instantly feared
that I had trespassed.

"Walter," she echoed. "I guess I should talk about him," she said,
and I surmised that she'd made the decision before coming.

She was quiet for a moment, obviously thinking about him. Not
wanting to interrupt or stare at her, I waited. She seemed terribly
sad, and she was pinching her lips together, rubbing them. Perhaps
because of that facial gesture she looked quintessentially Welsh to
me in that moment, and I thought of the old line about the Celtic
people, that "all their wars are merry and all their songs are sad."

Well, let's fight a war then, I thought, but with no idea how or
where.

Then she said, in a high-pitched voice, "Walter doesn't want
me."

"He told you that?" I asked her.

She nodded yes. "I asked him, 'Can I go along with you?' and he said no."

"Did he say why not?"

"He said no one can go with him."

I waited before telling her that I didn't understand.

"Walter was burned," she said. "Forty percent of his body was burned. Do you know what that is, forty percent of his body? He had three operations. He was in bed for most of two years. He didn't go out in the daytime between the ages of thirteen and sixteen."

"You mean in the fire where his father died?" I asked.

"That's right," she said. "In the fire where his father died. In the smoke, he woke up and he found the door, but his clothes were on fire. And luckily, someone, a neighbor, caught him and tackled him and rolled him over and over in a carpet.

"The skin on his arms and chest and legs was gone. His mother could hardly visit him in the hospital, she was so upset. He couldn't use his hands for a long time. That's when his mother took him. He was alone so long and in such pain. So that's why he doesn't want anyone now. Do you follow me?"

"Elinor, I do. I follow you perfectly."

"I want to get some water," she said. "My throat is dry."

I told her I would get it for her, and I did, and returned with a glass for her and one for me.

"He's really a hero, isn't he?" I said. "He kept on reading and studying and working. He never quit."

"Yes. He said he must have survived for a reason. I'm the only one who ever saw his body, and that took two years, and it was beautiful. It was beautiful, but he doesn't think so. He calls himself a zebra, with all those skin grafts. I told him it didn't matter. I'd rather be with him than anyone, but he said it wouldn't be fun, he said he wouldn't do that to me. So he left. I saw his body only the last time we were together. I went up to his room. I wanted to. I forced my way."

I told her, "I don't understand why he didn't want you to go to

Cleveland with him, or for him to stay here. I mean why you're not together."

"He said I needed someone to take care of me, I'd had it bad enough." For the first time, she was crying openly.

"What did you say?"

"I didn't know what to say. I was in bed with him, and I was holding him. He didn't want to take his sweater off for the longest time, that goddamned black sweater. I made him take it off.

"I told him I wanted to go with him, to marry him. But I didn't really insist. I never insist on anything. It was all that last night. I just felt so terrible for him. Not the way he looked, the way he felt."

"Is it too late?" I asked.

"I don't know. Can I go home now? I think I've said enough for one day."

I nodded that it was okay. "But please wait just a couple of minutes, and then if you really want to leave, you can."

She waited, but only to comply. She was silent for a few moments, and then she said, "I really do." Before she left, I told her to call me if she wanted to talk before our next session. But I knew she wouldn't. It wasn't her style to do that.

In our next session, when I asked Elinor more about why Walter had gone off without her, she answered at once, "He loves me. He wants me to marry someone successful, who can make me happy. He kept saying he wasn't worthy of me."

"Even if you're so happy with him?" I asked incredulously.

She nodded yes.

"It sounds wrong," I told her.

"It does to me too," she said.

I thought, it's wrong because happiness must be seized first and explained later, if ever.

"Maybe Walter said all that because he lacked confidence," I suggested.

"What do you mean?" she asked me.

"I mean maybe he was afraid he wouldn't make you happy for long, and you'd both be hurt in the long run."

"I know. I thought of that," she said. "After he was gone, I kept thinking that if I hadn't told him how bad my childhood was, and how I used to dream of a good life, maybe he would have been happier with me."

"He was happy with you, from what you say. He couldn't have been happier," I corrected her.

"I know," she said. "I could have given him so much."

"And that would have made you happier than anything else," I said.

"I never thought of it that way," she said.

She talked about little besides Walter during the sessions that followed. Walter was brave. Walter didn't care about money. Walter taught in a school that paid him a pittance, just so he could help impoverished kids: blacks and some whites. They could call him anytime, and he'd talk to them. It was like one of those "freedom schools" of the sixties; the kids could talk about whatever they wanted a lot of the time, as long as they worked on their reading and basic skills. Walter was like those boys who went down south and were killed. He actually looked a little like Mickey Schwerner. Walter was a genius, self-sufficient. No. Walter is scared. Maybe he's both. Walter needs me.

She toyed with calling him and begging him to have her go out there and join him. She could work as a nurse. Her parents would go crazy, but who cares? It would be her helping Walter, a poor, burned boy out there—she said that without sadness, and then added, "But we're all burned, one way or another, aren't we?" I nodded, and she said, "I certainly am."

"So, it's the burned helping the burned," I said, and then somehow we got on to the topic of her lifetime dream of meeting a man not burned but rich and capable, who would lift her out of her history and make it all seem nothing more than a bad dream. In Larry she had met such a man. What was wrong with her to disdain him?

Meanwhile, she and Larry argued more. As it became obvious to him that he was not prevailing with her, he resorted to reminding her how hard her life would be without him. She was forfeiting more than she realized. One evening, after she had refused to go home with him, he descended to pronouncing her less than competent. "You have a lot to learn about operating room nursing," he told her. "People can still see it, you're still young."

Hearing that, I recalled William Congreve's line about the fury of a woman scorned, and realized how sexist it was. But like arrows Larry's comments went in much more easily than they came out. Elinor's susceptibility to them went back to childhood, when whatever love and security she knew had included such barbs. For me to observe to her that Larry's appraisal of her skills went down as she pulled back from him meant nothing. She suffered, and though she continued to retreat from Larry, she still felt unready to call Walter and even less ready to join him in Cleveland, if that was what he wanted.

Summer came, and I worried whether Elinor would be all right during my vacation, but she assured me she would. Perhaps my distance in space and time from her gave me a different perspective. In any event, I had been in London for nearly two weeks when suddenly I saw her dilemma differently.

Naturally I never even toyed with trying to explain why she loved Walter. That they were soul mates was obvious, and in any event, as some philosopher said, only those who have never been in love try to account for any instance of it. Elinor was finally ready to give up the life her parents would have wanted for her. Nor was it the first time that I'd seen someone scuttle a master plan, a lifetime of painstaking preparation, the dream of living a certain way, for love.

But then I saw that Elinor's case was very different, and I got new insight into what Walter meant to her. After all, what is real salvation for a young woman who has been brutalized in childhood? Is it to join a man who is himself unscathed—a citizen of some finer world, capable, secure, complete—who will offer her safe passage from the past? This is the classic "rescue fantasy," ending with the couple's entry into the land without strife. Or is it better to rescue a man whose chances are even worse than her own?

I had been thinking that the latter journey was uncertain and much longer at best. But then I realized it isn't. It is shorter. For from the very beginning the rescuer knows that her every effort to save the other person is right—and so, in this case, salvation begins, the land is reached, with the very first step.

Such a solution-by-reversal wasn't so unfamiliar, once I thought about it. Aren't most parents giving their children the love and protection that they themselves yearned for? And many of those who adopt stray dogs or cats are saving themselves by proxy. Elinor could create a world for Walter, and dwell in it with him, with a far deeper sense of security than she could ever experience in a perfect world that was simply given to her.

Toward the end of August, Elinor drove through the Rockies with her nurse friend Jennifer, and then down to San Francisco, where Jennifer's mother lived with her fourth husband. Elinor and Jennifer had become close friends in recent months, though they struck people as quite different. Jennifer was garrulous, bubbly, loved to dance; she knew every innovation of fashion and recognized every movie star and half the extras.

But Jennifer too had chosen nursing to escape from a home that trembled around her. From the time she and her sister could talk, their mother had cried to them about men, programming them to love each new daddy and then to hate him.

Within five hundred miles of San Francisco, the sutures of Jennifer's composure began to rip, and over that last span of highway the two confided in each other as they never had before.

To Jennifer's question "If you love him, why don't you go to him?" Elinor had replied that she wasn't yet strong enough.

In my office I asked her what she had meant by that.

"Capable enough as a nurse, I guess. I have a lot to learn."

That seemed a strange answer to me. I told her I didn't see the relevance.

"I don't feel confident enough, but I'm getting there. Don't push me. I'm planning to call him. But not yet."

This time she didn't apologize for striking a tough posture with me, and I was glad. Later I sensed that I had been treating her more robustly because I felt her to be stronger. And her stopping me in my tracks when she felt pushed seemed to corroborate that she was.

That vacation with Jennifer strengthened Elinor. She had confided in someone besides me, and Jennifer, rather than mocking her, had totally understood her. Jennifer was an exile from a home terrible in another way, but who had emerged dauntless in her desire for a better life.

By then Elinor found continual excuses to keep Larry at bay, and he finally began to accept his fate, but not without his usual prophecies that she would find life without him much harder than she imagined.

At least once a week Elinor's parents would also try to dampen whatever joy was possible for her. Her mother did this by constant complaining—"That neuralgia of mine is so bad that I can't do anything I enjoy anymore." Or "I spend half the day getting special foods for your father. The doctor has him on a controlled diet for his gout and his cholesterol, and his platelet count is low. You know what platelets are."

The messages from both sides were curiously the same, intended as they were to instill guilt in Elinor and to immobilize her.

For a short time I concentrated on decoding those messages, holding them up to the light so that Elinor could read them explicitly as they were intended. I felt there could be no better way of depriving them of their inhibiting force.

Very possibly I would have succeeded, but the real problem lay within her. Others could sway Elinor only because she herself felt conflicted. Elinor often repeated her comment that not until she could prove herself as a nurse would she be ready to call Walter and see how he felt about her.

I had no doubt that she saw it that way. However, I felt absolutely sure that no mere accomplishment in itself could produce that sense of readiness. I knew only too well the Hamlet syndrome, in which a frightened person places preconditions on himself or herself, impossible ones if necessary—which are merely ways of justifying one's feeling of unreadiness motivated by some deeper reason. When Elinor kept repeating that she could call Walter only after she became "one of the best operating nurses around," I felt convinced that she believed it, though I just as surely didn't. However, it was not my place to doubt a dream.

Inspired at least in part by this dream of becoming worthy of life with Walter, Elinor devoted herself to improving her operating room skills. Certain surgeons asked for her routinely, but the most renowned ones, the veterans, had their own favorites in the different local hospitals, and it became almost an obsession of Elinor's that until one of those in the pantheon approved of her work, she had not yet arrived.

"What would amount to approval?" I asked her.

"If I worked with Dr. Webb, and it went well, and he told me he liked my work," she said. But she quickly corrected herself, and as those with obsessions often do, she instantly raised the barrier, making it harder to surmount. "No, approval would be if he called me and asked me to scrub with him."

"Well, that's not really up to you if they don't give you a chance, is it?" I asked.

"I guess not," she admitted. And by her look I realized that instead of reducing her requirement, as I'd intended by suggesting that it was unrealistic, I had simply demoralized her further by implying how little she could do to fulfill it.

Not surprisingly she had frequent dreams about surgery. Most of them were just instantaneous photographs of herself as part of the team, counting the sponges or gloving down a doctor or laying out the sterile drape while the surgeon looked at the X-rays. "Who was the patient?" I asked her, and she said she didn't know, but it was always a young male, she imagined.

In one dream snapshot the surgeon was worried; she saw beads of sweat glistening on his head. "I wanted to help him and I wanted to do it right," Elinor said. In that dream it was a very tense surgery, things went wrong, she was under awful strain; they all were, she told me, but she had the special worry that the patient on the table would wake up prematurely. Then somehow she knew that the lad was saved, she had assisted critically, and she woke up abruptly in the middle of the night, at first glad the operation was successfully over, and slowly realizing that she had only dreamed it.

I wondered about her fear that the patient would wake up. She had mentioned that it was a common, horrible worry that patients had, but groundless. Here she was one of the team, and in actuality a dreamer, who could conceivably wake up this time too soon, while the patient was still on the table, before the operation was over. If so, she would abandon the poor boy and never know the outcome of his ordeal.

In discussing the dream, I suggested that possibly she was the patient as well as a crucial member of the rescue team. "Can that be?" she asked me.

"Why not?" I assured her. "It was your dream, you can play as many parts as you wish."

Then I told her, "It's not so different in real life."

She waited for me to finish.

"Well, I was thinking, we're all the person we save and not just the savior, when we do something big for someone in trouble. And I think this may be even more true of you than most.

"Maybe that's something Walter can give you that a lot of people can't," I suggested, and I explained to her that besides the fact that she loved him, she knew he genuinely needed someone like her, more than say Larry did.

"What do you mean 'someone like me'? Do you think he's found someone else already?"

I assured her I hadn't meant to say that.

I recalled her other dream, in which she had persuaded a young man to leap overboard to safety with her.

At about that time I also remembered how distraught Elinor had become when the nurses tried to talk her into having plastic surgery on her nose. To do that would only increase her distance from Walter, for whom nothing more could be done.

That fall Elinor drew closer to her women friends but ended it with Larry. When they met in the hospital halls, they had little to talk about; she did her best to avoid him. She also spoke to her parents less, partly because they seemed so angry with her for letting such an opportunity slip through her hands. She poured herself into her work.

I knew she thought about Walter, though she didn't mention him. When she said, "I don't think Walter would really think I made it in my profession yet," I rebutted her, perhaps too sharply.

"I can't believe that Walter would judge you by how accomplished you are as an operating room nurse."

"I know," she said, but she sounded unconvinced.

I realized that Elinor had simply taken her own standard of readiness before she could call Walter and applied it to him, and that no merely logical argument of mine could have value. I wondered if she would ever really call him.

Meanwhile, I kept trying to lift out of her unconscious and make available to her a different kind of understanding of herself. She condemned any form of pleasure, even that of going to a good restaurant with a friend, always making the case that poor people were starving, that others were less fortunate. It was obviously fruitless for her to deny herself something of value merely because she couldn't bring the whole world with her on an experience. I realized that a fear of loneliness, of standing out, masqueraded as kindness in Elinor, though she also had an enormous true kindness. I sought to help her see this, but I didn't feel that I was making much progress.

However, one day, I could tell almost by the way she strode

into my office that she felt uplifted. She had hardly sat down when she smiled and said, "I got a call today from Dr. Donald Kulp. He wants me to scrub with him next week."

"Who's Donald Kulp?" I asked.

"Oh, he's one of the best-known surgeons on the East Coast. He's a gastroenterologist. You know, he does intestinal surgery."

"That's great. How did he get your name?"

"Dr. Jaffe gave it to him. She's that nice anesthesiologist I told you about. She works with him a lot. That was awfully nice of her to mention me. It's next Monday. It's a bowel resection. The man has a malignant tumor, but we're hoping it hasn't spread yet.

"Dr. Kulp asked me if I had any available time, and I said I did. I already wrote it in.

"This morning I looked up Dr. Kulp's doctor's preference card. He likes a lot of hand signals. He doesn't like to talk much when he works."

I could see she was excited. "What makes a surgeon really good?" I asked. "Is it experience?"

She thought a moment. "I guess experience has to do with it, but with the really great ones, everybody says you can tell the first day. The person works fast and very cleanly. He's sure of himself. And when he opens up a patient, you can see that it looks just like in the anatomy books."

She had mentioned her surgeries from time to time, but never so exuberantly. Two days before the operation was scheduled she mentioned it again and said she'd been reading up for it.

However, that Monday night, when she came in, her face looked like that of a woman who just found out she was damned on Judgment Day. At first she swallowed her words, and I couldn't understand her. All I could make out was, "The operation . . . I assisted Dr. Kulp today."

Something had gone wrong, terribly wrong during the operation, I felt sure of it. I gripped the arms of my chair as I waited, and the horrific thought went through my mind that she had blundered, and maybe even cost the patient his life.

Several times she started to talk but seemed to think better of it. When she seemed on the verge each time, she would shake.

"I think you should bring me up to date," I said, trying to sound light, but not too light.

"Well, it was just an operation, that's all," she said.

"Am I right that you're very upset about something?" I asked.

She nodded that I was right but didn't clarify.

"Elinor, the only way we can possibly put this thing together is if you go over every detail." I sought to encourage her.

"That would take all day," she said. And then a moment later, "Where should I start?"

"What did you have for breakfast?" I asked, in what I quickly perceived as a fatuous effort to reduce the tension.

"Coffee. Just coffee." She smiled.

"Was anything said before the operation?"

"Nothing special. Everyone was there. Martha, she's the circulating nurse, went out to get the patient. I was sterile and I was assembling the instruments on the back table. A lap set—"

"What's a lap set?"

"A laparotomy set. Do you want to know what's in it? There are different kinds of clamps. Kelly clamps, and mosquitos, and providences—"

"No, Elinor, I don't need a list. I don't even know what they look like anyhow. Just go on. Anything special so far?"

"Well, Dr. Kulp told me he uses a Garrick clamp. He was surprised I knew what it was."

She made a signal that looked like the "V for victory" sign used in the Second World War, which I assumed was Dr. Kulp's hand signal when he wanted that clamp.

"So it started." Elinor's voice went up very high, as it often did when she was tense, and again she was trembling. "Dr. Jaffe had the patient under, and Dr. Kulp swabbed out the abdomen with his prep sticks. How much detail do you want?"

I told her I wanted as much as she could remember.

She said, "I could tell from the incision he made, from the way he went down, first through the fat, and then into the muscle layer, that he was great. It hardly bled. When he hit the muscle layer, I could see a few bleeders, nothing special. Once in a while he would signal for the cautery, and he would touch a bleeder and it would stop fast.

"Everything was going very well up to that point. I was right with him. He would clamp off some muscle and cut through it and seal it with a suture. When he got down to the peritoneum, and exposed the bowel, I peeked over and it looked just the way it does in books, that was how cleanly he worked. There was hardly any bleeding.

"There was a lot of cutting and clamping, and I was in synch with him. He had isolated the area where the cancer was. He had the clamps in great. He had good bowel on one side and bad bowel on the other. He took his knife and was getting ready to cut out the diseased portion. I was getting ready for the anastomosis."

"What's that?"

"He'd have to suture the bowel together from the ends. But it didn't happen that way."

I knew we were coming to the desperate part; she balked, as if her power of recall refused to go forward and tell me the rest.

"The tumor was very deeply lodged. When Dr. Kulp lifted it out, he ruptured an artery. It wasn't his fault, it couldn't be helped. The blood came like you couldn't believe.

"Dr. Kulp couldn't visualize, he couldn't see, there was so much blood. Blood, blood, you couldn't tell where it was coming from. You've got to be able to visualize, but the field kept filling up with blood. Dr. Kulp was asking for additional clamps, for suction.

"Dr. Kulp was trying to find the bleeder, it seemed like forever. He was incredibly cool, but the resident was in a panic. He kept handing Dr. Kulp sponge rubber sticks for dabbing, but I knew they were worthless, there was too much blood, and Dr. Kulp didn't even take any.

"Then Dr. Jaffe indicated that the patient's vital signs were failing and that we didn't have much time.

"The pace was incredible. Just then Dr. Kulp reached up over his head to adjust the operative light—he had to see better—but he burned a hole in his glove. Everybody saw the hole except him, but there was hardly any time. I thought, 'My God, he's not sterile, I have to tell him. He can do what he wants.' So I did. The resident looked hysterical. But Dr. Kulp calmly held out his hands, and I gloved him again.

"Then, thank God, Dr. Kulp found the bleeder and clamped it off. I kept handing him clamps. You know, with arterial bleeding like that, you can't just cauterize. The pressure is too high.

"It was beautiful, watching Dr. Kulp work, and helping him after that. Clamp, clamp, cut, tie. Clamp, clamp, cut, tie. It was like we had worked together forever. We were in such a rhythm. The patient is fine. We don't think it spread, let's hope.

"Then, afterward, Dr. Kulp went out in the hall. He was so upset that he had to sit down. He pointed to the soda machine. He could hardly talk. I got him a Coke."

Elinor had told the story lightning fast once she reached the terrible crisis. It was almost as if she herself had received an infusion of blood from participating. But suddenly she looked at me as if she wondered who I was.

"Then Dr. Kulp put his arm around me. He said I was great. He thanked me." And here her eyes moistened. "He said he could never have done it without me, and that I was one in a million.

"He thanked me for telling him about that hole in his glove. I said, 'I was afraid to tell you. I didn't mean to tell you what to do.' 'Well, I'm glad you did,' he said. He said it took a lot of courage. He said, 'You're a natural.' Those were his words. He said he wanted to call me whenever he came to our hospital." Now she was sobbing uncontrollably.

I felt like putting my arm around her too, but I let her cry. She deserved the release of tears, after that prolonged strain of having helped save a life, of having to do everything right.

Her eyes still moist, she looked over at me. "I don't understand. I mean Dr. Kulp listened to me. He really listened to me." She stopped.

"You mean why didn't other people listen to you?" I asked.

She nodded. She was wiping her eyes.

"Like who?" I had her parents in mind.

But she said, "Larry. People like that."

"I guess you mean you're worth listening to," I said, just to embolden the discovery she was making.

Suddenly her eyes grew stern. "Who the hell do they think they are. Who the hell do they think they are anyhow? I'm good. You know what I mean. I'm good."

"I know you are," I said.

"I mean I'm good," she repeated, mainly to herself. She kept assimilating the idea.

A lot of thoughts went through my mind: that Dr. Kulp had really proved his greatness, that Elinor had finally found a top-level person who wasn't competitive with her, and that she would have to digest this discovery about herself again and again. I hoped she would reinforce it by demanding more from people, by expecting more from them. But we would always be ahead, we would have this moment to remember; it would stand as a precious counterexample to what she had been taught every day growing up, to what she had experienced. And I realized too that this was her moment, not mine, and that she would do with it what she wished.

As if discovering the idea on the wall behind me, she said, "I think I'll call Walter and tell him."

I nodded to indicate that I understood her, but I didn't say anything.

Afterward, I thought I understood why she had cried and had seemed so desolate when reporting a success. It was because from that pinnacle she had reached she had achieved a new vision. She had seen, however fleetingly, that all was permitted, that the world could be hers in a way she had not dared to imagine. She had cried at seeing the vastness of this new world. It was terrifying, though beautiful. And then, knowing Elinor, I imagined she had cried for all those who would never see it.

Nor had she reached that new height in one step. Dr. Kulp's show of confidence in Elinor was only her most recent corroboration, however significant. There had been others in the previous months. She had cemented friendships with people like Jennifer, who sincerely respected her and said so. She had been moving toward some people at work who thought highly of her, like Dr. Jaffe. And she had been removing herself from people like Larry, who, though well meaning, regarded her as a lifetime apprentice.

Then I thought about Walter, and I wondered if she were really going to call him. She had said so on a whim that she could dismiss as easily as it had come to her. But I knew there was more to it. The tearful joy of her sudden sense of worthiness was something she wanted to share with him. He had never been far away. Perhaps now more was possible for the two of them.

Not until near the end of the next session did she mention that she had phoned Walter in Cleveland. A man who answered at the number Walter had given her had said that Walter no longer lived at that address but was subletting space elsewhere. The fellow didn't know the new number but promised to find out and told Elinor to call back after the weekend. She left her name and urged the man to get the message to Walter.

However, in the next session, as soon as I saw that Elinor hadn't bothered to change out of her nurse's uniform, I realized that something had left her feeling defeated. When in good moods, she changed into attractive street clothes and high heels.

I was right. She had finally tracked down Walter's number and called him. He'd said he was pleased to hear from her, but he didn't sound nearly as excited as she had hoped he would be. After narrating to him her operating room triumph, she had said to him exuberantly, "You were the first one I wanted to tell. You're the only one in the world who knows how much this means to me."

He had congratulated her on her success, but he hadn't really shared it with her. Still unable to process in her own mind the terrible realization that Walter was so remote, she asked him if he had gotten her message. He told her he had. When she demanded to know why he hadn't called back, saying that she'd located his number only by luck, he said matter-of-factly that he was going to call her back "this week."

By then her heart told her that he wasn't responsive, but she couldn't let herself believe it. Elinor told Walter that she missed him terribly, but in reaction he just gave a nervous laugh and said that it was always nice talking to her. Unexpectedly she heard herself asking, "Is there another woman in your life?" And he shot back in surprise, "Of course not." She was sure he was telling her the truth. Then he said he had to run, that people were waiting for him. He made no offer to call her back at a better time.

Elinor was left with the terrible feeling that she had interrupted him, that Walter, the only man she had ever loved, experienced her phone call to him after months of separation as an intrusion.

She came in the next time again looking dismal.

There was a long pause, which I broke by asking her what was on her mind.

"I've decided that I'm going out to Cleveland. I'll only be seeing you a few more times," she said. "I applied for a job at Cleveland General and I'll probably get it."

Naturally I was surprised. I asked her what had prompted her decision.

"Well, I'm miserable here. There's no point staying here. I might as well be miserable out there." She smiled faintly, as if it might not make sense to me. "Maybe I'll bump into Walter once in a while out there. There's no hope if he's there and I'm here."

"Have you spoken to him about this?" I asked her.

Elinor seemed disconcerted by the question. She asked me, "How do you mean spoken to him?" Then without waiting for me to answer, she filled in quickly, "I told him I was coming. All I can say is that at least he didn't beg me not to."

I nodded.

But Elinor still seemed to be thinking about the question. Then she said, "Now that you asked, and I'm trying to remember, I guess

I don't know how I put it to Walter. Maybe I made it seem like I had a big offer there. Maybe I didn't put it right."

"You mean you made it sound like coincidence?" I asked her.

"I don't know." She wrinkled up her face at the implication that Walter might have told her to stay in New York if she had been fully open with him, if she had told him that she was about to uproot her life to be near him.

I had a sense that she expected me to oppose her. However, all I could do was make sure that she realized the implications, that she knew what her cards were before she played them.

I thought that if I didn't say the obvious, represent the argument for her not going, or at least for her reconsidering, I would be depriving her of something she needed from me. And so I said the obvious, anticipating that she had considered it and dismissed it.

"Elinor, I'm thinking, you're doing so well in your career—you're starting to get everything you want, aren't you? Surgeons are recognizing you, and you have new people behind you, like Dr. Kulp. Do you think you can transfer all this prestige that you're beginning to accumulate? Can you really pick things up out there?"

"Yes," she said at once. "A lot of it depends on recommendations, and I'm getting good ones from Dr. Jaffe and a couple of surgeons. Anyhow, I really don't care. I don't care about anything. All I care about is being with Walter."

Now the tears were streaming down, and she snatched a tissue from the box in front of her. I was moved by her tears, but I felt I had to go on playing the role of dissenting authority, if only to help her firm up her resolve to leave New York.

So I pursued my unpopular role still further. "What worries me," I said, "is that suppose you go out there and Walter doesn't want to be with you enough. Won't you be stuck there without anybody? And maybe the hospital won't be right for you."

For a second I thought she hadn't heard me, but then her mood suddenly changed. She spoke almost truculently.

"Hospital!" she said. "I'm the one who can make the hospital right for me. I'm not worried about that. I know that I can do the job," She looked around the room for a wastepaper basket and dumped the tissue into it.

"Walter's the only one I can't get through to." She wasn't crying anymore, she seemed angry. "I know he loves me, and if I ever doubted it, I could hear it in his voice the other day, even though he was trying to get me off the phone. I'm not going to let him do this to the two of us. I'm sick of having people tell me what I can and can't do."

She seemed to be feeling so much stronger and more organized that I opted to keep drawing her out. I asked her what she meant.

"Six months ago I didn't think any doctor would ever ask for me, and now look at them asking for me all the time. Walter's the only one who doesn't ask for me. How dare he say I can't love him because he's burned! How dare he tell me what I can do, and how dare he control both our lives this way. Who does he think he is, God? And I'm some little kid?"

She told me a little about the job in Cleveland. She would be working mostly with four surgeons, assuming that her references were in order and the job came through. But Elinor spoke as if there was no doubt that it would.

The last time she came in before she went to Cleveland, we spent much of the session talking about what therapy might do for Walter. "Could it get him over his fear of having a relationship with me?" she asked.

I told her that it could, but only if Walter wanted to go into therapy—only if he wanted to change. If he went merely because she insisted, the prognosis for his getting anything out of therapy was much less than if he wanted to change something about himself. And who could foretell in what direction successful therapy would lead Walter? One couldn't guarantee that he would want her after he changed. I thought my saying that might faze Elinor, but it didn't. She had absolutely no doubt that he loved her.

I had said and done all I could, and we parted wistfully that last session, with her vowing to stay in touch.

Three months later Elinor wrote to me telling me that she was doing well on her job and that she liked working in Cleveland. Concerning Walter she wrote, "All I can say is at least he's letting me talk about therapy to him." I assumed that they were seeing each other with some regularity, but she said nothing more.

That was two years ago. I think that she would have told me if there were any big changes in their relationship or in her life since then. But I have not heard from her since.

the

accident

THE PLAYERS AT THE MIDPOINT, A private backgammon club on Park Avenue in New York City, had two things in common. They could all afford the club's high fees, and they all greatly preferred winning to losing.

However, in their secret attitudes toward the game the members differed widely. Although everyone pretended to play backgammon solely for diversion, many had their own special motives.

Some of the players cherished the infantile belief that Fate would reward them ahead of the rest, giving them reparations for past injustices at its hands.

Others gravitated toward the game, ironically, because it provided them with regular doses of bad luck, about which they could complain publicly. They could gripe about bad rolls of the dice when their real complaint was that they were getting older or were unloved or felt unappreciated.

And a few real backgammon experts, who pretended to play only for fun, actually eked out their living by exploiting the mistakes of the other players.

I was one of those who wanted to win but saw the game only as a diversion. I always played for the lowest stakes possible.

I had the impression that this was also true of a man who often chose the same games that I was in—a quiet, mannerly man we all knew as Sammy. Sammy was a small man, about fifty-five, with whitish sideburns. He was slender, and he always dressed impeccably in dark custom-made suits.

On crowded Sunday afternoons at the club, Sammy and I would play in so-called chouettes, games designed to accommodate a lot of people at once. Half a dozen or more players would compete as a team, playing against an individual. In chouettes, the player whose turn it is to compete alone against the rest of the group is at a disadvantage, because the team can discuss its moves, pooling its knowledge against the single player.

As a team member, Sammy would sometimes give his opinion, but he always deferred if anyone disagreed with him, strongly favoring a different move. Unlike most of the players, Sammy never complained about his dice, and he never blamed another player even if the person had overruled him with a move that had backfired and cost Sammy money.

When, as often happened, bitter debates erupted at the table, Sammy and I would exempt ourselves and wait until they were over. Because the game was only a diversion to us, and we played for little money, nothing that happened seemed worth arguing about.

It wasn't until about a year after we'd met that I even found out Sammy's second name. One day we shared a cab uptown, and in the course of chatting we learned more about each other.

When Sammy told me that he was a psychoanalyst and that his name was Karpov, I was startled.

Dr. Samuel Karpov was a very eminent Freudian whose papers were classics in the orthodox world of psychoanalysis. But more than that, his name still rang in my mind because of a violent argument I'd had years earlier with a former classmate and friend, Alan Jenkins. My clash with Alan had come shortly after we had both received our doctorates from Columbia.

Apparently Alan had long been in analysis with Dr. Karpov by that time, and had begun further technical training at the institute over which Karpov presided.

Throughout our argument, Alan had cited Dr. Karpov's point of view so often that I had come away furious at this man whom I had never met. It was hard for me to believe that Samuel Karpov, this gentle soul, this Sammy whom I always enjoyed seeing at the club, was the giant to whom Alan had virtually turned over his mind.

My argument with Alan was so heated that it effectively ended our friendship. Obviously the real subject of our dispute was much bigger than the topic we were discussing.

But I am going ahead of my story. Some further facts are necessary.

Samuel Karpov was the luminary of a prominent psychoanalytic institute in Manhattan, one of the very few remaining centers devoted to preserving Freud's original views of therapy. Karpov was a highly respected man who wrote prolifically for psychoanalytic journals—his very name was an ensign of the old guard.

Since Freud's death in 1939, the great majority of therapists, myself included, have expanded our ideas in many ways. While we acknowledge our indebtedness to Freud, we have nonetheless modified our positions radically after trial and error. To most of us this has seemed nothing more than Freud himself would have done had he lived on. Over his lifetime Freud continually revised his own points of view, and since his time many innovations have been made.

Dr. Karpov's institute is one of the very few in the country that still teaches Freud's system exactly. Its members require that their patients lie on a couch, that they come for five sessions a week, and that they talk mostly about their past, as Freud's own patients did.

Even more telling, Karpov and his institute make assumptions about the psyche that the majority of other therapists consider too extreme, if not wholly unwarranted.

Central to the theory of these orthodox analysts is their belief that whatever people do they have unconsciously wanted to do. For instance, the man who says he wants to marry but never does must be shunning intimacy for some unconscious reason. The gambler who loses all his money must have secretly wanted to lose it—perhaps to punish himself or his loved ones. Of course, all therapists believe in unconscious motivation, but it takes an orthodox Freudian to insist that every outcome in a life must have been precisely what the person secretly wanted.

Five years earlier, my disputing that very idea, that what happens to people must necessarily have been their secret wish, was what led to the terrible fight with Alan. We'd cursed each other as politely as we could, and never spoke again. Nor would we—until the accident.

The night of our argument five years previously, Alan and I hadn't expected to see each other. A mutual friend had invited us, among about fifty others, to a backers' audition of a play in a fashionable East Side apartment. Aside from the sprinkling of theater people there to ballyhoo the play and read a few scenes from it, the guests were nearly all connected with the therapy profession, being practitioners or teachers in the field.

I could see why we were chosen. The protagonist was a psychoanalyst who solved a murder and explained his solution in the last scene.

The play sounded very static to me. I recall the protagonist saying at the end that the murderer wanted to be caught or he would never have left a telltale clue. In the play, when the murderer had denied that, the analyst-detective had explained, "You wanted to unconsciously. Nothing is pure chance, there are no accidents. The unconscious governs all. You could escape the police, but you could not escape yourself."

I was far from being in a position to invest in a Broadway play, but even if I were, this would certainly not have been the one. The characters were bloodless, and the plot was contrived. Mercifully others felt that way too, and its author, a man who had himself gone to the same orthodox psychoanalyst for two decades, turned his mind elsewhere.

In the year since I had seen Alan, he had grown a beard, and I hardly recognized him. He introduced me to his wife, Rosalind, and to a friend, whom Alan had apparently met at the institute. A half hour later, the four of us were having a late-night snack at a local restaurant.

To my surprise, they talked about the play in glowing terms. "The playwright's long analysis really shows," said Rosalind.

"Yes, it held together beautifully," the friend agreed.

I told them I thought it was just too pat.

"What is?" they asked me.

"Well, murderers make mistakes, and it doesn't imply that they want to be caught. This man had a dozen things to be careful of. Maybe he just slipped up—"

"There are no slips," Rosalind said flatly.

"You mean the only time a murderer ever gets caught is if he unconsciously wanted to?" I asked, underscoring their thesis in a way that I felt would surely get them to reconsider it.

"That's correct," Alan said.

I referred them to a detail of the plot. "Couldn't the arrival of the murderer's brother just when he was burning the letter have been an accident, or at least if not an accident, then let's say unforeseen?" I asked incredulously.

"There are no accidents," said the other fellow, whose name I forget.

"I know," I said. "I heard that in the play, but I don't think anyone still believes that."

"Dr. Karpov does," said Alan with the authority that Karpov's name apparently imbued him with.

I disagreed a little more, but they seemed to consider me naive. The waiter came, and we ordered drinks and some snacks. I can recall about the restaurant only that it was white inside—with white walls, white tablecloths, white tables, and white clientele. I said something to that effect and remarked that it looked like the inside of an egg, which set them off talking about rebirth.

Then the subject changed to the institute. They talked a little about its upcoming schedule and about a change in editors of its official journal. When they mentioned Dr. Samuel Karpov's name, it was with a stultifying humility. Alan and the other fellow were patients of his, and as members of the institute they also discussed their own private patients with him. Alan said he never agreed to take on a patient unless he had cleared the decision with Dr. Karpov first.

Rosalind, who was a social worker, was as respectful of Karpov as her husband was, and but for the orthodox rule that an analyst never treats both husband and wife, she said, she would have gone to him too. In that case, I thought, the three of them would have consumed fifteen hours a week of Karpov's time.

When Rosalind said something implying that she was proud that Karpov had considered her mentally healthy enough for Alan to marry, I put down my forkful of cheesecake. Didn't it bother her to see her husband so diminished in the ability to make judgments for himself? But I managed not to say this.

A little later Alan told me, "You really should consider studying at the institute." Then he added ruefully, "It's too bad that Dr. Karpov wouldn't have the time to treat you himself. I know his next three years are booked. But there are some excellent psychoanalysts there." He knew that I had already gone to therapists for years while I was getting my doctorate, but apparently they didn't count alongside those of the institute.

I thanked him politely and didn't comment.

Then Alan mentioned that someone we all knew well, a professor at Columbia named Richard Nager, was going blind. Nager, who could have been no more than forty, was a very warm person whom I especially liked.

"My God!" I said. "I didn't know that. How?"

"The official diagnosis is maculate degeneration," Alan said unemotionally. "But obviously there's more to it."

"More? What do you mean?"

"Richard had always avoided therapy, you know, which is why he specialized in statistics and research—"

"So?" I asked.

"Richard simply does not want to see things," Alan said very quietly.

"Doesn't want to see. What are you talking about?" I was aghast.

"That's correct," Alan said.

"Whose idea is that?" I asked. "Hasn't he been officially diagnosed? I mean he must have gone to a half dozen ophthalmologists if his eyesight is at stake."

"Oh, he has," Rosalind said, with no more apparent distress than her husband showed. I couldn't believe that they were all so detached and were using this pat explanation to keep themselves that way.

"My God, how can you say he wants to go blind? He's just had a kid after all those years. Don't you think he wants to see his daughter?"

"Possibly not," Alan said.

"What do you base that on?" I asked. I think I gulped down a second glass of wine without knowing it.

"Simple psychoanalytic theory," Alan said. "Freud has written a dozen articles explaining the unconscious wish in such cases. I've discussed it with Dr. Karpov, he agrees. He himself wrote a paper elaborating on—"

"Elaborating on what?" I was practically shouting. "On the idea that everyone who suffers, who endures a tragedy must, ergo, have wanted to suffer? I mean, that every woman who gets raped wanted to get raped? I don't know what you're talking about." I was addressing all three of them.

By then I could feel them looking at me as if I were a zoo animal, as if my being so emotional disqualified me as a member of their higher species.

I don't remember all the details of what followed, but they kept mentioning Samuel Karpov and his so-called psychoanalytic proofs of what they were saying. After a while I caught on that there was no arguing against the words of the master. It came out that Alan and Rosalind so revered Samuel Karpov, and his every conception, that they had just bought a house close to his, in a little town near Hastings, New York.

Then I said something I was sorry for. "I understand that he's a genius and never makes a mistake, but do you really think that breathing the same air molecules as he does on Sundays will make you people geniuses too?"

Alan put me in my place. "You seem upset," he said. "Maybe we should change the subject."

"Can I ask one more question?" I said, regaining my composure and resolving not to lose it again.

They nodded, a quiet jury of my self-styled superiors.

"Do you think that all the people who died at one time on the *Lusitania* really wanted to drown? Do you honestly think that they decided to go under, in consort, to end their lives together at that moment?"

Alan answered. "Actually I've read a lot about that, George. There had been warnings in the American newspapers that English ships in the north were in jeopardy. It was a choice to go on the *Lusitania*. Yes, the answer is that I do think these people—"

I saw where he was going and broke in. "Well, what about the *Titanic*?" I said. "The *Titanic* was a sheer pleasure trip. There were certainly no warnings about that. Don't you people believe in chaos, in tragedy, in the unforeseen? Isn't it possible that Richard's going blind is just a tragedy, a terrible tragedy, something we can't explain, that we can only feel sad about . . ."

"Let's not belabor the matter, shall we?" someone said.

A few minutes after that, Alan looked at his watch and said it was getting late, and I agreed. Though we finished up politely, we all knew that neither side would ever seek out the other again. In fact, there was little that we agreed on beyond the obvious fact of our incompatibility.

That had been about five years before Sammy revealed himself as Superman. Whether he had heard about me from Alan or knew my name from any other source, I will never know. If he had, he certainly didn't let on, but of course he wouldn't. Nor, I can say truthfully, did I care. Psychotherapists try never to prejudge people about whom they've heard from their patients, and I didn't want to judge Sammy by hearsay either.

We continued to play in the same games at the Midpoint, and I came to like him increasingly. As a partner he never recriminated, and he was a sportsmanlike adversary. He was unfailingly affable.

One day when I arrived, Sammy was playing with some guests of the club from Belgium and Switzerland who spoke only French. As I was always eager to refurbish my conversational skills, I joined their game. Sammy, who spoke like a native, told us that he had grown up in Paris, where his parents had fled to escape the Nazis. He seemed a little looser and more revelatory in French than in English. I had no trouble thinking of "Sammy of the Midpoint" as a totally different character from the Dr. Samuel Karpov about whom Alan had spoken with such whispered humbleness that I'd come to dislike him intensely.

Over the succeeding few years I found myself with less free time and went to the club infrequently. But whenever I saw Sammy there, he still seemed neatness and containment incarnate—he was always meticulously dressed, moderate in his speech, absolutely composed. Waiters in tuxedos brought food to the players, and sometimes a drink. But Sammy never had as much as a pretzel, not even after suffering a terrible sequence of rolls of the dice, which was when most people broke their diets by ordering a hamburger or by reaching into one of the bowls of M&M's that were posted around the plush suite. It seemed easy for Sammy to stay imperially thin; he almost looked impervious to the aging process.

About two years later the club changed location, and I got a letter to come to a backgammon brunch to commemorate the opening at its new venue. Backgammon had enjoyed a resurgence, and jet-setters were going to tournaments around the world. The new suite was even grander than the old one.

Sammy invited me to join him at one of the lunch tables, where he had in front of him a huge platter of food, which was unlike him. I knew the others there, except for a man who introduced himself as in from Monte Carlo. When a little later the man got up and left, someone whispered that he was worth a fortune.

"Diamonds," one person added.

Then Sammy looked up from his plate and whispered to us that the man had stolen his money in Iran and had fled with it to Monte Carlo. It had been alien to Sammy to gossip; now it was as if he'd shed his special identity.

The brunch was on a Sunday afternoon, and I had an appoint-ment at two, which left me too little time to play. I was astonished when Sammy offered to join a chouette of high rollers, people who played for a hundred dollars a point—at those stakes one could easily lose four or five thousand dollars in an hour or two. Making matters worse, there were a few players in the game who everyone knew were world-class competitors. Backgammon was their business, and they toured the world, fleecing the wealthy. Sammy or I might come out ahead in any given sitting, but we would lose everything over time if we kept playing with them.

The club provided stilt chairs so that those not actually playing could watch any game in progress, and I positioned one, ordered some coffee, and settled back to watch Sammy's game for the half hour I had left. When Sammy's partners rolled the dice, he eyed every throw as if his mortgage payment were riding on it. When it came his turn to play, he shook the dice cup so hard that more than once his dice flew out of it and tumbled across the floor. He waited annoyed while another player picked them up, and he never thanked the person who returned them to him; he was too concentrated on the game.

In spite of Sammy's sense of urgency, which was unlike anything I had ever witnessed from him before, luck went against him. After twenty minutes I peeked at the score sheet and saw that he was behind more than two thousand dollars. He looked wild-eyed. The two professionals in the game were used to seeing people unravel in front of them, and they gave Sammy mock encouragement. "You were very unlucky." "I think you played the position perfectly."

Finally it became the turn of a very well known actress to roll the dice. She was a woman everyone liked, and she played the game purely as a diversion. For her the stakes were truly not daunting. So far she'd been lucky, and was ahead even more money than Sammy was losing.

Before she took the dice cup, Sammy, who was to be one of her partners that game, whispered, "Keep up the good luck."

"I'll do my best," she said.

The game was tense and drawn out, and the stakes escalated as the two sides doubled and redoubled each other. The actress was having a wonderful time. She talked to her dice and discussed her moves with her partners—mostly with the two experts but also with Sammy, who exhorted his preferences. The man from Monte Carlo, also their partner, was on the phone. He seemed to regard the game in progress with only passing interest, though he too had a lot of money at stake.

The game reached the stage where the next few rolls would decide the winner, and the stakes doubled once more. The participants now stood to win or lose thirty-two hundred dollars each, and double that amount if the game ended in a gammon.

Overhearing that the stakes had so escalated, the players at the other tables held up their games to watch this one, and the owners of the club came over too.

The actress loved the theatricality of being the one to roll the dice for her side. The two experts studied the board closely and did their calculations while affecting nonchalance. Sammy was on his feet, watching the dice the way a pyromaniac watches a fire he has set. Only the Monte Carlo fellow remained indifferent, actually turning his back to the group and walking away so that he could concentrate on his protracted phone call.

Delighted by the onlookers, the actress kissed the dice with a loud smack as she dropped them into her cup. Then she shook the cup and spilled them out over the table.

A five and a three! How was she to play those two numbers? Conservatively? Or should she make a move that would decide the game on the very next roll? She favored the dramatic act. If her opponent rolled a two, the game would be lost. However, if he didn't, her move would win the game. She moved the checkers appropriately and left them in their new places so that her team could consider her suggestion. The move would not become official until she picked up her dice.

Unexpectedly Sammy stood up. "You can't possibly do that. It's insane," he said. "It's almost certain you'll lose the game that way."

The actress turned toward one of the experts and asked him what he thought.

"I agree with *you*," he told her. "I think it's our best move. We're favorites to win, and we're not favorites if you play safe."

Now Sammy was shouting. "I don't understand you people. Why on earth would you take such a risk?" He sounded perplexed and furious.

"Sam, really, I think this is the move," said the other expert. "It gives us our best chance."

"Okay," said the actress, reaching for the dice.

"I beg you, please don't touch the dice," Sammy implored. "Please don't. I beg you not to pick them up yet."

Sammy blocked the actress so that she couldn't reach them. His eyes watered, and he gestured broadly, as if crazed by fear and seeing himself as terribly misunderstood. In minutes he had become a man plucked from his home by the special police and about to be carted away to his death. He was Peter Lorre in *Casablanca*.

"I'm sorry, I don't agree with you," said the other professional calmly. "And my money is on this game just the way yours is."

"Please," begged Sammy a final time. "Wait, let's get our other partner's opinion."

With a gesture of despair he called across the room to the man from Monte Carlo. "Jacques, put down the phone. Come over here. We need your decision on a very important move."

Jacques gazed indifferently in the direction of the players and saw the actress at the table, representing his interest in the game. "Whatever she wants to do is all right with me," he said softly. "She's beautiful. I love her. I'll follow her anywhere."

"Thank you, darling," said the actress, scooping up the dice.

The opponent instantly rolled the number he needed and won a double game. Sammy and the members of his team had each lost sixty-four hundred dollars.

I thought, clearly this was not his institute. Things here did not always go just the way he wanted them to. But then again he knew that. Or did he?

The actress smiled warmly and said sorry to her partners, who, whatever they were really feeling, smiled and commented that it was okay. The professionals were specialists at losing gracefully. They wanted to teach others the way. The man from Monte Carlo shrugged his shoulders indifferently and returned to his conversation.

The players quietly set up the board for the next game.

Then the bystanders, who had been ambling back to their own games, froze as they heard Sammy shouting at the top of his voice. "Goddamn it! I don't understand why you people don't listen. What's wrong with you? I quit."

And he stormed into the club office, presumably to write out his check for his losses.

While going down in the elevator with another low-stakes player, I expressed surprise that Sammy had changed so much.

"Sammy has been like that for a few months now," the man said. "He gambles for thousands of dollars and he loses control. He blows up like that a lot. We're getting used to it."

I could hardly believe it. "What's gotten into him?" I asked. "I'm amazed."

"We think he's had some kind of tragedy in his life," the man said. "I have no idea what it is, but he's cracked. Utterly cracked."

The man went on. "Maybe something happened to his wife or one of his kids. Whatever it was, he really has lost his bearings. We're all trying to figure it out."

I wondered along with the fellow what it could be.

Sammy didn't actually quit the Midpoint, though perhaps he'd intended to momentarily. He continued playing, and though I never saw him as distraught as he'd been that Sunday afternoon, he had other, very poor interludes. Sammy was certainly not the same compact, restrained figure that he had been when he'd joined the club.

Over those years since I had argued with Alan, I would see him on occasion in the street or in a store. We would nod to each other politely but not stop to talk.

However, at about the time Sammy lost his composure, I sensed that Alan was thawing toward me. Once he detained me on Broadway with an anecdote about his oldest son, of whom he was very proud; another time, he complimented me for a book I had just had published.

I felt relieved that we were speaking more freely to each other, but took for granted that time alone had been the healer and gave it no more thought.

Then one day at the club I overheard a member telling Sammy about his daughter, who was about to finish medical school and study psychiatry. The man said that his daughter had talked about the brilliant Sam Karpov.

"For a while I didn't realize it was you. When I did, I told her I knew you very well, that we belonged to the same club. Boy, was she impressed!

"You're a director at the —— Institute," the man said. "Do you think she should apply there? It's really an honor—"

Sammy's face suddenly looked sour. "Martin, may I please stop you," he said. "I'm not a director there anymore. I was for twelve years, but I've stepped down."

"You have?"

"Four months ago. And from the journal also."

"Is that so!" said the man. "Why, if I may ask?"

"We thought it would be best," Sammy said. "The board and I."

He stopped abruptly, and his face seemed in shadows. But almost at once he forged on. "However, I would definitely advise your daughter to apply. The institute is excellent for psychoanalysis, though of course, I am not in a position to recommend her."

"Oh, I wouldn't want that. Maureen wouldn't want that."

I had eavesdropped past my limit and moved off. From a distance, I saw the man smile and Sammy try to smile back. But Sammy couldn't really.

There could be no doubt of it. Sammy had been found guilty of something awful. From that self-contained scheme of things he had been thrust from grace, like Hyperion from the heavens. But what could Sammy possibly have done that led them to demote him?

In spite of my better judgment, my mind capriciously spewed forth inane possibilities, one after the other. Had they caught Sammy embezzling funds? Or having an extramarital affair? Or having sex with a patient? Nothing made sense to me. Yet they had found him guilty of something, I was sure of it. Whatever it was, poor Sam Karpov had lost everything.

Suddenly I conceived of Sammy's gambling and rudeness at the club as akin to the behavior of a man who drinks because his whole life has taken a terrible turn for the worse.

I felt my curiosity piqued to a degree that I found almost unbearable.

And I realized that, almost surely, there was one person who could tell me what had happened—my old friend Alan.

Only a few weeks later I was delighted when, hearing my name called in the street, I turned around and saw it was Alan. It was a brisk September day in New York City, and Alan was talking with another man in a street café. He introduced me to the fellow, whose name was Barry, and we shook hands, and then Alan invited me to join them for coffee if I had time. I did, and sat down with them.

I was surprised when Alan said to Barry, "George was the first person who was really on to Sam Karpov."

"I was?" I said.

"Yes," Alan said. "We were just talking about the incident."

Barry, who was evidently also connected with the institute, said, "We have a big job ahead of us. We have to reexamine everything Karpov ever wrote for the journal, in the light of what we now know about him."

"You see, Karpov chaired the National Council on Freud twice," Alan said to me.

"I gather he doesn't edit the journal anymore," I said, trying to show as much conversance as I could with whatever they were talking about.

They both smiled.

I felt like asking them directly, "So what the hell did Karpov do that was so awful?" But the two of them seemed more likely to divulge something if they thought I knew it already.

Apparently the whole institute was buzzing about it.

A waiter put a cappuccino in front of me.

"I don't know if you should drink that stuff," Alan said solicitously.

"Probably not," I agreed.

"How did you know that Sam Karpov had so much unconscious violence in his makeup, George?" Barry asked me. "Alan told me that you had him pegged years ago. That's quite remarkable, since you never met him."

"Yes, Rosalind was very impressed when she thought it over," Alan said. "You sure took a strong stand against Karpov."

A strong stand, yes. But not against Karpov, I thought. However, if they wanted to misremember me as a genius, they had that right. It wasn't my obligation to refute them.

"So I was proven right," I said. "How long has it been?"

I'd meant since our debate. But Alan answered, "Five months. It was April seventeenth. That's five months ago, and I guess you know the rest."

"Well, I'd really like to hear your version," I said noncommittally.

Then Alan told me. "It happened at seven twenty in the morning—we're still trying to figure out the significance of those numbers. It was a Saturday, and I was headed to New York City for the spring psychoanalytic convention at the academy. You know, it's our all-day program, followed by a party at night.

"Roz was coming in for the afternoon papers. I especially wanted to hear the eight thirty paper on the letters between Freud and Fliess, so Roz stayed home with the kids. Thank God she did. Karpov was scheduled to be the discussant of that first paper in the morning.

"I took our white Chevrolet. There's a winding road where we are that leads right into the Taconic Parkway. It's about twenty minutes to the parkway. And when there's a heavy fog, as there was that day, you have to be very careful. You really can't see more than ten yards. So I was going real slow. I was listening to the news on the radio, then bang!"

He rapped his hand on the table, making a sharp, loud noise.

"What happened?" I asked.

"Thank God, I came out okay. After that terrible noise my head whipped back violently. I was stunned. Then I realized that a car had crashed into me from behind. For a minute I was afraid to get out of my seat and try to stand up. I guess I was in shock. I wasn't even sure it was over.

"When I turned around, I saw the fog lights of the car. Then I saw it was a black Mercedes. And I knew, even before Sam Karpov got out to see if I was all right. He had deliberately smashed into me."

"Deliberately!" I gasped.

"Well, of course, it was deliberate."

"What did he say?" I asked.

"He asked if I was okay. I walked around a little, and I guess I was. But he had smashed my trunk, he really folded up the rear end of my car. He said he was terribly sorry. He said he didn't see me until the last few seconds, and when he did, it was too late."

"You don't believe him?" I asked.

"Obviously he was trying to kill me, or at least injure me."

I recalled that out of idolatry Alan had gotten a house near Karpov's. They had both paid for that proximity.

"Are you saying he knew it was you in the car?" I asked Alan.

"Knew? He knew unconsciously. Of course he did. He must have known."

"Why on earth would he do it?" I asked.

"That we really don't know . . ."

"So maybe it wasn't deliberate," I said.

Barry interceded. "Karpov himself, by the time he got to New York City, realized that it must have been deliberate. Even if Alan wanted to stay in treatment with him—"

"Which I didn't," said Alan. "I'm not crazy—"

"I was saying," resumed Barry, "that even if Alan were willing to continue, Karpov realized that with such murderous instincts he should not be treating Alan. Or anyone else for that matter."

"Yes, my analysis with him stopped abruptly," Alan said. "Naturally I told the institute what had happened and why I couldn't deal with this man. He might kill me next time, God knows how! I couldn't entrust my formative years to him."

"So you left him," I said.

"Yes, and so did a lot of other people when they heard. The important thing is that the institute insisted that he resign as control-analyst and that he not chair any more presentations, at least not until he works this thing out."

"And no more connection with the journal," Barry said.

"I can't believe it," I said. "It's like a quarantine. You're treating him like a man with the plague—"

"His unconscious *makes* him a plague," Alan said. And then with fury: "He's out. I'm sure he'll leave the institute entirely."

"You won't be seeing his name anymore," Barry said. "He's had to resign from everything. He knows he's a very dangerous man."

I resisted any impulse I had to mount a defense for Sam Karpov. Alan, and the whole institute for that matter, had already indicted him and sentenced him to his ritual death, and Sam Karpov had no doubt that the sentence was just.

So Samuel Karpov, who had lived by the sword, had died by the sword of interpretation, I thought. He had pleaded guilty when he was probably innocent, because he had no word for "innocent" or for "accident" in his lexicon.

From what I gathered a few months after that, the institute did, indeed, rip the stripes off Samuel Karpov's sleeve. He remained a member but was no longer seen on the podium at meetings, and his name was removed from the masthead of the journal. New trainees chose others of the old guard to treat them five times a week. Samuel Karpov's long waiting list, which would have kept me in the wings for three years had I wanted to see him professionally, had melted away.

According to Alan, Sam Karpov took his demotions with stoic resignation. A few years later, when I read about evidence uncovered about a Celtic man found in a bog, which proved that he had offered himself up for ritual slaughter so that the gods would bar Julius Caesar from Ireland, I thought of Sam.

Only at the Midpoint, and possibly in other places far away from the institute, was Sammy very much alive. Apparently he had money enough to go on gambling loosely, which he did. He became a welcome figure despite his outbursts, being one of those who lost a lot more than he won. The professional players, who were not allowed in a low-stakes game, would sit around watching TV and chatting, hoping for the arrival of Sam or a few other players like him.

When Sammy came in, they were on their feet, smiling and acting as if they were just starting without him and he was a welcome addition. They chatted with him amiably and would ask him if he'd been busy, and if he'd gone on vacation. He might have surmised from their precise memory of how long he'd been absent from the club that they relied on him for his money. But if he did, it seemed not to matter.

During the games they would congratulate him on how well he had played, and afterward, especially if he'd lost a lot, one of them would offer to drive him uptown. "Are you ready to go, Sammy boy?"

Sammy did his best to act restrained with them. He was, after all, older than most of them and he was a professional man, a notable analyst. But he evidently delighted in their company. It crossed my mind that he would doubtless have preferred to start a new institute, with the backgammon crowd as his trainees and followers. And if he had spilled money among them as liberally at his institute as he did at the club, I am sure that they would have followed him readily.

About a year later Sammy calmed down at the club and returned to playing for lower stakes.

I continued to see him there on occasion. His status at the institute slowly returned as he went on producing new papers and propounding the institute's theories, and as the story of his accident lost its novelty over the years.

Sammy himself never doubted that he'd acted with unconscious ill intent. But now he presumably imagines that he understands what the problem was and that he has defanged himself. He would not have undertaken most of his old responsibilities at the institute unless this were so, for Sammy was always an honorable man.

I for one am glad that Sammy did not ultimately ruin his life from the security of his silent tank, his Mercedes.

Just why he threw himself to the mercy of luck after the accident is something that perhaps Sammy himself is best equipped to understand. I like to think that underneath Sammy really did believe in chance but was too committed to his extreme position, that unconscious motivation accounts for the effect of every human action, to plead "bad luck" even in his own defense. If so, he may have joined the ranks of those who gamble because they believe that luck owes them something for having mistreated them.

All this was fifteen years ago. Sammy, I am glad to report, now well into his seventies, is still practicing, though he has severed his connections with the institute. Since I am no longer a member of the Midpoint Club, I don't know if he still plays there, but I'd like to think that he is more at peace both at work and at play.

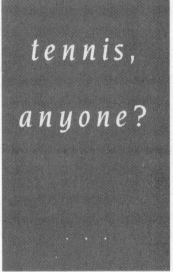

tennis, anyone?

IT WAS A BLEAK GRAY TWILIGHT with the day's snow still falling. Drifts were already up to the curbs, leveling the sidewalks with the street. The city lights gave off blurry images at best. What traffic there was crawled cautiously homeward, and only intrepid pedestrians were out.

Tricia Lester had arrived at my office and introduced herself a few minutes earlier. She had brushed a few flakes of snow from her long ranch mink coat and then removed it, revealing a superb body, about five six, lush and lithe, in a cream-colored blouse, brown wool slacks, and brown boots, whose cuffs were turned down just below the knees. She had a haughty but beautiful face with high cheekbones and hard, emasculating blue eyes. She had said, "Richard's always late," and scowled.

I dabbled with papers on my desk, not wanting to begin before he got there. I was aware of Tricia's big gold earrings, which caught the light with their twisted knots, and of her wedding band and another ring, both cold with diamonds. Her comment, "Do what you have to, doctor. I'll wait," felt presumptuous, though I could not have said why.

I was relieved when the doorbell rang. Richard, six feet tall, with dark wavy hair and a very handsome face, introduced himself. I ushered him in, and he sat on the couch near her. He was formidable in his Dunhill suit, with its very narrow pinstripe, cut precisely for his well-formed shoulders and for no one else on earth.

He smiled at her. "The driver was late."

She didn't grant him the movement of a facial muscle. She asked him, "Is John out there now? He'll have to take us home before we go to the airport."

Richard just nodded. His black shoes were highly polished. He and Tricia were both accustomed to being delivered door to door.

Hardly turning to look at him, Tricia said with disgust, "That jacket doesn't fit you the way it should. You gained weight since you bought it three months ago."

The temperature was about the same inside my office as it was outside, and they weren't even there to discuss their relationship, which seemed to be living up to their expectations. They had mentioned that they were coming to talk about Tricia's mother, and to reach a conclusion about what to do with her.

We arrived at that topic quickly. Tricia summarized her mother pithily. "She walks around everywhere in a rumpled old raincoat, carrying a tennis racket."

"A tennis racket?" I echoed.

Richard explained. "Yeah, winter or summer. She swings it. She goes into a panic if you try to take it away."

"She won't even check it in a restaurant. She looks great going through the snow with it. It's as warped as she is by now," Tricia said.

"No," said Richard. "Not really. She keeps a plastic cover on it."

"I think she really lost touch about five years ago, doctor," Tricia confided. "We're doing our best with her. After all, she is my mother. And my sister in Chicago doesn't give a damn about her. But we've got to live our own lives. We're trying to make this marriage work. It's my third."

"And my second," Richard volunteered.

Tricia said, "She's really becoming a heavy burden."

"A burden?" I asked.

"You should see her. It's hard to have her come into our building. Our friends tell us we shouldn't put her in a home. But they don't really know what the problem is—"

"Now wait a second," Richard broke in. "Arthur knows it. He has a full-time nurse for his mother."

"When did she get that army raincoat?" Tricia asked sardonically, ignoring Richard. "During the war?"

"It must have started raining one day, or snowing," Richard tried to explain. "And she went to an army-navy store and bought it."

"Yeah, seven years ago, and she never takes it off," said Tricia. Then turning to me: "So anyhow, I found this wonderful nursing home an hour and fifteen minutes from here—in Connecticut. She'll be much happier there."

"She'd be trapped there. Like an animal!" Richard said.

"She won't mind."

"How can you say that?" Richard pleaded.

"We're pretty trapped with her now," Tricia shot back.

I asked her what she meant.

"Well, for example, we would have left a lot earlier if we didn't have to come here. We'd be in the Caribbean by now."

Their itinerary was five days in the sun, then a week in Rome and Milan and another in London—to survey the latest fashions and do some shopping. Both had inherited their wealth and had greatly increased their capital, Richard as an investment adviser and Tricia through a very successful ski shop with three outlets.

Tricia's father had apparently made his money after divorcing her mother and had remained close to both his daughters until he died.

"I was hoping that you would have an opinion about whether we should put her away," Richard said to me, while Tricia's eyes panned the walls of my office as if she were evaluating my net worth.

"Is she difficult?" I asked them.

"Not at all," Richard said.

"Has she lost a lot of memory?" I asked.

"Not at all," Richard said again.

"Would you say she's confused?" I asked Richard.

"Not much more than she's ever been."

"Not confused!" Tricia's eyes glinted. "Wait until you meet her, doctor. You have to see her. She dresses like a pig. It's sad but it's true, and she waves that racket."

"She gets around. She gets around," countered Richard defensively.

"Can she handle money?" I asked.

Tricia snapped at me contemptuously, "Money! She doesn't need money. She's so unkempt and overweight—"

"What's the difference?" said Richard.

"I know *you* obviously don't give a damn about weight. You used to. But I guess you're planning to leave me anyhow."

He didn't respond.

"Really, why do you say that?" I asked her.

"That's the way men are. I should say that's the way this man is. They want younger women after a while."

"That's happened to you before?"

"It's happened to everyone, hasn't it?" She laughed mockingly. "Doctor, I'm not your patient. My mother is the one we're worried about." The cold light in her eyes gave me the fantasy that she wanted to beam her mother onto another planet—or out of existence entirely.

"She'll be sleeping with the damn racket soon," Tricia went on. "She's going to whack someone with it, I'm sure."

"Has she ever actually threatened anyone, or come close?" I asked.

"No. Not yet," Tricia said in a sinister tone.

"I'll have to see her," I said.

I had the obvious thought that mere embarrassment over her mother was hardly a reason for Tricia to imprison the lady, doddering or not. But I was concerned that if I confronted Tricia, I might be pulled off the case at once, dismissed as incompetent. I needed to temporize if I was going to exert any impact.

"Then mainly it's the potential danger of her swinging that racket," I said, as if summing up.

"That's right," Richard replied. "If she would put that racket away and just act a little more restrained—" He stopped abruptly.

I turned toward Tricia and asked her, "If your mother stayed away from you, and just looked rumpled but without the racket, I mean if she didn't look outright crazy . . ."

She smiled. "I didn't know you professionals used a word like 'crazy.'"

Richard turned toward her and said almost pleadingly, "I guess if she just slowed down and wasn't a burden, and put that racket away, we could leave her alone."

Tricia rose to her feet and flexed her back. "Damn it, I wish I had worked out today, before going south," she commented apropos of nothing, and I knew I was being dismissed for the day.

"Okay. We'll leave it at that for a while. Have her call me," I said.

Richard peeked through my shutters and confirmed that his limo was right out front.

After Richard and Tricia were gone, I realized that, curiously, they had been much more open with me than many couples are in a first session. Tricia had unhesitatingly displayed her contempt for her mother, and her own fear of being abandoned by Richard— by all men. The two of them hadn't pretended to be harmonious in front of me, though I would have bet that they tried to pass as the ideal couple to others in their circle.

I puzzled out that, paradoxically, their very disdain for me had accounted for their easy openness with me. Because they'd considered me a mere functionary and far beneath them, they had felt free to voice whatever came to mind. They had come to me to get insight, but it hardly mattered what judgment I might form of them.

I remembered an observation by Richard Wright, the black writer, who as a boy had worked as a bellhop bringing drinks and sandwiches to whites in a Southern hotel. Wright had observed that the women didn't even bother to cover up when he entered the room. So profound was their conviction that blacks did not count as people that they readily allowed him to see them in their nakedness. I concluded that in this case I was the servant in much the same way. However, maybe I still had some leverage to help a person even worse off—Tricia's mother, whose future depended utterly on the two of them and now perhaps on me.

It was another harsh misty night, bleak and slippery, when Tricia's mother came in. Rita was a bulky woman, well into her seventies, with a big-boned coarse face and sorrowful brown eyes. Her straight gray hair was cut short, and a brown army raincoat covered her whole shapeless body. In her left hand she clutched a heavy old-fashioned wood tennis racket in a transparent case.

After I introduced myself at the door, she said in a voice louder than she probably realized it was, "I've seen doctors, but not this kind of doctor."

She seemed oblivious of my previous patient, a young woman, who was in my waiting room bundling up against the icy evening.

Inside my office Rita sat in a corner of my couch, tennis racket still in hand, waiting for me to begin.

Not knowing how to start, I mentioned that Richard had arranged the appointment for her.

"He's a nice guy," she said.

"He is," I answered.

There was a long pause, and again not knowing what to say I felt like an actor who forgot his big speech on opening night.

She took her racket out of its case and adjusted her grip on it.

"I guess Tricia and Richard are in Europe by now," I offered.

She responded, "I hope Patricia likes the hotels she's staying at."

"Why, doesn't she usually?"

"Well, I haven't heard from her since she went to Europe, and she usually doesn't like the first hotel. She switches around a couple of times," Rita said flatly.

She spoke without expression, almost as if she were reading and didn't understand her own words.

In an attempt to move things along, I mentioned that Tricia had been eager for her to see me.

"Yes, she's a wonderful person that way. She cares so much about everybody," Rita said.

She told me some facts about Tricia and her other daughter, Dorothy. She spoke of them both fondly, and sometimes moved her head in the exaggerated way that so often bespeaks a loss of control in the elderly; it is a disinhibition sometimes due to weakening of the ever-regulating frontal lobes.

For a while after that she just sat quietly, staring down at the dead center of her racket, which she tilted so that it faced her.

"I hope she stays with Richard, he's such a nice person. They're both so nice. They're the only people I see," Rita said.

Had she any idea that her daughter was planning to put her under permanent house arrest? It didn't sound as if she did. But possibly her fulsome praise of Tricia and Richard was a desperate response to a fear that they would.

During a slow half hour she still didn't mention how she spent her daytime hours or bring up her likes or dislikes.

She mentioned Tricia's two daughters now living with Tricia's ex-husband, Frank, in Florida. "They're two darlings. I talk to them on the phone anytime I want to. I can call collect. Frank pays." She seemed proud.

But then a shadow came over her face. "I don't like to bother them too much, though. They have their own friends."

She looked at me directly, through her watery eyes.

Then suddenly her mouth set in a grim line, and she stopped talking altogether.

As if in response to a thought that she did not convey, she peered at the strings of her racket again and then swung it slowly, making an arc of no more than ten inches. She did this repeatedly, as if memorizing the correct stroke.

I had resolved not to mention the racket. It was just too obvious, and if I had any hope of not becoming part of the multitude to her, I'd decided, I had better not bear witness to her behavior by even referring to the racket, which seemed virtually an extension of her hand.

However, still looking down at the strings, she said, "I guess you've noticed my tennis racket."

"Well, yes. Actually I had," I said. But that was as far as I went.

There was another long pause, which I ended by asking her if she wanted to take her raincoat off and hang it up.

"No thanks," she said, politely but with a crispness suggesting that she'd felt molested by my even asking the question.

She seemed to be getting more melancholy as the minutes ticked by—as if she were sinking into a vortex of I didn't know what.

As I watched her move her racket repeatedly through its slow pendulum, I felt stymied as to how to reach her.

Half to myself I said, "Oh, I see you're a lefty."

"You've seen me play?" she shot back, with an elation so sudden it surprised me.

"Possibly," I said.

"Yes? You remember me? Were you ever in England?" she asked, beaming.

"I was. Many times," I told her.

"Wimbledon. No, you wouldn't have seen me play the match in Wimbledon against Doris Hart. You're too young. That was an incredible tournament. Pauline Betz was in it, and Helen Wills Moody. Have you heard of her? Actually, she was only Helen Wills then." There was a twinkle in her eyes.

"What year was that?"

"Nineteen thirty-nine. I used a racket just like this one. We all did."

But suddenly she stopped and looked off, out of the window. I wondered if she had lost her train of thought or if she was mentally back there, playing in the tournament.

I decided to wait, and in a minute the twinkle returned.

"I looked at the draw sheet to see who I had to play," she said, as if it were yesterday. "My first opponent was from France, I can't remember her name. She was a damn good player. I beat her easily, though. She sure was a good sport about it. Gee, I'd really like to remember who it was. I bet you knew her."

"And you played Doris Hart, you said?"

"Yes. It was a beautiful day, without a cloud in the sky, and everybody cheered Doris Hart, naturally." Rita was still smiling. "She had beaten me twice before, but I felt that if I could keep the ball deep I could beat her. I won the first set, and she won the second.

"We took a break before the third set, and she talked to her coach and I talked to Mario, Patricia's father. Mario and I had been married about two years. He didn't know much about tennis, but he said, 'You can definitely beat her.'

"She beat me in the third set, and you know what she said?"

"No, what?" I asked her.

"She said, 'Rita, you were terrific. I don't think I'll have to face anyone better than you in the whole tournament, because there is no one better than you are.' "

She paused, as if responding to the story, and I saw that her whole face had softened. The grim line that had been her mouth had given way to full-sized lips; her eyes were active.

"You must have felt bad about losing," I commented.

"Yeah, I really did," she admitted. "But you get over those things. The main thing is to *play*. How many people can say they got to the quarter finals at Wimbledon?"

"Very few," I granted.

"It's something I'll never forget," she said.

Then Rita asked me if I played tennis.

I told her I did, but she broke in and announced that she had been ranked thirteen in the world one year. Her asking me had merely been the politesse befitting a champion, it didn't really matter how much or how well I played. She mentioned another good player whom she had beaten.

I asked her if she still played once in a while.

"Who? Me? Now?" she asked. "I gained too much weight, I'm too slow. Maybe if I got serious and lost fifty pounds. But I'll admit something to you. I'm not sure I could beat anyone with these new graphite rackets."

She told me again that she was left-handed, and added that she had a great serve.

Our time was up. Obviously Rita was toting that racket every-where as a pretext to talk about her past. I was astonished that Tricia had never even mentioned that her mother had once been a high-ranking tennis player. How could Tricia omit such an ob-viously relevant fact? I had assumed from Tricia's presentation that the racket was some inexplicable aberration having nothing to do with anything in Rita's real life.

But now I saw that the racket was very meaningful to Rita. She banked on people's seeing it and bringing up the subject of tennis. The instant someone did, she could return to the world in which she had excelled and been happy.

She readily agreed to come back in a few days, and we set up another appointment. It seemed advisable to set up one session at a time rather than to broach a weekly schedule. Her knowing that she could stop at any time might be important to her, and besides, I wasn't sure she could remember a regular schedule.

I wrote down the time of our next meeting on a card, which she took from me. I was certain of one thing—she was looking forward to more tennis talk next time.

During the days before I saw Rita again I came to feel increasingly that it would be terrible to incarcerate her. Obviously she was forgetful, and she was obsessed by memories of the past. But the intrusiveness of such memories often accompanies forgetfulness in the elderly, and Rita's present life was a vacuum that cried out to be filled. She had doubtless lost many brain cells that once functioned for her, but I didn't feel that she was seriously senile or confused. According to Richard when he'd first called, her physician had found no sign of Alzheimer's or of anything unusual for a woman her age.

I saw Rita essentially as a stranger in the modern world, with no allies. But idiosyncratic as she was, she still fared quite adequately. She locomoted well through the city, she enjoyed her walks and her freedom. So far as I knew, she wasn't dangerous to herself or to anyone else.

I could certainly see why Rita would be irritating to Tricia. To the fastidious and socially conscious Tricia, her mother's appearance and behavior with the racket were a disgrace. But it would have to cut much deeper than that for Tricia to be as pitiless as she was toward her mother. What had seemed to me at first to be irritation on Tricia's part now appeared to be contempt for everything that Rita valued, including playing tennis. Tricia certainly knew as well as I did what her mother used the racket for. And as desirable as the racket was to Rita, it was almost that undesirable to her daughter, who must have mentioned it half a dozen times to me.

I felt urgently that I had to forestall Tricia's packing her mother off. For Rita, who still pictured herself a near superstar, going to a home where she was restricted would be a pointless and horrifying ending. Not only would Rita feel herself a prisoner, but the house rules of the Connecticut institution would almost certainly demand that the racket be taken away from her. I could already picture myself calling to say that I was her therapist and imploring management to permit her to take the racket with her everywhere.

I realized that in order to save Rita I would need a much better understanding of Tricia, in whose hands the decision rested. But this would be difficult because Tricia was so reluctant to talk about herself. Tricia had been right when she had said that she wasn't my patient—her mother was. By definition our patients are those who choose to come to us, and not always those whose behavior we would like to change. It was a delicate predicament.

The next week Rita began by asking, "What should I do now?"

"Just say anything that comes to mind," I told her.

She was silent for a while as she gazed at my plants and then at my globe of the world, which lights from the inside. She looked furtively at me and then down at the strings of her racket as she said, "You know, I was thinking, I forgot to tell you something last time."

"What was that?" I asked her.

"Allison Danzig, the man who writes about tennis for the *Times*, mentioned me in an article after my match with Doris Hart."

"Really? What did he say?"

"He said that I have a very hard forehand and that I cover ground surprisingly well. I wish I had that article to show you."

"I believe you."

"Even so, I wish I had it."

She returned to talk about her tennis exploits, and as I listened I kept looking for openings to inquire about the rest of her life. It wasn't easy to edge in. She was running through a set speech about matches she'd played, and I felt up against a surface as smooth as glass. But finally I found a place.

Rita had mentioned a wonderful party after a tennis tournament, and I asked her about it.

"I wore high-heeled ankle strap shoes and a gorgeous black straw hat. Mario was with me—"

"How long had you known Mario?"

"About three years by then. We'd been married almost that long."

"You were still happy together?"

"I was, I guess. But he wasn't."

"Why not?"

"He used to call me selfish because I played tennis all the time. But I had to. You can't be a top player without practicing and playing in the tournaments." She nodded indulgently, as if I would surely understand.

"And what did he say?"

"I think he was angry with me for not going to his mother's funeral."

"You didn't?"

"I couldn't. It was the week of the Florida Open. Mario went."

She told me Mario was a bruiser of a man, a former wrestler, who was very close to his family, none of whom liked Rita. Mario, who drove a truck, had met Rita when he went to watch his brother play in a Parks Department tennis tournament. He was smitten by her and proposed to her in three weeks. She married him but continued her routine of practice and total involvement with the game.

For a while Mario would shuffle his schedule to go to tournaments with her. "If it wasn't for me, he might never have gone to Europe at all," she said with a lordly look.

Their daughters were born during their first three years together. From the beginning, Mario begged Rita to cut down on her tennis schedule and give the babies more time. But even when Rita was not on the road, she paid a minimum of attention to them.

On occasion during that session, when Rita mentioned an event, I would ask her where her daughters were at the time. She would always answer with sovereign finality, and in almost the same words, "Oh, they were at home. With a woman we hired."

With ten minutes to go I almost welcomed Rita's returning exclusively to the topic of tennis. I felt that I had caused her to suffer by my interruptions with personal questions. She could go on only so long without the esprit of her tennis past.

She told me her best win was over Jinx Falkenburg. "She was good, and her brother once got to the finals in Forest Hills," Rita informed me. "I was working a lot on my second serve."

"Do you watch tennis on TV?" I asked her.

"No, I never do. I told you the game has gone down, now that they're using these very light, fast rackets. It's no fun anymore."

She looked disappointed when I told her the time was up.

After she left, it occurred to me that Rita had no idea how much she had told me about herself. Perhaps she had changed a lot less in the last half century than I'd imagined.

When I saw her again, Rita seemed even more averse to talking about her private life than she had been. She needed the nutrition of nonstop tennis talk, which she sometimes iconographed by moving her racket appropriately. Once she stood up and held it flat out in front of her to convey how she'd dropped a ball just over the net against an adversary.

The glint of pride in that perfect placement did not leave her eyes as she added about that opponent, "She's dead now. She died about two years ago."

Rita was anything but lovable up close, and I had to remind myself that her predicament was the same as it had been when I hadn't yet gotten to know her so well.

Our fourth meeting fell on the day that Tricia and Richard returned from vacation, and I knew they would be calling me very soon. In that session Rita rounded out the picture of having spent a long, isolated life, one entirely without friends. She told me that when Mario had asked for the divorce, she had readily given him custody of their two daughters. He had afterward gone into the used-car business with a brother and "made gobs of money." She told me, "I never saw him after that."

"Did you miss him?"

"Not really."

"Why do you think he wanted a divorce?"

"I can tell you why. It's because I didn't like sex."

I got her to resume her account of her life at about the stage when she and Mario broke up. Rita had continued playing in tournaments. "In those days if you wanted to go on in tournaments, you couldn't take money to teach. You would lose your amateur status. A man I knew was ruined because he gave someone a lesson. The local pro turned him in, and he could never play in tournaments anymore."

"So tournament tennis was for the rich, or at least those with some other means of support," I said.

"It was, and after Mario left, I couldn't go to many tournaments. I had to save up for one or two a year."

Mario's alimony payments were thin, and soon afterward Rita's career petered out. After quitting tournament play, she tried giving lessons, but she had trouble keeping students. She took odd jobs working at tennis courts, and then worked in a store. She finally got a job minding a table-tennis emporium while the owner was off giving lessons, she kept that job until her retirement.

Rita told me, "After Mario made his money, he spent fortunes on Tricia and Dorothy. They had the best schools, summer camp, rich clothes. He took them to Europe. When he died they were very upset. He left them millions."

"Did he ever remarry?"

"No. He never did."

She hadn't brought up the topic of her daughter's return from Europe, so I did.

"I guess Tricia will tell you all about the trip," I said.

"Not really. She doesn't tell me that kind of thing, and I don't ask," Rita said with a resignation that sounded very long-standing.

"How come?" I pressed.

"My daughters are disgusted with me. The way I dress. And I talk to myself sometimes."

"Do you?" I asked.

"I'm not aware of it. They tell me I do."

After that session, when in my waiting room a wise-guy young man saw her with her tennis racket, he smiled at her and said, "Tennis, anyone?" Rita acted as if he weren't there.

I wasn't surprised when I got a message that Tricia had called. She left word on my answering machine that she would be home all evening.

When I got back to her, she asked me to wait until Richard picked up the extension. Then she said, "I really think this experiment has to be over."

"Why?"

"My mother threatened someone with her tennis racket while we were away. We just found out about it."

"Who?" I asked.

"The manager of the Red Apple, our supermarket. Martin Hickey, if you need to know his name," said Tricia bitingly. "She's going to hurt somebody very soon. We can't have her raising her racket to people."

"Do you know any more about it?" I asked.

"Yes, a security guard stopped her and told her to leave the supermarket with the racket. She started to swing it. They would have pressed charges, but they knew her, and they just told her to leave."

"I think Tricia's right," I heard Richard say.

"Well," I said, "I certainly agree we can't let her hit anyone with that racket. Or threaten someone. But I was hoping . . . maybe if she would give it up . . . I mean, if I could get her to put it away, to leave it home and walk through the streets without it, it would be a lot cheaper . . ." I could hear myself faltering. Cheaper? I thought. That wasn't the point at all. I realized I'd compromised myself to the degree of appealing to Tricia on the only grounds on which I thought I had a chance to persuade her. The real issue was freedom versus the loss of it—and almost as important to Rita, it was racket in hand versus being deprived of it.

I changed my approach, knowing even as I did that I was treading on more slippery ground. "Maybe we owe her just a little more time—"

"Doctor, I owe my mother nothing!" Tricia said. "She was never a mother to me: I shouldn't even call her mother . . ."

"I know she's been terrible to you," I granted. "I gather she's always been a very selfish person, and how hard it must have been for you and your sister. And I realize that if it weren't for your father you never would have made it. God knows what would have happened."

"She told you that!" said Tricia in absolute surprise.

"No. But it's obvious from what she did tell me. You could hardly have had a worse mother unless she left you in a garbage can—"

"She just about did. What do you think of that, doctor? What do you think of that?"

"I know. And I agree that you don't owe her anything. But if I can get her to leave that racket home, at least most of the time—"

"Most of the time! She'll kill someone with it. I hate the damn racket anyhow, even if she never did anything with it."

"She did plenty with it, already," I agreed.

"What do you mean?" Tricia asked.

"She neglected you with it, didn't she? She neglected you for tennis. She chose the racket over you."

"She did. That's exactly what she did," said Tricia, momentarily softening. Of course, Tricia had always known it, though perhaps she'd never quite thought of it that way.

"But you made it," I added quickly. "I'm sure you have problems. We all have. But you still have all your chances in front of you. That's the big thing."

Somewhere along the line I realized that I was breaking my own personal rule never to do therapy during a brief phone call. Too much can go wrong when you don't see the person or have time to clear things up. But afterward I consoled myself in remembering Tricia's words that she wasn't my patient. It wasn't really therapy. I was negotiating for time.

"Just give me a few weeks, please, and let me see if I can get her to leave that racket home," I said. "I want to find out exactly what happened. And what your mother thought was happening. Maybe you and Richard can come in one more time in a month or so, and we'll decide."

"My mother's the star. She's always the star," Tricia said, and I could feel her beautiful, cold eyes rejecting me and my plea.

"Please—"

"Both Richard and I are very busy." She was retaliating in kind. Her mother had always been very busy over the years when Tricia had needed her most.

But finally Tricia agreed to put off the decision for a while longer and give me some more time to work with Rita. Perhaps I could help her improve enough to go through life without her "damn tennis racket."

We agreed that after that brief trial period Tricia would come in and talk to me before reaching her decision.

I told Tricia, "I know you really don't owe her anything. Not a thing. It's really very generous of you to go this far."

After I hung up, I hoped that Tricia wouldn't call me back and change her mind.

Immediately I wondered what could induce Rita to surrender her conversation piece, the prompter that brought people to the one topic that allowed her to live in her glory.

I pictured her talking to strangers in stores, on buses, and in the streets. She could relive her life a little with them, one after the other, until they tired of her conversation and moved on. It was something she could never do with her own daughter, she had forfeited that. And now my task was to persuade her to surrender the tennis racket itself.

Only then did I recall having heard Richard say at the end of the phone call, "Thanks, doctor. We really appreciate it." The memory of his words buoyed me up.

The incident at the supermarket had turned up the heat in the case considerably. Suddenly I faced an unpleasant time pressure. I had planned to avoid broaching Rita's giving up the racket for as long as I could, so that Rita would continue to talk and I wouldn't unsettle her into clamming up.

Obviously Rita's need to get people to talk to her about her past was part of a much deeper problem. Her lugging the tennis racket with her everywhere was only a symptom.

Ideally I would have left the symptom alone for a long stretch while I sought to deal with her isolation—and with the self-centeredness that had estranged her from everyone she knew. But this had become a case in which so-called symptom removal had taken obvious precedence. I would have to remove the symptom fast or she would be gone for good.

It was imperative that I zero in on the topic of her giving up the racket right away. Moreover, I would have to get Rita to tell me what had happened at that supermarket, in case she really was dangerous, which I still didn't believe. I hoped that she wouldn't feel that I was in league against her, and I gave a lot of thought to how I should broach that topic. But it seemed that nothing short of direct questioning would do.

In the next session Rita seemed eager to give me more details about the various jobs she'd had in the pro tennis world after she had retired from tournament play. She spoke especially about her most responsible and best-paying job. A man she had once played mixed doubles with, a highly ranked player turned teacher, had paid her to watch over his courts when he wasn't there and to rally with people when they had no partner. But Rita said that within a short time she found out that he was receiving complaints about her.

"People said I was eccentric," she told me, but she had no idea why. Before the year was out, the man had fired her, and after that she went steadily downhill in the nature of the jobs she was able to pick up.

As a lead-in to the topic of her racket, I inquired whether the rackets she'd played with back then resembled the one she was clutching at the moment.

"Yes, certainly," she snapped. "And they don't make these heavy Spalding rackets anymore."

"Yes, the racket you're holding really does look heavy," I said, going along with her.

After a pause I asked her why she carried it around with her everywhere.

She replied at once, "For protection."

"Protection!" I echoed. "Rita, do you need protection here?"

She looked warily around. "No, but you never know for sure."

"What could happen? I don't understand."

She writhed in her chair and closed her hand tighter on the racket. "Well, I don't want it to get stolen," she said.

I plunged ahead. "Stolen. Do you think I'm going to steal it?"

"You never know. People do want to take it away from me."

"They do? Who?"

"I don't know. I like the feel of this old wood racket. I grew up playing with this kind of racket, you know. It's the exact size and weight of the racket that Sarah Palfrey Cooke used to use. She was a great champion."

Rita held the racket in the forehand position to check its balance. "I really like the feel of it," she said.

"Can I try it?" I asked.

Suddenly she clenched it tightly and put her handbag over it on her lap. "No, it's really mine, doctor. I don't want anyone stealing it." A look of pain came over her face.

She just sat there, as if the hideous possibility of the racket's being stolen, the ultimate horror for her, was reverberating in her mind.

For the moment I withdrew from that line of questioning, though I knew I would have to resume it soon.

She was guarding the racket in her lap now, and I imagined that she would have died before relinquishing it. I wondered if it was this racket in particular that meant so much to her or if any racket of the period would have been as precious.

Watching Rita look at me so suspiciously, I experienced a flash of annoyance at her. As always when I feel angry or annoyed with a patient, I took pains to examine why I felt that way. It stands to reason that if I feel a certain way about a patient, others might too. Using this fact, I can often learn the effect my patient has on other people by pinpointing exactly how the patient makes me feel. It's especially important for me to identify annoyance so that I can step back from it and avoid involuntarily saying something in pique that I would regret later.

In seconds, my reaction became clear to me. I felt like telling her, "Keep your racket. Get locked up. It would be fitting justice for your self-centered life. Don't you even realize that I'm the only one who is on your side?"

At that moment I felt sympathetic with Tricia, who must have been mistreated by her mother repeatedly, just as I felt I was being mistreated now. I certainly believed that Tricia had not been wrong in saying that she didn't owe her mother a damn thing.

But then I looked over at Rita, at her puffy square face and matted hair, as she clutched the racket and pouted like a little girl, and I realized that it wasn't my role to judge her true deserts and treat her accordingly. She was suffering as palpably as any innocent victim does. Of course, I knew too that very often the most disagreeable people find themselves in the worst plights, especially in later life. And whatever the cause of her strife, this woman was utterly maimed in judgment.

As a therapist I couldn't help only those people who in my opinion had lived exemplary lives, and here it devolved upon me to use my best skills to offset the harm that Rita had done to herself and to help her find the best possible life.

Now she was regarding me with challenging eyes.

I forced myself to smile at her.

She seemed to relax a little, and then she said, "At home I have some photos of myself when I was at my best. Should I bring them in? Would you like to see them?"

"Sure," I said, recovering.

"I know you may not believe this, but very few people could beat me back then," she said.

"I believe you," I told her.

Rita came in the next time with two old photos of herself on the tennis court. One was a newspaper clipping and the other was a snapshot. She told me the woman standing beside her in the newspaper clipping was Margaret duPont, who Rita said was an excellent player. In the clipping Rita wore a white blouse pulled down off her deeply tanned shoulders and a full skirt with a gay print. She was not especially attractive even then.

She beamed as she read me the caption, which said that she and Margaret duPont had just won a women's doubles tournament. The day that photo was taken had evidently been as bright a day as her firmament let shine.

In the snapshot Rita was standing next to a boulder of a man with curly black hair and what looked like a broken nose. She identified him as Mario.

After we looked at these two pictures, she told me that she had others in her purse and asked me if I wanted to see them. Of course, I was curious, so she took them out. In one, from the forties I supposed, her hair was done in an upsweep and she was wearing outlandishly high heels. I imagine that she was trying to look glamorous, but actually I felt sorry for her—she appeared a bit ridiculous.

While handing me another picture taken on a tennis court, she pointed out her two tiny daughters.

"My daughters don't like to look at these pictures," she told me. "They refuse."

I nodded noncommittally.

It was a sorry array of photos, mangled and rumpled, and all with either too much exposure or too little. The dreariness of their totality was accented by Rita's enthusiasm about them. Virtually every photo pertained to tennis in some way. But I noticed that she never had a racket in hand in any of them, and I seized the opportunity to return to my objective.

I commented, "Rita, you don't have a tennis racket in your hand in any of these. How come?"

"I don't know. I guess I just didn't feel like it," she answered coyly.

"Do you think you could put the racket over there while we look at these pictures again?" I asked her on a whim. I had to keep trying.

To my astonishment she said, "I'll leave it right here on the table." She placed it carefully on the coffee table between us with the handle only inches away from her hands.

I backed away in my chair, to dramatize my absolute nonintention of stealing her racket. She pretended not to notice, but I was sure she had.

"Why don't you pass the pictures over to me so I can look at them under the lamp?" I said. "I can see them better there."

The light didn't add much. But Rita obviously didn't notice the photos' unclarity. The world and time of those pictures was what counted, and it burned in her mind, a shimmering land, as she commented here and there. "That woman was a good player." "That girl beat me in the Ohio Open." "You see that pretty woman. I beat her in straight sets. Mario was there. He said he was very proud of me."

When our time was up, I said to her, "We have to stop. You'd better put your pictures away carefully, and don't forget to take your racket."

At the very least I was increasing her awareness of her behavior with the racket.

It seemed like real progress that Rita had willingly put the racket down in front of her, and I was glad for that. In some curious way, I felt she trusted me and might trust me further if I could find some way to approach her tactfully. But I was still far from convincing her to leave the racket at home.

And, of course, I still had to ask her about that incident in the supermarket. Had she raised the racket in anger at someone? Would she really have hit him with it? She was well on in her seventies, but still it wouldn't take much strength to break a kneecap or a skull with that racket. Rita could injure someone badly and destroy her own life before she knew it.

In my waiting room the next time, the young man who'd commented "Tennis, anyone?" smirked when he saw Rita with the racket again. I imagined that he was just the sort who could get his head broken with it.

She brought the racket into my office as usual, but this time when I asked, "Can you put it down here?" she said angrily, "Not really."

That felt like a setback, and I wondered if Rita had done some thinking about the risk entailed in parting with the racket even for a few moments, and had decided against it.

"Are you sure you won't?" I asked, to gauge how firm she was in her conviction.

"I'm not putting down this racket and that's all there is to it," she said.

"Okay, okay," I said. "Why are you so angry, Rita?" I asked. "Has anyone else asked you to give it up recently?"

I realized instantly that my remark had been a not very subtle invitation for her to volunteer the supermarket incident.

But she didn't respond. She just looked at me with expressionless eyes.

I told her directly, "Your daughter's afraid you're going to hurt someone with that racket, Rita."

Still no response.

"Is she right?"

"If they try to take it away from me," Rita said.

"Something like that happened recently, didn't it?" I pushed. "In the supermarket."

She nodded yes. Then she told me without hesitation. "Some kids started asking me where I was playing. They were laughing at me. One of them tried to grab the racket, and I raised it up and I told them, 'I could smash you to pieces with this. You better not come too close.' The manager was standing there and he tried to grab my racket, but I wouldn't let him."

As she spoke, she reared the racket, presumably imitating her gesture toward him.

I asked Rita what had happened next.

"A couple of clerks came over and told the manager to calm down. Then they made the kids leave the store. It was a good thing too. Then the manager told me to get out. And I said, 'I certainly will as soon as I buy my groceries.'

"So the clerks went through the store with me, and they sent me to the head of the line, and I paid for the groceries and I left. That was all there was to it. I don't like people to comment about this racket."

"You *don't*?" I asked incredulously. "But you like people to talk about tennis, don't you?"

"I *do not.* I can't stand it. I didn't say one word to those boys. I never talk about tennis."

"What? You don't?"

"Why should I? Just because I have a racket? They never saw me play. The hell with them."

"But you talked to me about it . . ."

"Yes, because you know about tennis. And you might have seen me play."

By "tennis," she meant the tennis of a half century ago, about which, actually, I knew almost nothing.

For the first time I fully appreciated the relevance to Rita of my having commented that she was a lefty after I'd observed that she cradled the racket in her left hand. She had granted me access to her tennis past only on the assumption that I must have seen her play. Either she had decided that I was a little older than she'd thought at first or she had momentarily blanked out on chronological time.

Rita made a few more remarks about the incident at the grocery store and then went on at some length about her refusal to discuss tennis. She was so adamant that I was finally absolutely convinced that she was not using the racket as a device to initiate such conversation.

It astonished me to see that I'd been so utterly wrong about the function of the racket—not about its status as a vital organ to her but about exactly what that status was. If the racket wasn't simply a conversation piece, why did Rita rely on it so desperately? I felt stymied and wholly at a loss for the answer to this. But I had to rally myself.

Ideally I would have gone deeper into Rita's history for alternative reasons why she might need the racket, but I pulled myself up short. Such investigation was a luxury I couldn't afford. Now, besides the fact that the racket's presence was goading Tricia into sending her mother away, Rita's attachment to the racket was beginning to present problems to society. I would have to get it away from her.

I decided from then on to treat Rita's toting that racket around as a bad habit. I would approach her as I would anyone who came to me afflicted by a seriously self-destructive behavior pattern, like smoking or excessive drinking or taking drugs. Rather than spend months or years looking for root causes while the patient destroyed himself or herself, I would concentrate wholly on helping the person give up the behavior.

For the rest of that session I mostly listened, and observed Rita. She kept an even firmer hold on the racket than she had in our first session. Evidently she had reverted to distrusting me.

After she left, I identified in myself a sharp concern that she would never come back. I asked myself what cause Rita had given me to feel this way. Not finding any, I realized that I had been merely projecting onto Rita my own sense of futility about being able to help her, and my worry that she would soon be whisked away forever.

When Rita next arrived, I was surprised to see that she had dyed her hair auburn. Clearly she had done it herself—there were patches of orange, where her hair had been very white. She brought it up almost as soon as she sat down. "Look at my new hair color. This is the color my hair was in my playing days," she informed me.

After some chitchat I plunged in, asking her directly why she brought the racket around with her everywhere.

"It's important. I want it," she replied. Then she nodded, as if deciding that her answer was accurate and complete.

"I guess you know Tricia is really upset by the racket," I said.

"That's too bad," Rita snapped.

"What would happen to you if you went out without the racket, the way you used to in the old days?"

"I don't know. I don't like to think about it." Her mouth shut firmly.

"Rita, we've got to think about it," I insisted.

"Why?"

"Well, there's some danger that they don't want you to have it."

"What do you mean? They'd take it away from me?" She squeezed the handle, as if ready to die fighting with it, the way the old Viking berserkers would grab their battleaxes when they were surrounded and death was near. Rita made a tragic appearance. I could imagine that even Tricia might have been moved by it.

I backed off from telling Rita precisely what was in store for her, but I could not let the topic evaporate.

"I'm just asking what would happen if you didn't have the racket on the street with you."

"Why are you asking?"

"Oh, just to get an idea of exactly why you bring it places, why it's so important to you."

"It is. That's all," she said.

I heard myself putting a question to her that she had already answered, just to be sure.

"Is it that you like to talk tennis? Because if it is—"

"No. I told you. I never do," she said in a raised voice, precisely as she had before.

Next I considered asking her why she'd been able to put the racket on the table that day we went over the photos. But I instantly rejected such a question. It would make her feel under microscopic surveillance. No question that makes a patient feel watched minutely is ever worth the answer it yields; more often than not, people react by pulling back and telling you less, and I felt sure that Rita would do just that.

That evening I thought about a story Rita had told me a few weeks earlier. It was not so much her remembrance of the story itself that got me thinking, but my recollection of how she had told it.

Rita mentioned that she had watched the champion Helen Wills Moody get furious with an opponent and refuse to shake hands after a big match. In describing the incident, which had happened forty years previously, Rita had seemed so freshly astonished at it that it was as if she had just witnessed it. Rita had blushed, perhaps imagining that Helen Wills Moody was just about to get into trouble for her discourtesy. The incident had felt so immediate to her that she'd actually closed her eyes for a few seconds, as if contemplating how the newspapers might write it up.

She was living in the past, that was obvious, and the story was a prime instance of it. But how did the racket fit in? The old questions bounced around in my mind as they often had. What was the racket protection against? It had to be a prospect so horrendous that Rita would do anything not to be parted from that racket.

Suddenly an answer came to me in a form so simple that I had trouble understanding my own wording of it. That racket *was* Rita's past. She was suffering from the kind of brain deficit that left her unable to think abstractly, to conjure up what was not. Rita had little faculty left beyond what the great student of the brain Kurt Goldstein called "the immediate claim of objects."

Only by holding the racket could Rita go on feeling that she had a past. She could summon up nothing of her past without it. Thus the *racket itself* was her history, her prime, the glorious morning of her life.

To Rita the horror of being cut off from her past and cheated of it loomed worse than pain, worse even than dizziness; indeed, it threatened a kind of perpetual dizziness, a whirling through the winds with no possibility of landing anywhere, of being someone. We who can think abstractly find this hard to understand. I know I did when first working with brain-damaged people. But imagine waking up one morning an amnesiac, with no memory of whatever was good about your life, of anything you prized.

I realized how wrong my original conversation-piece theory had been. It had presupposed a much subtler and more manipulative person than Rita was, a person much more in touch with what she wanted and more capable of maneuvering for it. If there had ever been sham or subterfuge in her, it was long gone.

In reality, if Rita were alone in a room, she would want that racket every bit as badly as when she was out in public. In the asylum she would cry for it—to use it not as a bridge to others, but as a bridge to herself.

I wondered, could anyone, knowing this, still wish to deprive her of it?

And the answer came to me at once, yes, and perhaps for good reason, if she was going to clout someone with it.

In the next session most of our time seemed to slip away with Rita chatting about her daily routines. Listening to her required little real concentration, and one part of my mind kept trying to comprehend what life must be like for someone who needs a concrete object to stand for an intangible.

As always, we finished the session with a bit of tennis talk. Rita headed for the door with her racket firmly in her possession. But this time, perhaps because now I saw the racket as her past, her life, her wisp of hope, I no longer found it so objectionable or even odd.

A few nights later the phrase came to me that Rita was literally "holding on to her past." An ill-meaning person could rob her of what to the rest of us is absolutely safeguarded against theft. The phrase made it still more comprehensible to me why Rita would fight in a frenzy to keep her racket.

But I also knew that however hard Rita fought, in the end it would be up to Tricia to decide whether the racket would be taken away from her mother or not. And I suspected that even if I could explain to Tricia what the racket really meant, it might not affect her verdict at all.

I pictured Tricia sending Rita to a home. Those burly attendants who came to pry the racket out of Rita's hands, hardly noticing her desperate efforts to cling to it, would have no idea what they were really doing. How could they possibly realize that in seizing it they were crushing poor Rita's picture-making mechanism, her inner life itself?

I was feeling very gloomy about Rita's prognosis, as if what I'd come to realize about her relationship to that racket had doomed her utterly. The racket didn't merely represent an obsessional habit—it was an intrinsic part of her being. I didn't see how I could get it away from her without doing her great injury, and Tricia was surely not going to let things go along as they had.

But then I recalled something that suddenly took on great significance. The only time Rita had parted from the racket in my presence was the day that we were looking through her photographs. Rita had willingly deposited the racket on the coffee table while we devoted ourselves to those old, tattered snapshots. As I thought about her unusual behavior that day, an idea came to me.

Because time was running short, I immediately called Rita on the phone to set my plan in motion. She wasn't especially surprised to hear from me; her expectations in general were rather foggy. But she immediately perked up and tuned in when I asked her to bring back the photos she'd shown me.

"All of them?" she asked, sounding very pleased.

"Yes, all of them," I told her.

When in the next session Rita presented the photos to me once more, I immersed myself in them with her immediately. I read the caption about her and Margaret duPont aloud, and I commented about some of the other players and asked her some questions.

Once again, at my request, Rita willingly deposited her racket on the table in front of her while we perused the pictures.

I was elated to see that she reacted exactly as she had the first time. She seemed to have the same relationship to the photos that she had to the racket; both were embodiments of her past, so that to some extent at least, the presence of either one lessened the need for the other.

My idea was to employ a technique known as "symptom substitution"—the deliberate replacement of one symptom by another. Such replacements are often employed in helping people break self-destructive habits—for instance, many hypnotists give their subjects a hand gesture to engage in when they want to smoke, finding that the substitutive act helps a great deal. And one reason physical exercise helps most dieters is that the very activity substitutes for overeating in discharging anxiety.

No symptom is precisely the same as another, so replacements are necessarily imperfect. But to the degree that Rita's photographs and memorabilia were serving the same function as that tennis racket, it seemed to me Rita could use them as a replacement.

And if these harmless samples of her past were serviceable even as a partial replacement of the potentially lethal racket, perhaps a much more elegant set of memorabilia could accomplish even more. My plan was to assemble such a set, and I used this session to get the information from Rita that I would need to do so.

I introduced the subject early in the session.

"You must have had plenty of pictures taken of you when you were a top-notch player," I said. "How come you only have these few?"

"I had others, but they got lost."

I nodded.

Rita mentioned the Allison Danzig article again, and told me that she'd been included in a book on Pauline Betz and in many other articles. She had been included in group shots in *Life* magazine and in *Look*. "Once when I won a tournament in Springfield, I got a whole writeup," she said.

"Springfield, in what state?" I asked.

"Massachusetts, of course," she replied.

"What about other magazines? Did they ever mention you?"

"Did they!" she answered at once, startled that I didn't know. "*Time* magazine mentioned me, what do you think of that?"

"When was that?"

"In an article on women players." She couldn't say anything more about that article, and those were the only references she could remember. In any event, I had enough.

That evening I called a young graduate student who had done some work for me previously, and I gave him an assignment.

"I want you to track down every photo, every article, every reference, even every phrase about Rita—anything that ever appeared in print about her."

It seemed fitting to me that the researcher was a student of theology: it felt to me as if we were doing something spiritual, almost mystical, in an effort to replace that racket by an even stronger, more tangible substitute that might signify Rita's past once we put it into her hands.

When Rita came back the next time, she told me that Tricia and Richard had returned; they had brought some groceries over to her apartment and had spent a little time with her.

"They were all dressed up, and they had to go to a dinner party, so they couldn't stay long." Rita didn't say a word about their trip.

A few days after that I received a note from Tricia and Richard with their monthly payment for Rita. The note said that they would contact me soon.

My researcher needed time to assemble his nostalgia kit, but I pressed him to hurry.

I'd seen Rita twice more before he came over with what he had gathered and promised more material to come.

By chance, Richard called that night and put Tricia on the extension.

She said, "I'd like to have our meeting about mother. We want to make arrangements. What do you think, doctor?"

"I'd still like more time, of course," I said. "But I think I have some good news for you. I have an idea that your mother can really behave herself—"

"I hope that by behaving herself you mean throwing away that damn racket," Tricia shot back.

I think I surprised Tricia when I asked her to come in alone to see me.

"You mean without Richard?" she asked.

"Yes."

"Why? He'd like to come in with me."

"No, Tricia. This one time it's important that you come in yourself. Is that okay with you, Richard? I don't want to exclude you, but there are times when it's important for Tricia to stand alone—"

"Of course. Of course," Richard said. "It is Tricia's mother."

"Yes, it's really Tricia's decision," I said.

Tricia said, "Doctor, I can't possibly make it this week. I have to go to my store in Chicago—we have inventory." She spoke very fast.

"No hurry," I said. "Suppose we set something up for three weeks from now. I can use the time to help Rita a little more."

I heard Tricia whisper sharply to Richard, "Hand me my schedule book." A moment later she was back on the phone, sounding cosmopolitan as she told me, "The Monday, Tuesday, and Thursday of that week are just impossible. It will have to be the Friday."

I agreed to schedule a session late on that Friday afternoon.

After hanging up, I realized that Tricia was obviously scared. She relied on Richard a lot more than she cared to admit. Her trendy, sharp style—that snappish certainty of hers—was a lot readier to give way than I'd imagined. I was glad that she had put our meeting off so far. Rita and I could use the extra time.

In requesting Tricia to come in without Richard, I was simply following my usual practice of always seeing people alone when big decisions are to be made. At such times people need the space and privacy to air all their thoughts, to make available to themselves as many pieces of the puzzle as possible before arriving at their decision.

However, as the days passed, I began to see why it was especially important for me to talk to Tricia alone. It was not farfetched to believe that Tricia's future with Richard might well be affected by the decision she was to make about Rita.

Because Richard had made the first call to me, and because in my last conversation with the two of them he had seemed much more sympathetic to Rita than Tricia was, I felt sure that he strongly wanted Tricia to grant Rita amnesty. The idea of Tricia's locking Rita up and throwing away the key was unpleasant to him. Doubtless Tricia's decision concerning Rita would affect him profoundly.

Tricia made no secret of her anger toward Richard. I had no way of knowing whether that attitude was warranted by the kind of person he really was. For all I knew she would be better off without him. But I felt sure from the little she had said that she wanted him. I sensed that her disdain for Richard masked a desire for him to cherish her. Tricia had certainly been deprived of mother love, that was obvious. From there it took no great leap of imagination to assume that she might be contributing to her problems with Richard by showing what seemed like an inability to love.

I had seen many situations in which people resolved uncertainties about a lover, one way or another, as a result of observing how the lover treats other people. To a person shaky in belief, the sight of a lover abusing a waiter or waitress or neglecting an animal can confirm the idea "This person is dangerous. I will never be safe with this person." I felt sure that Richard's own willingness to commit himself to Tricia would be strongly influenced by what she decided to do with her mother. I would do my best to convey to Tricia this ramification of her decision, that in sparing Rita she would perhaps be sparing herself the estrangement that seemed dangerously likely otherwise.

Over the following week I could hear myself pleading with Tricia: "I know you don't owe Rita anything. Richard knows that too. But sometimes when one person in your life feels unloved, that person identifies with someone else you don't seem to love. Richard may get more out of your kindness to your mother than you imagine. He'll surely see a quality of caring in you, and that matters."

I could hear myself refining my presentation as I went over it. I would explain to Tricia, "Don't you see, it's not just a strategy. I'm saying that if you stick with people, you'll start to feel that relationships last. You'll see yourself differently. I want you to live in a world where people cherish each other and stick together, where they overlook a little because it's lonely out there . . ."

However, before I could make this presentation, I still had ahead some critical interviews with Rita, who, I hoped, would prove a star witness in her own defense.

Rita had once said that she was born on Saint Patrick's Day, which was about ten days away when I told her I had a birthday present for her.

"I've collected some clippings and quotes about you, and some photos," I told her, "and put them in an album. Here. This is for you."

She hesitated when I handed her the black gilt-edged book. But when I opened it to the first page, she snatched it from me like a greedy little child.

There was the article by Allison Danzig in the *New York Times* about her match with Doris Hart. She recognized it at once, and read it in front of me.

Instantly she went on to the next piece, another reference to her match with Doris Hart.

About then I asked her to put the racket down on the table, and leave it there while she looked at the album.

She put it down without a thought. Then she plunged back into the book. This time she chanced to open it to the two-page spread about her in the *Springfield Sunday Republican*. She had won the Springfield tournament easily.

Where my researcher couldn't get clippings or photos, he had photocopied them, and where he couldn't do that, he had typed up passages that he had read on microfilm. Rita didn't seem to care what form the reference took, and possibly didn't even notice whether she was reading an original newspaper account or a typed version of one.

Once or twice I could see that she was blushing, as when she read a reference to herself in *Time* that described her as one of the teenage players to keep an eye on.

In all there were about a dozen actual newspaper pieces, five or six newspaper photos, and about a half dozen typed reports, such as the one taken from the microfilm copy of the book on Pauline Betz.

Rita was utterly unaware of my presence as she went through the book. She seemed to get younger with every page, and at the end she looked cherubic, as if the lines of life had not yet been drawn.

"Can I have this?" she asked me.

"Definitely. I got it for you," I told her. "But I want to ask you a favor in return. Is that a deal?"

"Sure," she said.

"Good," I said. "I will ask you for one. But not today."

I wasn't sure she heard me.

Rita again began reading the article by Allison Danzig, this time aloud. When she read the part where Danzig had written that she'd played well enough to win but that it just wasn't her day, Rita reddened like a little girl getting praised in front of the class.

"I moved gracefully, but I didn't cover enough court," she said to me apologetically.

When I told Rita that our time was up, she asked me, "Do you want to see these articles again?"

I said I did, and added that I had a second copy of the scrapbook in my possession, in case hers ever got lost.

"Don't worry. I won't lose it," she assured me. "When should I come here again?"

"The day after tomorrow, if you want. Same time."

"Okay."

She never thanked me for the album, or even came close, but I hadn't expected her to. She'd probably had no sense of gratitude even in her best years. In any event, what I had offered her was her inalienable right, a connection with her own personal history, and that's something that the rest of us don't need a stranger to bestow on us.

Rita came in the next time with her racket in one hand and in the other a preposterous-looking old-fashioned handbag. It was big and gray, with a red floral design that seemed to be made out of pipe cleaners sewed on it. If Tricia had ever seen the bag, she might have bought it from her mother just to destroy it.

Rita unfastened the wooden clasp and pulled out the album. She was about to open it, when I gestured toward a chair and said, "Leave your racket there."

She complied without a word.

"Rita," I said, as casually as I could. "Do you think you could go for a walk around the block without your racket if you take your album with you? You can leave the racket here with me."

She didn't respond.

"Rita, this is the favor I said I was going to ask of you when I gave you the album. That was the deal."

She looked at me blankly.

"Take your purse and the album, and go for a short walk and come back. Leave the racket with me."

She hesitated.

I insisted. "You have your album now. You don't need the racket the way you used to."

"Please don't ask me to do that."

"Rita, you can keep the racket. No one's asking you to throw it away. But keep it at *home*," I said as firmly as I could. "You'll always have it. But you can't bring it with you everywhere."

"Doctor, why are you doing this? Why are you so cruel?"

The time had come when I had to say something directly to her about the real threat facing her. I'd done all I could to ease her task of getting rid of the racket, by providing a near equivalent for it. But she would have to do the rest, using will power of her own, and the only way I could convince her to use that will power, it seemed, was to inform her of the real stakes of the game.

I didn't want to injure her wantonly, but I was afraid that if I lacked persuasiveness, she might let her last chance for salvation pass her by. Rita was a little foggy at best, and I realized I had to be blunt.

I braced myself and said, "If you don't separate yourself from that racket, Tricia and Richard feel that for your best interests they'll have to put you in a home for the elderly. They're extremely worried about your having that racket all the time. Rita, you know if you go to a home, they'll *take* the racket away from you anyway."

She sat silently for a moment as if she were thinking it over. Then, almost slyly, she said, "I knew my daughter wanted to do that, but I won't let her."

That surprised me. So Tricia must have mentioned it to her already.

I promised Rita that if I could, I would try to talk Tricia out of it. But I added, "You'll have to cooperate with me and leave the racket at home."

"Not today," she pleaded. "I don't want to leave the racket in your office while I go out. Next time I'll leave it home in my bedroom when I come here. Okay?"

"Do you promise?"

"Yes."

"Good," I said. "You'll see that you don't need it. Come back without it tomorrow. It's very important."

During the rest of the session I reminded her of our deal so many times that she finally shot back at me, "Okay, okay. I hear you."

I was sure she had heard me. But I knew that she never would have consented if the album hadn't already given her a solid sense of security.

The next day I was elated to see Rita arrive without the racket. I thanked her for not bringing it. She smiled faintly.

She was holding her purse on her lap, and I knew that the album was inside of it. "Why don't we look at your clippings?" I asked her.

"Not today," she snapped. With a sudden motion she grabbed the gawky purse and clutched it with both hands, as if it were a living thing that could run away.

I was delighted to see that the album was now as precious to her as the racket had been. At least part of my plan had obviously worked. It remained only to see if she could transfer totally to the album and dispense with the tennis racket entirely.

Our time was running out. I was to see Rita only once more before Tricia would come in and reach her verdict.

When I handed Rita her appointment card for the following Tuesday, I reminded her once more to leave the racket home.

"Of course," she said. I think she was delighted that I had made no claim on her precious purse.

As Rita left, I actually felt that she looked strange without the racket. I had the thought that she was like a recent amputee. But, of course, the only real change was that Rita now had a retractable past instead of an appendage. There was nothing basically different about Rita herself: she had only switched symptoms. But if that exchange stuck, and if I could press her case with Tricia, it might prove worth her freedom.

By Tuesday when Rita came in, again without her racket, I was slightly more accustomed to seeing her that way, and I had the impression that she herself was adjusting to being without it.

I handed her another newspaper article, the last that I'd been waiting for.

Rita glanced at it, and her eyes lit up. But then she quickly secreted it beneath her purse on her lap.

I felt sure she would pore over it later. But in front of me Rita didn't even dare to open her purse and risk her past flying out and becoming lost forever.

The photos and clippings combined embodied Rita's past more compactly and comprehensively than the tennis racket ever had. They represented that tiny fraction of a centimeter lodged in the brain that in the rest of us can be activated at will when we want to remember who we are and where we came from. Rita, lacking the power to direct her own mind to do this, would probably have to squeeze that atrocious-looking handbag many times a day.

I assured Rita that on Friday, when I was to see her daughter, I would make the strongest case I could for Tricia's allowing Rita to stay in her apartment.

"I'm very proud of you for not carrying that racket around with you," I said to her. "You're doing everything you can to stay out of trouble. Please, make sure to leave the racket home when you see Tricia from now on."

Rita promised that she would.

Although most deliberate symptom substitutions feel less satisfactory than the original symptom, at least for a time, the purse containing that album seemed to take hold at once.

I was beginning to feel quite hopeful that I could prevail with Tricia, that Rita had earned her freedom.

That evening Tricia left a message on my answering machine. Because she was due to come in that week, I imagined that whatever had prompted her to call needed quick attention, and I got back to her at once.

After we exchanged pleasantries, Tricia said, "Doctor, tell me what I owe you because I'm writing out checks. My mother won't be seeing you anymore."

I was taken aback. "There's really no hurry," I said. "You can pay for her on Friday when you come in."

"Friday? Oh, no. I won't be coming in Friday. I'll be in San Francisco."

"You will?" I said. "I thought we had an appointment to talk about your mother—"

"There's nothing to talk about."

"Tricia, I want you to know that your mother has given up that tennis racket for good. She has changed—"

"That's good," Tricia said with ostentatious unconcern. "But it doesn't really matter what Rita does."

"Well, I meant as far as your decision goes—"

"I've made my decision, doctor. I'm sending her to the . . . home in Connecticut."

"Why? Has she done something else?"

"Not that I know of."

Falteringly I asked Tricia if she could possibly wait before deciding. Maybe she could come in and talk to me first. I had some insights that certainly pertained to her life as well as to her mother's.

But she would have none of it. She repeated with such asperity that she was not my patient that I felt almost beggarly.

Sensing her haste to hang up the phone and have done with me, I tried one last time. I made a brief but strong case for Rita's improved behavior, and I pleaded the humanity of letting her keep her freedom. When only silence greeted me, I suggested that maybe Tricia would feel more comfortable coming in to my office with Richard. The two of them could look at the problem together.

"Together!" Tricia echoed with what seemed like mock amusement. "It's really not your business, but for your information, my marriage to Richard is over."

Then she told me that Richard had moved out a few days earlier and had already served her with papers asking for a divorce. "The whole idea of keeping Rita near us was Richard's anyhow," Tricia said. "He was just using my mother to torture me. But no more.

"They're picking Rita up on Monday," she said. "I'm going to my San Francisco store for a week, and by the time I get back, she'll be gone.

"That's why I called you. Don't tell her if you talk to her. She's not supposed to know. My lawyer has arranged the papers for them to take her. I've already signed for her."

I knew this meant that Tricia had procured the signatures of two physicians and a judge in New York State. And realizing that she must have lugged Rita to those handpicked physicians and gotten their signatures without consulting me, I felt dismayed and faintly irritated at not being included.

On the following Monday, throughout the whole morning, images came to me. I pictured two burly attendants arriving at Rita's building and going upstairs with the doorman, who would let them in. I closed my eyes at the thought of her resisting them, skipping to the moment at which they were escorting her through the lobby, without her racket but, I hoped, clutching that precious purse of hers. They would direct her into an ambulette and drive off.

I never again heard from Rita, Tricia, or Richard. They had passed through my life with the brief intensity of a dream, and vanished with the abruptness of waking up. One could argue that Rita's own daughter convicted her of neglect and that Rita's sentence to the home was punishment for having abandoned her daughter in her most critical years.

But that seems too pat. A cosmic injustice was done to both of them, in that neither developed the faculty of caring for another person. Wherever neglect gets passed down over generations, some individual must go first in giving more than he or she received. Some creative artist in the realm of loving must invent such generosity for himself, or herself. Only when this is done can the chain of neglect be broken. But here, unfortunately, it was not.

the

nonentity

. . . .

I TRIED TO CONCEAL MY HORROR as he spoke, this clumsy-looking man with the wide ears and expressionless face. Artie Henshaw seemed a lot older than thirty-seven, maybe because he plastered wisps of hair over his bald spot and his skin was so pale.

"Anyhow, my brother was in the other room showing Tony how to throw a football, or something like that, and I was alone with her. She stayed in the room with me. She likes me. A really nice little girl, nine years old, with a sweet smile. 'Uncle Artie, are you ever going to get married?' she asked. 'Sure, Sylvia,' I said. 'Someday.' 'If I were old enough, would you marry me?' 'Oh, I don't know,' I said.

"Then, suddenly it came again, that terrible fantasy of my strangling her. I looked at her delicate little neck, and pictured my hands around it. And I had this fear that her mother wouldn't return in time and I'd be alone with her. And in a minute I would do it, in *seconds*. I'd put my hands around her neck, she'd let me, and I'd crush all those arteries and little bones, and it would be so easy.

"And they'd come back into the room, and she'd be dead. They'd know it was me. Who else could it be? A few seconds would change everybody's life.

"Sometimes I imagine myself doing it and then saying something like 'I have to rush downstairs, I'll be right back,' and leaving through the front door. They'd find her. Doctor, it's just too much for me. I think I'm insane."

I inhaled deeply but quietly. I knew he was scrutinizing my face for any reaction. Above all, I had to show none. Whatever I felt, top priority was not to disturb the data, not to drive him underground toward concealment by a show of horror, and I listened as noncommittally as I could.

I felt like a gambler who had drawn the death card and didn't want to let on.

I asked him, "What happens in actuality?"

"I back away from her. When Janet goes out of the room into the kitchen, I go to the kitchen too. Sometimes when it gets real bad, I go to the bathroom."

"You've never actually touched her neck?" I asked, trying not to respond to the cards in my hand.

"Once, six months ago maybe, she followed me into the bathroom. I was looking in the mirror, to see if I was insane, to see if anything showed on my face. I saw her behind me. I yelled at her to go away. She got scared. She left, and after that, during the evening, she was afraid of me, but I apologized, saying I was nervous, and the next time she forgot it."

"Artie, have you ever actually touched her?" I repeated.

"Well, no. I never allow myself to be alone with her. I sometimes want to just touch her shoulder. When they're all there, she sits on my lap. But sometimes when the urge is strong—no, it's not even really an urge. An impulse. No, not even that. A *picture* of myself ending everything."

"Do you ever have sexual feelings toward her?" I asked.

"No. I thought of that. I thought about that. Never. I don't like sex with underage girls. No, definitely not."

"What kind of partner, I mean what kind of situation do you think about when you masturbate?" I asked him.

Such questions are often easier for people to answer during the first session, or at least early in treatment, than they are later on, once a relationship has been established.

"I think about older women, someone who will take care of me, who admires me. Never a little girl, I swear. Never a little girl! I'm thirty-seven. I like sex with women my own age. Even older. A woman who will mother me. Drive me around. I love that. A woman who feels lucky I'm there. I mean a woman who thinks of me as a young, virile man. Up and coming."

I wondered if that last phrase of his had a conscious sexual overtone. I asked him, "Does this happen every time you see her?"

"No. Sometimes when I go over there, it doesn't happen at all. I pray that it won't. But lately it's been terrible."

Artie and his four-year-older brother, Dan, were born in Casper, Wyoming, the only children of a couple who married at forty and worked in a grocery store until they retired. Their parents, both still living, were always uninspired and afraid of the world at large. "They still have no idea why we left Wyoming or what Dan does for a living. It was a miracle that we both went to college."

At the end of the hour he told me his brother would be paying for his therapy. "We're very close. Send the bill directly to Dan. You sure charge a lot."

He started to jot down the address, but I told him that I don't like sending bills to a third party. He could arrange to get the money as he wished, but for the sake of his commitment to therapy and his relationship with me, he should pay me directly. And indeed, I preferred that at least some of the money actually come from the patient if he or she can afford it.

"And the good Lord made them all" was the phrase that came to me the instant he had left. It flashed through my mind that I should have told him, "If any kind of violent urge gets very strong, call me." I might have given him my home number if I were as sedulous as I'd sometimes been.

Then why hadn't I? The next few patients preempted my attention, and the question was lost and not recovered until I closed up for the day and headed downtown through the lower part of Central Park.

On a cobblestone stretch near the pretentious restaurant Tavern on the Green were a couple of dray horses eating out of feed bags, each yoked to a black hansom cab. Tourists would pay for a trek around the lower loop of the park. As I approached, a driver, apparently displeased by his sorry breadwinner, slapped the nag hard on the withers. My immediate impulse was to knock him down as I found myself running toward the man, who was portly and about sixty, with a bulbous red nose.

Even before I could reach him, three or four other people were there, shouting curses at him. He deferred, though I assumed he would be brutal in private, and I redoubled my opinion that whatever justification humans once had for sentencing innocent horses to a life of hard labor before the era of the horseless carriage, we surely have none today.

Then the thought that evil could be committed by such peripheral people, such nonentities, made me think of Artie, morose, expressionless, gray—and possibly a murderer.

Why hadn't I told him to call me if he needed to? I'd made that offer to dozens of patients in extremis and had never been sorry. Few had availed themselves of it, but to the last man, woman, and child they had been moved by it and felt me to be an ally, and they'd often reported sometime later that my willingness to be there if needed was valuable. If anyone overused the privilege, I could always rescind it. No, I hadn't extended it to Artie because he repulsed me.

By his potential violence? I asked myself. And I was sure: not at all. There was something about him, grim, disappointing, demanding without asking for anything outright, that revolted me.

Then I recalled Hannah Arendt's phrase "the banality of evil" and felt sudden terror that Artie would indeed kill that nine-year-old girl, kill her because he loved her and could not endure what I suspected to be his own sexual desire.

I toyed with calling his brother but decided not to, yet. Artie had said he wouldn't be going over there until the following Saturday for brunch. I would see him on Friday and could decide then.

Only at that moment did I let myself realize that his disappointment about my fee and his comment that it was steep bothered me too. His delegating me to send bills to his brother, though I had resisted it, rounded out the picture of a person who, even in dire straits, wordlessly rebuked me for making a living and thought of me as a servant.

When I checked with my office at ten thirty, there was a message from him. He had called my office an hour after leaving me. "Do me a favor," he said when I phoned him back. "Please don't mention to anyone what I told you tonight. Nothing. Please. It's very important."

"Of course not."

"Promise me that you won't."

I could understand his concern.

"Artie," I said. "I promise. I won't do anything unless I talk to you first. But *you* promise me you won't really do it."

"I promise."

That seemed good enough for now. But as soon as I hung up, I realized I'd lied. Suppose he seemed likely to do it. Would anything on earth stop me from turning him in? No way, even if he objected. If I felt really sure he'd do it, he'd have to kill me to silence me.

My phrase "talk to you first" must have been a deliberate ambiguity, one I hadn't contrived consciously but a piece of casuistry nevertheless—a device perhaps that I had unconsciously adopted to have Artie substitute talking for acting. His secrecy had prompted mine. He was hiding his true self from his brother, and here I was—concealing my reaction from him. As if dissimulation were a contagious disease.

On Friday he told me about his early life. His parents seemed to define the color gray, offering the kids nothing by way of encouragement or education. Artie had idolized Dan, his generous, capable, popular, flamboyant older brother. By high school age Dan was a matinee idol type. He did odd jobs at a radio station in the late afternoons, cultivated his voice, and to the amazement of all the kids in Casper, he sometimes actually filled in for the DJ's on the air.

By fifteen Dan was part owner of a secondhand car, a Dodge, a junk heap that his partner, whose dad was a garage mechanic, was able to keep going. Having a car would have been nothing in a middle-class neighborhood, but it was prestige in that circle, and Dan took groups of kids swimming and dated the prettiest girls anyone had ever seen in person. When an acting troupe came into Casper, Dan was there, offering his services—as messenger, grip, anything.

The glory and the greatness of boyhood belonged to Dan, who like Dylan Thomas basked in it and "went his lordly ways." And he readily shared it with his younger brother, who soaked in as much of that splendor as he could. Dan had helped him with homework, gotten him a job, taught him how to comb his hair and walk, and how to dress.

As Artie said this last, I mused that the leather patches stitched onto the elbows of his jacket, to give the impression of robustness, simply didn't work. Surely Dan hadn't told him to wear them. There was simply no spring to Artie. No matter how hard his brother must have tried, Artie was jowly and double-chinned and pale. One might as well have tried to make me an opera singer. But such cynicism hardly makes a therapist, and indeed, I realized, there had to be more than a mere misfiring of messages to bring about this result.

Then I looked at Artie's arms—too thin for his body—and I had the notion that he had never lifted more than a ten-pound weight, and that, at most once. But even those feeble arms, I thought in disgust, would be more than enough to strangle a nine-year-old child.

I said, "You're going over there tomorrow. How do you feel?"

"I'm tense."

"Can you control it?"

"Yes."

That would have to do, though of course, it didn't reassure me much.

It still seemed possible that behind those violent impulses of his lay a sexual attraction, one utterly intolerable to him. If there were such an attraction, and if I could surface it to his consciousness— if he could acknowledge it, then maybe he wouldn't have to keep translating it into those violent impulses. But how could I surface it?

Once again I tried—this time, more obliquely than I had the first time. "What does little Sylvia look like?" I asked him.

The vagueness of his answer surprised me. "Look like? I don't know. Just a girl. She's cute, I guess. She's not very tall for her age."

"What color are her eyes?" I asked him.

"Gee, brown I think. I really don't know. She's dark-haired."

He brought up his brother, Dan, again, and Janet, who Artie said adored Dan. "If he told her he could bring the dead back to life, I'm sure Janet would believe him."

"Do you like Janet?"

"She's okay. She takes a lot of his time. But she's okay."

This time I remembered to tell him that if the urge felt out of hand, he should call me at once. "Just don't act. Don't touch her. Call me if you have to, and I'll get back to you as fast as I can."

He nodded but didn't thank me, seeming to take my offer as his due.

By then I had started doubting that his murderous urges sprang from anything sexual. Almost surely, if he had harbored erotic feelings for little Sylvia, he would have described her with much more subtlety. Eros evokes far more sensitivity to the physical features of the beloved. Unless Artie was feigning opacity, it seemed unlikely that he'd been observing her over time through the lens of obsessive sexual desire.

But if he wasn't suppressing a sexual urge, then where did the violence come from? And how dangerous was he really?

He came in next time very agitated.

"There were a lot of people there, and it was terrible. I couldn't believe it, it was so awful. I think you're making it worse.

"She sat on my lap after dinner. They were taking some photographs. You told me to watch *everything*, and I did. After dinner Dan walked over to Janet and he whispered something to her, and they both laughed. I couldn't hear. I thought it was about me. I felt my heart beating. Like they *knew*. They knew all the time! They asked her to sit on my lap to test me. They were watching me!

"Then Janet brought some dishes into the kitchen, and Dan followed her. But only halfway. He only followed her halfway. He waited in the hall. He was watching me, because I was alone with the kids. I can't tell you how terrible it was to think that he could read my thoughts, that he had caught me.

"But I didn't let on. I didn't say anything. I had the most incredible urge to strangle her right in front of them. To defeat them. That laugh of his, I kept hearing it.

"But I fought it off. I ran into the bathroom as I always do. Not ran. Walked, but it didn't seem to matter because I thought they knew. It didn't seem to matter. I guess I must have run because Dan laughed again. He said, 'Boy, you really have to go. It must have been a good meal.'

"I didn't say anything. When I was alone, I did what you once told me to. Do you remember? I asked myself every thought that came to mind. And you know what? I imagined I did it already, I just did it. I just killed her! And they were looking at me, astonished, terrified. So terrified they were unable to talk. They couldn't even punish me. They didn't want to. Dan couldn't kill me. That wouldn't help.

"And I could picture myself telling Dan, 'Yes, I did it. Yes, I did it. I'll pay the price. Willingly I'll pay the price. Life imprisonment. Anything you want.'

"But they were too numb. Dan was numb. He looked over at her lifeless body, and he couldn't act. There was no one to call. It was over for them. Who could they call?"

After that unanswerable question, Artie paused.

I commented, "It was over for her too."

"What do you mean?" he asked, almost as if that hadn't occurred to him. Then he said, "Oh, I know. But somehow I don't think about her. She's dead. But I don't think about her. That's it. I mean that's it."

"Then what?" I asked Artie.

"I had to get out of there. I mean I really had to get out of there. So I told them I was exhausted, and I went home."

"Could you sleep?"

"It wasn't easy. I . . . uh . . . uh . . . I . . ."

"You what?" I asked him.

"I must have jerked off about three times, and took a drink. Finally I could sleep. When I woke up the next morning, I had no desire in the world to hurt her. It was all like a bad dream."

"What did you think about when you masturbated, what sexual fantasy did you have?" I asked him.

"None!" he answered instantly and decisively.

"Come on. That's not so," I said. "You're a man. Men always have some sexual fantasy with orgasm. Maybe you forget."

"No," he said. "I don't forget. Maybe I just don't want to talk about it."

"Please, it's important," I said.

"Maybe sometime. Not now."

"Was it about Sylvia or any little girl?" I asked him.

He smiled. "*No.* That I can tell you. It had nothing to do with Sylvia. I told you I don't like little girls, at least not sexually. It wasn't about Sylvia or any other little girl. That I can assure you."

"Then why can't you tell me?"

"I will. I just don't want to. Not now. Things are tough enough," he snapped.

By the time he left, I believed him that the fantasy wasn't about Sylvia. I wondered: Could it be that Dan was on to him? Or were we facing a rather common paranoid sense of transparency, based on guilt?

Then the terrible thought came to me that Artie might have come closer to harming her than he let on. If Dan really did suspect him, maybe it was because Artie had actually done something this time, like putting his hands on her neck—or worse. He'd lied to Dan. Why not to me?

That weekend I couldn't stop wondering whether, after all, I had the obligation to break confidentiality and contact his brother. Suppose he killed her and I'd known it was coming. I'd be to blame, partially. Partially? Maybe even *more* than he was, because I was of sound mind.

Of course, no one could *prove* he'd told me; I could always deny it, no matter what he said after getting arrested. But *I'd* know it, I would always know that my mistake had cost a life.

On the other hand, who was I to play God? No. That didn't hold. I *was* playing God by *not* moving and doing something real —for his sake as well as for poor little Sylvia's. For Sylvia, who was living closer to instant death at age nine than she could possibly have imagined.

Students of psychology and psychiatry all study instances in which the practicing therapist, perceiving a threat to someone's life, is responsible under the law to take preventive action. Just as social workers, teachers, and family doctors have a legal duty to report evidence of child abuse, a therapist is obliged by law to sacrifice confidentiality and do something if it seems likely, or even very possible, that his patient is about to commit murder.

The most famous case in which a therapist defaulted, one that still comes up on state license exams quite often, is now known as the Tarasoff case. Tatiana Tarasoff was a young woman murdered in California in 1969 by a patient who had confided his intention to his therapist. The murderer, Prosenjit Poddar, who had come here from India, was a rejected suitor of the young woman and became obsessed with her.

Poddar, while a voluntary patient in psychotherapy at a university hospital clinic, announced his plan to murder Tatiana when she returned to California from her summer vacation abroad. Though he didn't actually name her, his therapist knew who she was and could have gotten in touch with her or her family.

Instead the therapist conferred with two colleagues and then contacted the campus police, asking them in a form letter for their help in restraining Poddar. The campus police brought Poddar in, but quickly released him on the basis of his promise not to harm the young woman. Apparently the therapist and his supervising psychiatrist continued to fear that Poddar would make good on his threat. Hoping to dissociate themselves from him, they took steps to recover their letter from the campus police and destroyed it, along with all their therapy notes relating to Poddar.

Poddar disappeared for a time. Then when Tatiana Tarasoff returned home after a vacation in Brazil, he murdered her.

Not surprisingly the victim's family filed suit against Poddar's therapist and the psychiatrist who was in charge of the case. The family lost the first round in court, but on appeal in California, that verdict was reversed and they were granted the right to proceed against the therapist and the psychiatrist who had sorely misadvised him.

According to the verdict, the professionals had failed to employ "reasonable care" in assuring Poddar's confinement by going only to the campus police instead of to the actual police. Moreover, they had neglected their legal duty to inform the intended victim, who might have taken measures to protect herself. At the very least they might have contacted her family.

Tatiana Tarasoff's family argued further that the botched attempt to control Poddar might actually have been incendiary and aggravated the man's condition. On the one hand, by reporting him and thus destroying his trust in therapy, they cost him a chance to improve in treatment. On the other, by not taking a firm enough measure, they allowed him the freedom to do his worst. Incidentally, by the time this decision was reached, Poddar had returned to India.

The Tarasoff case remains a blazon to practitioners, a reminder of their responsibility and their challenge in cases like the one I now had on my hands. However, such a case would surely never have become a legal problem had not the therapist and the psychiatrist written that note to the campus police. That first measure, which although insufficient perhaps showed better intention than if they'd done nothing at all, in the end doomed them, along with their second fatuous and self-indicting act of destroying documents that had already been seen by a number of people.

All this went through my mind, though, of course, public law can at best only mirror what any decent human being can easily recognize as just. In my case I had no concern with the law per se. I knew that no one could prove in a courtroom that Artie had confided his purpose in me. Moreover, I had done nothing either to provoke him to murder or to make him despair of therapy. But, of course, none of this assuages the soul, any more than the knowledge that a thing is common practice mollifies guilt if one feels one has done harm. Our being even the unwitting accomplice to a murder echoes inside of us, and, as Gandhi put it a half century ago: "In matters of conscience, the law of the majority has no place."

So there I was, risking a child's life on the one hand, but reluctant, on the other, to run to authorities with comments confided to me in good faith and to use them to inflict havoc on a possibly innocent man. I would almost surely destroy the only real relationships Artie had were I to tell the brother he loved and the niece who worshipped him that he was a fiend, deadlier to them than the wicked-est enemy they'd ever had or imagined.

I tried to picture myself calling Dan—I knew enough to find him in the phone book—saying ominously, "Beware of your brother." How does one proceed in such a case? Would I do it over the phone or ask him to come to my office? How incredibly astonished he would be! He might look at me as if I were mad.

Still, even that consideration, if I were truly convinced of the danger, should not deter me. Then, pursuing my own ratiocinations, I wondered: How could I know if it *was* deterring me? As I sat in my living room holding the problem, mulling it over, it was hard to tell whether that instrument ticking in my possession was a time bomb or a clock.

In the end I think I decided against intervening then and there because Artie himself seemed so frightened of his impulses. He could imagine absolutely no justification for what he had the urge to do. He himself appeared as horrified of his fantasy as anyone else would be if he'd disclosed it to them. He reacted to his own urges exactly as if they were someone else's.

Had he offered the slightest pseudo-logical reason why Sylvia was in the way, or worse yet, why she ought to die, I felt sure I would have contacted the authorities. Conceivably he harbored such a reason, and I resolved to watch for one. But so far he was utterly different in that respect from the psycho-murderers I'd seen and read about.

For some reason I thought of those who'd assassinated our presidents, convinced that God or posterity would reward them—Lee Harvey Oswald, and John Wilkes Booth, whose last words were, "I died for my country." Anyone talking with them before the act, hearing their philosophy, could see the basis of justification, the structure of thought, the launching pad for the missile that these men were to fire on an unsuspecting target.

In waiting and watching, while I delved further, I resolved to myself that even the vaguest suggestion of such thinking would hurry me to Artie's brother—and then, possibly, to the police. But, though I listened carefully to his every word, I found no hint of such delusional thinking.

I recalled seeing a *Twilight Zone* episode in which a man with the sudden power to read minds becomes aware of an elderly bank employee's scheme to run off with three hundred thousand dollars when the bank closes that day. The mind reader can hear the man's thoughts as plainly as if he were making a speech—the contemplated switching of satchels just inside the door, the slow walk to a waiting auto, and the purchase of a one-way plane ticket to a distant clime.

The mind reader reports him to the police, who close in on the man and seize his satchel. But it's empty.

The poor employee is aghast and confesses that he has, indeed, plotted such a crime. He explains it roughly this way: "But I've been rehearsing this robbery, just this way, for the last twenty-seven years. Every day I say to myself, 'It's all set. This will be the day.' But I just can't do it, and I leave the bank promising myself, 'Maybe tomorrow.'"

Never was I more acutely aware of how thin a thread separates resolution and action than during my work with Artie. How many of us have imagined ourselves committing suicide, jumping in front of an oncoming train, or driving straight into head-on traffic, feeling what seemed like resolve, before continuing ahead on our accustomed route? Moments afterward, our "hairbreadth escape," our brush with the newspaper headlines, becomes again as unrelated to the real world as if it had never occurred.

I asked Artie to tell me whatever he could about his urges: What were they like? When would they come? What had gone on that day?

One evening at his brother's house, he'd gone almost insane, the impulse was so strong. Dan, Janet, and he were watching a tennis match on TV, and Sylvia was breaking in with a lot of questions of her own, geography questions mostly. It crossed my mind that she was inventing them because she felt excluded. Her father had told her several times, "Okay, this is the last one. Now we want to watch the tennis game." But he kept answering them anyway, and so did Artie when he could.

Then the doorbell rang unexpectedly, and Dan and Janet ran to answer it. Left in the room alone with Sylvia, Artie pictured the worst; he could feel tension in his hands, and he flexed them, as if he were strangling her. After a few unbearable seconds of this he stood up and rushed to the door, feigning curiosity about who was there. A little later he got over it.

He remembered being outraged, moments before he'd felt the urge, not at Sylvia but at Dan.

"Outraged, why?"

"Well, I like Sylvia, but they let her boss them around. They let her take up the whole evening. And couldn't Janet have gone to the door herself? Why did Dan have to rush after her? It was only a neighbor telling them some bullshit about a tenants' meeting."

So Artie felt a mighty possessiveness of his brother.

He wanted too much from me too. He took for granted that I would talk to him on the phone at length whenever he called. I stuck with him because of his delicate balance, but he never thanked me. He would often start talking fast at the end of a session to keep me there.

And he was competitive with my other patients.

He always seemed startled when my next patient rang the bell, and once I heard him mutter, "Damn it." Another time, my patient after him, a woman, graciously held the door open for him as he was leaving. Artie strolled out without acknowledging her.

Obviously such thanklessness must have been a great liability in his life, but I elected not to mention it until I had studied it more closely.

That he felt excluded by society was becoming apparent, and he clung to those few who showed him even a semblance of warmth or caring. But murdering Sylvia . . .

Even more than I'd initially realized, Artie had grown up as little more than a limb of his older brother. As a child he would play catch with Dan, who bought him a baseball glove and a Baltimore Orioles cap. He would pitch to his brother, just the two of them, in a local lot, and they had fantasies of going to the big leagues together—a pitcher-catcher, brothers battery. It had been done before, his brother told him, looking at the record book.

But Dan didn't follow through. His interest in baseball waned by the time he got to high school, and Artie felt abandoned. That perfect pitching motion Artie was working on would be allowed to die. Artie would never have quit on his brother. He himself was loyal even to his toys—the row of soldiers that had brought him pleasure, which had consoled him when he was lonely, and the portable radio that he and Dan had listened to but which no longer worked, he kept carefully on a special shelf in his closet.

His own steadfast allegiance to these inanimate comrades perhaps enforced his feeling of disappointment as he began to see less and less of Dan. He would watch his brother breeze in and talk about the radio station, or the school play, or the high school newspaper, of which he was financial secretary. Dan would go to wealthy folks to ask for money for the paper and end up having dinner there and making new friends. Artie was alone, and would have to content himself with stories of his brother's celebrity and accomplishments.

By the time Artie was in high school, Dan was going off to Yale. "His average wasn't so good, but they gave him a scholarship because he did so many things in high school," Artie said.

Still, Dan hitched rides back for every holiday, and though he saw a thousand friends in Casper, he would always spend time with Artie. But Artie didn't see it as nearly enough. Dan confided in him, "I've been to New York City. We may end up there. We may run a business. I don't know what kind yet. But we could be rich."

Not the wealth that economists talk about, but the wealth of the comradeship with Dan inspired Artie. The promise of going to a big city, and of spending more time than ever with his older brother stayed him through long periods of isolation among school-fellows, of nonparticipation in school events. When his teachers recognized him as Dan's brother, he felt proud and repulsed at the same time. He was nothing like Dan, and he knew it. But he was sure he would be someday—that he *could* be, if only Dan would bring him along, would continue talking to him, would keep the faith, remember his own promises, and never doubt that Artie, his kid brother, had talent—and loyalty. Above all, loyalty. At any moment, Artie would have willingly died for his brother, and he expected Dan to feel the same way about him.

After Yale Dan had come back to Casper, but didn't take a job there. He paid his share of the rent but was seldom home. It was obvious he would soon be off for good. Though he still told Artie, "We'll be in business together, somewhere," he'd become critical of Artie. "You've got to wear better clothes. Fake it. Look rich, if you can, and you'll *be* rich if you do. . . . Lose some weight."

Artie was dating a girl by then, a few years older than he, sullen, not attractive. "She was actually afraid to meet my brother," Artie said. "But she finally did. She said he was charming. He told me he liked her, but I knew he didn't. He was just trying to encourage me. I stopped calling her, and she never called me.

"Then he told me he was leaving. I asked him, 'For good?' and he said yes. I couldn't believe it. I felt like all the music and the talking and everything in the world stopped. I guess he saw I was very depressed.

"We were all in church. Dan always went on Sunday, wherever he was. He wasn't religious, I mean he didn't talk about it if he was, but I guess he was. He would always ask me to go. He used to tell me to go, over the phone when he was at Yale.

"Anyhow, he said he'd been praying for something, some chance to go after what he wanted. He said to me, 'I asked God to give me a chance, and he did.'

"I remember when he told me. I felt terrible. There was a big stained-glass window with a figure of Jesus. I used to look at the little flecks of red, blue, and white, the light was coming through. Jesus' robe seemed to shine. When Dan said, 'I'm going to New York City,' I kept looking down at my hymnbook so he wouldn't see how upset I was.

"He whispered to me, 'Don't worry, we'll be together soon.' But I guess I was really crying. I remember putting the book back on the rack. I didn't say anything. He was praying.

"A little later he said, 'I'll be sending for you as soon as I can.' All I could think of was how high that church ceiling was.

"Outside, he told me that he was starting with a big theatrical agency. William Morris. I'd never heard of it. 'It's a little job, but they're giving me a chance,' he said. 'If I'm good, I'll make it.'

"After that, he was busy getting ready to go. My parents couldn't understand what an agent was. It sounded crooked to them, but we told them it wasn't.

"Before he went, he asked me how much money I could save a week. I told him nothing until I finished college, but if I worked full-time in the department store, maybe a lot. 'Okay,' he said. 'I'll save some for you, if I can, and you'll come to New York City once I get set.'

"His last day in Casper, he asked, 'What do you want to do, kid brother?' And I said, 'Nothing, I'm busy today. I made plans with a friend to go driving in the country.'

"He looked disappointed. He said, 'I'm leaving tomorrow. You can't break it?' I told him, 'No. I promised him.'"

I asked Artie why he hadn't spent that last day with Dan.

"I was mad at him, I guess. I don't know. I forgot all about it, but he mentioned it to me a lot of times after that. He said he was nervous about going to New York, and I should have spent his last day with him. Anyhow, he took an early plane, and he left."

Dan did eventually send for Artie, posting money for his trip and offering to pay for him to live in New York City while he found a job and went into therapy. For three years Artie had refused to do the latter, saying he didn't need help, though he lost one job after the other.

"By that time my brother had left the big agency and was on his own. He was making a fortune managing actors and directors and TV writers. He was lucky. He came here at a good time. The field was wide open. But he didn't really have time for me."

That didn't seem fair.

"I thought you said he took you out to dinner at least once a week and talked to you all the time. What do you mean he didn't have time?" I countered.

"I know, but it was different. There were other people around a lot. It wasn't the same."

"And he certainly backed you with money," I said.

"I know. But he had a fortune. Do you have any idea how much money he makes?"

I didn't.

"About two hundred thousand dollars a year. He can afford it. And half the time we went out together, it was with one of his girlfriends around."

"That bothered you?"

"Not at all. He'd dump them, one after the other. I mean he'd be charming, have sex with them, then he'd change his mind about them. They were all beautiful. Sometimes they'd call and ask me if I thought he still wanted them. How the hell would I know? But I'd say maybe. I knew he wanted me to string them along. There was one, Alice, she's a big actress. Absolutely beautiful. She was in love with him. She invited me out to dinner. People thought it was a date. She was desperate about him. But she got over it."

On a whim I asked him, "Did you ever have an impulse to strangle any of them?"

"Not really. I knew he didn't really love them. He was just using them."

What was he saying? Could it be that *he'd just told me his motive* —in so many words? If Dan had loved those women, then Artie might have wanted to harm them. There seemed no other reading of that answer.

So *jealousy* was the driving force, whatever else was involved! And Sylvia was only a pawn in this game of kings and queens. Her father loved her, and that took him away from Artie—that was enough.

It made sense to me. Without being conscious of it, Artie had relied utterly on his brother, he had counted on Dan to supply him with his whole adult life. He was really furious at his brother for letting him down, but he couldn't afford to face that. And so he blamed Sylvia. Sylvia was in the way. Now, in unguarded moments, his muted rage toward his brother and yearning to have him back were assuming this monstrous form. He would have his brother to himself—no matter what. I recalled Macbeth's line "The near in blood, the nearer bloody," and no one was nearer in blood than Sylvia.

But though this made sense, I cautioned myself not to bring up the topic of jealousy until I had done more delving. The test would be whether the times when he might resent Dan but didn't do so openly became the very occasions when he felt his most murderous impulses toward the girl.

Sure enough, on a night when he felt very wanted, and actually needed, by his brother, he had no such impulse.

That whole evening, Dan was distraught over the loss of a client, an actor he'd discovered Off-Broadway and nurtured to the brink of stardom. Over dinner, Dan reviewed his recent dealings with that actor. He had several times asked his wife and Artie if they thought he'd done anything wrong. Janet assured him that he hadn't. "Some people are just like that." Artie kept consoling him too.

That night, Dan had taken Artie into his confidence, he'd talked to him as an equal, even needfully. After Janet had gone to bed, Artie and Dan had stayed together until midnight, drinking bourbon, just as in the old days. At the door Dan had said, "Thanks, kid." This was what Artie had come to New York for.

In my office he realized he had gone the whole evening without even a thought of hurting Sylvia.

I concluded that because that evening Dan had belonged to him,

Artie had been able to accept Sylvia and all she stood for. He'd had no need to compete for his brother or to punish him.

But then came a night when anyone might have felt excluded —both hurt and angry. In the afternoon Artie had suffered a setback in his real estate job. He'd blown a sale, and his supervisor had told him that his job was in jeopardy. He could hardly wait to talk it over with Dan, and they were finally discussing it with great animation when Janet crashed in and said, "Sylvia wants to play something for us before dinner."

All conversation stopped abruptly. Sylvia sat down at the keyboard, looking adorable, and played. The family applauded her, and so did Artie. Then Tony, their little boy, got center stage. During dinner Dan commented several times on how beautiful his wife looked. "She's the kind of woman Gainsborough would have loved to paint." Janet beamed.

No one noticed Artie's presence at the table, and he felt even worse than he had in the afternoon. When Sylvia asked Artie what he was going to get her for her birthday the following week, he said simply, "Something beautiful."

All evening he could see the cords and veins in her throat. She went to sleep soon afterward, and he repeatedly pictured himself slipping into her room and strangling her in her bed.

In my office Artie broke into a sweat telling me about it. "I was afraid to drink anything, afraid I'd lose control. I wanted to stay because I wanted to talk to Dan alone. But I couldn't. I had to go home. It's as bad as ever."

Though he still saw no correlation, by then I was sure that I had found the crucial one.

And I could piece together more. His murdering Sylvia would simultaneously satisfy many ends. He would remove one who stood between him and his brother. He would punish his brother for deserting him—punish Dan the worst way he could think of. And perhaps most important, he would establish himself as a force in the world, make himself unforgettable.

Was there also sexuality in the picture? He'd had only occasional fantasies of harming Sylvia's brother and none recently. I couldn't be sure—not nearly as sure as I was of his raging jealousy of Dan.

Once I knew what to look for, his jealousy seemed to announce itself everywhere. For instance, one evening Sylvia had gobbled down her dessert of apple pie, knocking part of it onto the floor. When her father had scolded her, she'd replied that it didn't matter, no one was there.

Dan had cautioned her that it did matter, Uncle Artie was here. He'd added that, besides, "An Englishman has good manners, even alone on a desert island." Artie had felt a rush of desire to strangle Sylvia almost at once.

What had touched it off? To my surprise it was neither her remark nor her father's rebuke. Rather it was Dan's adage about the Englishman! Artie remembered Dan's using exactly that example with him when he was small. He'd treasured the comment. Hearing it offered to Sylvia now seemed to signify that his own time of grace had come and gone.

When I realized what actually had bothered him, I felt rather fed up with him and hopeless. What could I do for him if he resented every hardship, even those that are universally shared, like the consequences of getting older?

Artie seemed unable to accept the fact that his relationship with his brother had changed. True, he was no longer the adored child in the family, but another person would have accepted being now the respected brother and uncle.

Furthermore, Artie readily translated his every discomfort into a desire to inflict misery on others. It was as if he refused life's contract. To be human requires being a good sport. Whoever invented the aging process, with all its vicissitudes, stipulated that. I realized, of course, that in the end Artie was the one who suffered most. His inability to embrace life excluded him from many of life's pleasures. He made himself unpleasant to be around and found himself at best on the periphery with people, the only exception being with his own family. Also, the symptom of his having those murderous impulses was a private curse. I felt sorry for him.

But that feeling too was short-lived when I thought again about his tremendous potential to become violent, even to commit murder. I couldn't possibly relax until somehow the charge had been defused.

My strategy was fast dictating itself. Artie would have to discover that the real quarrel was with his brother. It was Dan who had opted to come to New York City, who had chosen intimacy in the form of a wife and children, who had centered his life in them and in his work. Dan had, indeed, dropped a curtain on the past. Artie would never again be his sole love—or even his primary one.

I would have to help Artie reach this discovery and accept it—to free Sylvia from his wrath.

Then, even before I could get started on this, I was in for another surprise. Corroboration of his yearning, or at least what I took as such, came from an unexpected source.

Artie told me about those sexual fantasies, those illicit visions he'd had during masturbation. They concerned men!—or more precisely, an imaginary older man making love to him, adoring him, wanting to touch his body. Artie would become a teenager again, and that worshipful, appreciative older man would compliment him on his youth, on his penis, and then bring him to orgasm.

"Anyone you know?" I asked him, and he mentioned a man who had once tried to pick him up during a bus ride in Casper. He'd been only thirteen. The experience repulsed him, and he hadn't told anyone about it. In actuality he'd never had sex with a man, or wanted it.

Was he secretly homosexual? Though he'd enjoyed sex with the two women who'd consented, he'd sometimes wondered. One can always posit homosexuality. But doing so would add nothing to our understanding. Either way, one can surely call it an "eroticized older-man fantasy." Through sex with a man who would care for him, "still teenage Artie" could truly possess what reality refused to yield, the undiluted love that Dan had offered him when he was young.

How could I get him to see this—to redirect his disappointment to its real source—namely, his brother? No matter that his expectations of Dan were bizarre, or that he was utterly thankless for what his brother had actually done for him. For him to appreciate the depth of his disappointment in his brother would, almost surely, be to exonerate Sylvia.

And after that? What he might see from there was his quarrel with life itself, its promises to him broken, its refusal to unfold for him as he'd always imagined it would. And, finally, if we continued together, he might realize that life owed him nothing, that this glorious coincidence of being is no more than that. He would appreciate that his own life was a barren island because he had left it so. From there, by whatever means he chose, he could till the soil, expecting less and giving more to people until they mattered—and until he mattered too. That would be the master plan, if we had time.

I had reason to suspect that Artie himself realized things were not perfect between him and his brother. He told me that one night Dan had come out in a terrycloth bathrobe and fancy slippers. "I guess it was a hint that it was getting late and he wanted me to go home." When I asked him what he then did, he told me self-righteously, "I stayed another half hour. It was only eleven."

I could virtually see the tug-of-war between them—Dan not wanting to injure Artie's fragile pride, feeling sorry for him, and Artie, afraid of the dark once he left, seizing any excuse to stay. The idea that Dan would want him to go home even at midnight humiliated Artie, and, I imagined, fired his hatred of those privileged to remain behind.

But there was no questioning that relationship. When I tried to, he shut me up fast. "It's perfect." He flatly rejected the idea that either of them could ever be dissatisfied with the other. Apparently he needed the relationship too sorely to look at it.

I actually found myself hesitant to mention Dan's devotion to his own family. Who could tell? Artie's reluctant acceptance of this, along with seeing himself as an outsider, could turn him into an uncontrollable hazard. He might deny his wrath to me, but suppose it broke through? Would he seek revenge in the only way he had ever contemplated it? By murdering a child? I didn't think this was likely. But the stakes were too high for me to gamble.

So there I was, afraid of tampering with his outraged and outrageous picture of himself because he needed it so badly. Yet obviously he would have to alter that picture if he was ever to rid himself of his symptom and to move ahead in life.

Ironically, Artie liked Sylvia. On his impulse-free days she delighted him. His unsuspecting brother commissioned him to take her and her best girlfriend to the zoo on a Saturday, and they had a wonderful time. It was as if the joyous public surrounding them protected him from his impulses. But he'd been afraid to go back to the apartment with them and wait for Dan and Janet to return.

In front of Sylvia's building, before sending her and her girlfriend into the elevator, he'd asked if they'd be all right until Sylvia's parents came back. They'd told him, "Of course."

"Thank you. I had a wonderful time," Sylvia's friend told him politely, as if reciting her parents' words.

But Sylvia threw her arms around him and kissed him on the cheek. "Thank you, Uncle Artie," she said, with the ostentation that only childhood allows. "Can't you come up?"

"Sorry, I have some paperwork to do."

Going home he was aglow with joy. But moments later he felt sorry for himself because he couldn't go upstairs with them and lengthen a lovely afternoon.

I felt bad too. His sorrow was contagious. Yet his decision was surely right. Why tempt the fates? Though I never truly got to like Artie, I saw him that day, and in other moments, as a Titan doing battle with demons; he never allowed them footing, though he could not repel them from his shores.

Once again I wondered what accounts for the difference between those who remain tormented by impulses and those who act on them. One might call it sanity, but that's just a word, and besides, it seems cynical. I preferred to think of it as character.

I recalled a patient I'd seen in Norwich State Hospital who'd committed himself; the poor man confined himself in a few feet of space in the corner of the ward, where he cowered and muttered that he didn't want to kill his neighbor, but why were they telling him to do it? He kept up a dialogue with an imaginary person: "Will you please stop telling me to do it?" Without character that fellow might have quenched the fire of his affliction by taking a life.

No such men were John Wilkes Booth or Alexander Berkman, whose stories always fascinated me. A crucial motive of Booth's was sheer envy of his father, Junius, and his brother, Edwin, both greater actors and far more celebrated. Booth sought fame. His allegiance to his beloved South was a small motive, if any: Booth had chosen to stay in the North during the Civil War. His killing Lincoln was a patricide and a leap to celebrity. His greed for fame was such that had the South won he might as easily have assassinated Robert E. Lee.

Berkman, after shooting the steel magnate Henry Clay Frick, coolly told Frick's wife, who had rushed into the room and saw her husband on the floor, "Madam, I did not kill your beloved husband or the father of your three children. The man I killed was Frick, the vicious industrialist, who has exploited thousands of workers."

Fortunately Berkman was wrong on all counts. Frick lived, and Berkman was caught and imprisoned.

By the same token, Artie might have announced that he hadn't strangled Sylvia—he liked her and was sorry to see her go. The person he killed was the interloper who had dared steal his beloved brother from him. But though he had bent reality plenty, he was not to be confused with a murderer—and he would not be, if I could get through to him.

I sensed that things were going downhill with Dan. He and Janet, perhaps finding Artie too sticky, too demanding, seemed to be pulling back. They were still pleasant but had begun to limit his visits to once a week and no longer had him over with other people. I wondered if he'd dominated their time too much, or been too possessive. Whatever the reason, they had almost surely talked it over and agreed on how to handle him.

I too felt pressured by Artie, and could appreciate Dan's dilemma, that of not wanting to injure his brother but resenting the need for constant vigilance. Like Dan, I'd been overcareful about what I said and did so as not to offend him. And he was a past master at being offended. He still scowled when I had to end a session, and he still resented paying me, as if I should see him for nothing.

Early one afternoon I was stuck in a cab in downtown Fifth Avenue traffic a half hour before our appointment. I kept glancing at my watch, and then I realized that I was far too nervous over being a couple of minutes late for Artie. Pictures actually ran through my mind of Artie's going home because I wasn't there on the dot. I imagined him not even calling me later but waiting for me to call *him* and apologize, and when I did, he would make the most of it, acting crestfallen and pouting as if I'd deliberately stood him up.

Whether he would have done exactly those things or not I don't know. But he surely induced that expectation in me.

How I expected Artie to act was instructive. It gave me a more vivid picture of how I perceived him than I could have stated before that, if asked. In that sense my feelings were diagnostic of him. Admittedly, if I felt that everyone would behave that way on the very rare occasions when I was late, then those feelings would have been diagnostic of me, indicating perhaps an unsureness about my status with people. But I didn't ordinarily feel that way. I went down the list of my patients, asking myself what each would do —or at least what I would expect them to do—if I were late for our scheduled appointment. Most would be lenient and understanding. A few might worry about my welfare, since I am habitually punctual. Another few might get confused and doubt that they'd gotten the appointment time right. One person other than Artie would become irate, I decided, but he would forgive me fast. Only Artie would make such capital of my mistake.

It was easy to see that I was reacting to Artie much the way his brother did, except that everything was more intense in that relationship, so that if I were feeling confined, Dan must feel himself in a straitjacket, catering to Artie as he felt he had to. Such extreme generosity as Dan's eventually gives way to a feeling of obligation, and then to disgust. Dan must have been well into that last stage, and I was entering it.

Naturally my identifying with Dan wasn't especially surprising. Dan had poured a great deal into Artie's life and gotten little back. Artie was angry with both of us for not giving even more. I found myself hoping that they could fight it out and clear the air. After everything came out, no matter how much it hurt Artie, he could see how to improve his life. He would have to stop sucking so much from others and take responsibility for himself.

The more I savored the idea of their fighting openly, the better I liked it. Dan must surely be at wit's end; he'd given Artie everything short of the oxygen in the air they both breathed. Not only was Artie unappreciative, but he'd made nothing out of all that largess. Anyone just coming to New York City, with a well-honed sense of obligation and a willingness to work, would find people far more welcoming than Artie had.

It seemed obvious that if they fought openly, Sylvia would profit in the long run. Artie would stop seeing her as the person who stole his brother away. But what about the short run? If nothing got resolved for a time, and he felt worse, might he steal into her room and strangle her?

Suddenly this all seemed like the daydream it was. It wasn't Dan's province to bring Artie's rage out into the open toward him. It was *my* obligation to level with him, and to let him get as angry as he chose toward *me*—to help him discover reality with me. I myself would have to stop tiptoeing around him, to stop catering to him, and evoke the quarrel, if there was to be one, with me. He might as well start where the stakes were not so crucial.

I resolved from then on to be very different with him—to give him his due, but nothing more. If I felt he was being unfair with me in any way, I would make an issue of it. Not that I'd be cruel, but I'd stop pampering him. I would ask for my fair share of everything. I would play *real life* to Artie's little sulking boy, until he outgrew the role.

Maybe he'd hate me and walk out. But even then, Sylvia wouldn't be at issue. At worst, he'd still have Dan. At best, he could see, when the dust cleared, that he'd been cheating himself out of a life by expecting another person to give him one.

My new approach felt especially called for because my pampering him thus far had done him no good anyhow. I'd been as futile as Dan in my effort to lift him. I felt lighter immediately as a result of this resolve.

The traffic loosened, and I got there at five to the hour. He was already at the door.

We went in, but instead of bringing him right into my office, I told him in the waiting room to please have a seat, that I had to make a call.

Sometimes when a patient arrived early, I would begin right away, but Artie had made a constant practice of being there ahead of time to squeeze the maximum out of me.

In my office I was already annoyed at myself for even bothering to give him an explanation. I should have told him only that I'd be with him soon. The humorous thought came to me that I'd already given him plenty of extra time in the cab, but that I couldn't help.

Once inside, he talked about his job, renting apartments, and complained that the people didn't give him enough information. He especially hated his supervisor, Florence, an older woman, who always seemed to put him last—she preferred women to men, though she liked his friend Carl and favored him. They gave Carl more money for his listings in the newspapers.

"What does she see in Carl?"

"He plays up to her."

"How?"

"He bought her a birthday present. He always talks to her husband about sports when he calls."

I was silent.

"I know what you're thinking. That's not what I want to do. That's the way New York is. Payoffs! That's what it is."

"So, Carl will just do better, and that's it," I said. "Artie, if that's your system, you have your honor. Why should you get her a birthday present?"

"I don't even know when her birthday is."

That I would have bet on.

I said, "If those things really mattered, you'd find out. Does Carl rent more apartments than you do?"

"Yeah. That's because he gets better ones. I don't believe in birthday presents, anyhow."

"Not even Dan's, or Janet's, or the kids', or your parents'?"

"Not really. They remind me of mom's and dad's, and the kids', and I send my parents flowers. My father's retiring this year."

"They'll have enough?"

"Dan talked him into it. He's going to help him out."

"A pretty generous guy, Dan," I said.

Artie darted a fierce look at me. I was different, not against him but more objective.

At the end of the session, on the dot, I told him I'd see him next time. He was reluctant to stand up, but I did and headed toward the door.

"No one's here yet," he told me.

"I know," I said, taking pains not to add anything beyond "Have a good weekend."

I think he went out stunned, as if he'd taken an exit from a movie theater by mistake and was now out on the street trying to adjust to the brightness and open space.

Afterward I was surprised at how hard it had been for me to stay spare in what I said, not to put down bridges for him to cross in conversation.

Nothing dramatic had occurred, but he was acutely aware that something had been removed—things were not the same with me, and I was sure he knew it.

————

Over the following weeks he sometimes looked at me strangely, but he never actually mentioned that anything was different about me. I couldn't tell what he was thinking. I don't think I was ever wanton or cruel with him; I simply refused to sympathize with his complaints.

I could see better than ever how he converted pain into anger. He detested anyone who, he felt, was celebrated or even accepted by society. He told me he hated Grand Central Station, and when I asked him why, he said that it was because of all the sloppy sentiment people showed in public.

His few friends over the years had been boys who, like himself, missed out on everything social. They would sequester themselves during big events, like Christmas or the afternoon of a high school football game, mocking the majority for its enthusiasm—always two boys together, never three. Artie would have been too jealous of a third. Artie and his few friends were rejects from the army of youth on its march to maturity, rejects pretending they had defected.

As if demanding sympathy from me, he complained more than ever. And he had plenty to complain about. His job was going badly. He would oversleep—his alarm clock sometimes couldn't rouse him. Finally he'd retained a service to call him and wake him up in the morning. One morning the paid service had apparently defaulted, and he was furious; they'd nearly cost him his job.

I kept reminding myself not to give him sympathy, it had never helped him. When I had the impulse, I said nothing.

I could sense that things were coming to a boil. The evening after one session, I had vivid mental imagery of Artie doing his worst. I started at the thought of getting a phone call from the police. "We have an Arthur Henshaw here. He says he's a patient of yours. He's just killed a little girl."

Apparently I was afraid that the rising barometer of his anger at me could convert into rage against Sylvia. I felt sure it was my own paranoia. Even so, I was actually relieved to see him the next time, and realized that I couldn't afford to let up or my whole approach would be a waste of time.

He began the session griping about his job, about Dan, about his landlord—about everything except me. Then he said, "On the way here, I saw an old man lying on the steps of the church, all curled up with a burlap bag next to him. One of those street people. We don't have them in Casper. I said to myself, 'This is me. This is where I could be.'"

I kept quiet.

He went on, "But I guess that can't happen."

"I'm sure Dan wouldn't *let* it happen," I said, perhaps too ironically.

He looked at me, surprised—like someone who had just been short-changed at a lunch counter.

I let some more time pass.

"Do you really think that could happen to me?" he asked.

"Well, I doubt it," I said, still not being very helpful. I hesitated a moment, weighing his hypothesis. "I guess if Dan died, and Janet had to scrimp to support the kids, they might not be able to—"

"You mean it's up to him!"

"I didn't say that."

"What *do* you mean? You just said I'd be a street person if my brother didn't take care of me."

"No, Artie, being a street person was your idea. I was only considering it."

His expressionless face had come to life. I pretended not to see him staring at me angrily, granting me seconds to explain myself as if he were the Pope and I were facing excommunication.

"Artie," I said, "you have two ways out. Either Dan will save you, or you'll save yourself."

"What do you mean, 'save myself'?" He was chewing his lip.

"I mean, study why you're not independent or happy, or have enough money or the friends you want. Why you just don't get what you want."

"Well, why do *you* think?" he asked sarcastically.

"I haven't got one sentence for you, Artie. Or even a little speech.

But we could figure it out. You could have ten times what you have now."

"And you think I'll be a street person?" He was daring me to say it again.

Well, if he dared me to, I would. "Who knows? Maybe that guy you saw on the steps there had a brother he counted on too much. A brother who didn't come through."

"What are you saying?"

"If he did, he should have counted on himself, studied what he was doing wrong, and fixed it. He might have had all the talent in the world."

He was smiling with fury. "But that guy's a schizo. He's nothing like me."

"Well, then I'm wrong. If you're sure."

Suddenly the sluices burst. "You son of a bitch! You've been kicking my butt for the last month, you fucking Jew bastard."

Even though I'd wanted him to fire at me, and was in a sense ready, it was more of an outburst and came quicker than I'd expected. It wasn't easy to stay composed. But I had to.

"No, I haven't," I told him a moment later. I wondered what the words "Jew bastard" meant to him.

"You have. You *have*. You've been watching me go down the drain. And you haven't done me a fucking bit of good. I misjudged you. Oh, how I misjudged you. I *really misjudged* you. I guess you think I'm a murderer. I guess you hate me for what I told you about Sylvia."

That I couldn't let pass. It was blatantly false. "No, Artie, I don't," I said. "I respect you tremendously for that, as a matter of fact. You're a hero to me for the way you've been fighting this thing."

He looked at me quizzically. I had meant every bit of it.

Then, without another word, he got up and walked out.

I knew even as he left that I was going to call him. I had to call him.

"Well, what do you want?" he asked over the phone that night.

"I want us to keep working together. We're just getting started," I told him.

My fear that he'd think I was merely soliciting a customer was dispelled by a softness in his voice. "I'll think about it."

"I'll expect you next time," I said.

For the first time he was late—ten minutes late. An old trick, which many angry patients discover for themselves after announcing that they might quit. He'd wanted me to sweat it out. And I did.

I made a little speech saying that I thought we had a real relationship, and if he didn't like something I did or said, he should tell me at once. "Tell me off, if you want. Don't pull any punches. But let's keep working together. I want you to have a good life, I really do. And you can. If we stick it out."

I didn't count on his believing me then and there, I knew I'd have to prove it. But it was important to say.

When I asked him why he had been late, he looked at me grumpily. "What's the difference?"

"There's a big difference. I was expecting you."

"That's your trouble," he snapped. "You're oversensitive. If you don't like my face when I walk in, you complain. Everything bothers you."

"Maybe I am sensitive. But I'm never going to get to a point where you don't matter. So you might as well get used to it," I told him sharply.

For months I made it a point to mention even his slightest mistreatment of me—his walking into my office dourly, without saying hello; his attempts to overstay; his snide comments whenever he had to pay me.

But I couldn't get him to think about these things. I realized that if a comment or two by me could make a difference he would have changed long ago. Usually he would cut me off when he saw where I was headed. "You're oversensitive" or "Everything bothers you" or "I can't say *anything* to you."

"I know, Artie," I remember saying. "We're the same, in a way.

A lot of things bother you, a lot of things bother me. I think a lot of things bother everybody."

But I could never be sure if he'd heard me.

On the good side, I think he sensed that I was robust and could take it. He seemed to enjoy lacerating me, though he didn't again refer to my religion.

Once I actually brought it up myself. He had whined, "Why are you like that!" And I alluded glibly to his past accusation. "I'm one of those New York Jews. That's the way we are. Maybe other people are like that too."

I couldn't see that I'd accomplished anything, so far as heightening his sensitivity to people was concerned. He was far from accepting the premise that he'd have to run his own life. However, during those few months, he had no impulse to strangle Sylvia or anyone. Doubtless, his struggles with me took precedence. Even more important, I think, he was for the first time taking liberties that only a child assumed with an adult. He was enjoying a freedom of expression that he'd never had before. In reality he had less to envy, so far as Sylvia was concerned.

Then one day he seemed to switch his focus. He began complaining as usual, but relating those complaints—to Dan.

"Do you think I enjoy worrying about dinner and paying the rent at my age? I mean not being able to afford a good restaurant except once in a while. I never should have come here. Dan really fucked me up."

I resisted any impulse I had to defend his brother, as he went on, "He shouldn't have brought me here if he doesn't want to stick with me.

"I don't understand why he did it," he muttered. "I don't understand why he did it."

When Artie was gone, it crossed my mind that Dan had, indeed, complicated his life, though unwittingly. Actually Dan's miraculous escape from the torpor of his early life had beckoned Artie to ascend heights that he was unready for. It had made flying over the flatland of their childhood seem plausible. Without Dan's example, and without his offers of help, Artie would not have aspired so high or become so indignant. And the obvious coda to that thought was: Nor would he have felt so envious, or evolved those murderous urges toward Sylvia.

Now that I was no longer submitting to Artie's petulance, I liked him a lot better, and I felt sure he liked me better too.

The next night I answered the phone. A slurred voice didn't identify itself. "I'm never going to see him again. I'm never going to see . . . I swear I'll *die* before I ever talk to him."

"Who is this?"

"Artie. Artie. Can't you tell? Don't you know me? It's Artie."

"Oh, hello, Artie, how are you?" I said, trying to sound casual. "Let's start all over. What are you talking about?"

"I don't wanna start all over again. I'm telling you it's over. Over." He spelled out the word "o-v-e-r"—"I'm never going to talk to him again."

"Who?" Of course I knew.

"My brother. Daniel, my brother Daniel."

"Artie, have you been drinking?"

"Not really. Not really. I just want to be clear. I'm never seeing him again. And I'm never seeing you again. Am I being clear?"

"Not really. Please, Artie, don't drink any more tonight."

"Well, maybe one more."

"Are you home now?"

"Yes, I just got home. I just came up in the elevator. And before that I just took a cab. And before that I left the home of my . . . brother . . ." He gulped.

"Artie, I'm glad you called. Do you want to talk now, or tomorrow?"

"Tomorrow. I'm a little talked out right now."

"All right, tomorrow," I said to the disembodied voice.

So the trouble between Artie and his brother was finally coming to the surface. I was glad that he was at last fighting his battle

where it really belonged. I was glad for Sylvia's sake, of course,
and for Artie's in the long run. But though I told myself that the
ultimate therapist would have welcomed this, I slept nervously.

In my office Artie had a lucid memory of the evening, though he
began in the middle. He said, "I told him, 'You always mock me
with your money and your success.'"

"What did Dan say?"

"He said he didn't know what I was talking about. I told him,
'Yes, you do. Every time you buy something expensive, something
you know I can't afford, you show it to me. You ask, "Do you want
to see my latest acquisition?" What can I say?' He had on this raw
silk jacket he'd just bought."

"Is that how it started?"

"No, before that we got up from dinner, and he whispered to
me, 'Say something good about the dinner to Janet, you never do.
It hurts her feelings. At least thank her for the dinner.' I said to
him, 'You sound like my analyst. And you know what he said? He
said, 'I hope that analyst is helping you. I don't see any sign of it.'

"I was furious, and he said he was too."

"Why was he so angry?"

"Oh, he said that when he gave me that cologne he bought for
me, I didn't thank him. I asked him if it was a hint."

"When was that?"

"A week ago. He said it bothered him. He told me I was hard
to take. Can you imagine saying that to your own brother, when
he has everything and I have nothing?

"I don't know what happened next, but he said I was getting fat
and starting to look just like my father. It was the family genes.
'Only he's retiring and you're supposed to have your life in front
of you.' He said he hoped I'd have some class."

"What did he mean by that?"

"I don't know. But I guess I was shouting. I told him, 'You never
should have invited me here if you didn't want me.' He said, 'I did
want you, but you want too much. You're a *leech*—that I didn't

know.' I said, 'How dare you call me a leech!' Oh, and another thing he said, he said, 'Now I see you, you're just like daddy, with those thick-framed glasses that cut into your nose. And still you don't see anything.' He kept screaming, 'You don't see *anything*.' And I told him, 'I do. I see a lot more than you want me to see. You're a phony, Dan. You're a phony.'

"Then Janet got into the act and told us to calm down. And Dan said, 'I'm not going to calm down, darling. You're right, it is like having three children instead of two!' Do you know how that hurt? I knocked a few dishes off the table, and he said to Janet, 'You see, that's just what I was saying.' I said, 'I told you it was an accident.' "

"Did you pick them up?"

"No one did. I told him, 'You're just using me to show off,' and Janet was crying, and he put his arm around her, like it was all my fault."

"Where were the kids?"

"They were in their rooms. I told him to fuck himself. I just started shouting, I don't know what. I told him I didn't need him. I could do anything I wanted without him. I told him I was never going to see him again. I had another drink. He nodded to Janet, I saw it, and she took the bottle away. So I got up and walked out."

"Did he say anything else?"

"Yeah, he said, 'Say good night to the kids. They'll hear you, they're still awake.' "

"Did you?"

"I don't remember. Anyhow, I slammed the door and went home. So here I am."

"You went to work today?"

"Yeah, of course."

I just nodded. I had to assimilate all this. "What next?" I asked him.

"I don't know."

He stuck to his resolve not to call his brother. I would ask him continually how he felt about Dan, and he would answer, "Relieved."

Once, when I asked him to explain, he told me, "He had his way for a long time. I'm glad I did it."

"Did what?"

"Finally told him what he's like."

Meanwhile, he got to his job on time and seemed to be working more responsibly. I suspected that with his brother gone, and less hope of redemption from that quarter, he felt he had to shape up.

He met a young woman while showing her an apartment, "Marsha, a black-haired beauty" was how he described her, and he began dating her. His depictions of her were so superficial—he had no idea what she felt or wanted or liked or believed in—that I didn't expect it to last long. She had just come to the big city from the Midwest, and by comparison he seemed to know the ropes. I could virtually sense her discovering that he was infantile and dependent, and I worked hard to help him refrain from acting that way. But of course he couldn't grow up overnight.

Before long he heard she was going to some parties and dating other men, and he got intensely jealous. He made snide comments to her about his rivals, which, it seemed obvious to me, would only hasten his descent. For the first time he mentioned his brother to her, glowingly, implying that he would soon go into business with Dan. She didn't respond.

When he criticized Marsha for going out with these other men, I asked him, "What have they got that you haven't got?"

To my surprise he said, "Everything. They have nice apartments. They're better-looking. They have friends, places to go—do you want me to keep going?"

"Do you know them?" I asked him.

"No, but I can imagine."

"How did they get that stuff?"

"I don't know."

I was pleased for the chance to underscore these questions, and

I kept in front of him the idea that much more was possible, and actually feasible, for him. If he attended to self-improvement, he could hardly fail to achieve a great deal, fast.

Without Dan in the picture he was doing much more for himself than he had. I theorized that as long as he'd relied on Dan to furnish him with a ready-made identity, he'd felt no need to construct one of his own.

Marsha's existence opened up his dreams, if not his reality, and I was happy for the dream as a start. He would listen to what I said, not attentively but at least he'd hear me out, and he was distinctly more willing to try on his own.

But the inevitable struck. Marsha dropped him, telling him that she was in love with another man and gratuitously praising that man.

For another few months he struggled, forcing himself to go to some parties and to initiate conversations. He got a better grip on his job and collected a few men friends, some of whom were divorced but had social lives with women. These men would have dinner or go to sporting events or play softball in the park. Artie wallowed in his status of having just broken up with a beautiful woman and still being slightly down. But he was making more money, and he bought some fancy fall clothes for himself.

Then he told me his brother had called and virtually apologized. Dan had put the kids on the phone. "We all miss you," Sylvia had said, and Tony wanted to show him a toy boat that he could control by radio-remote from the shore. "We're going to the lake in Central Park this weekend."

Finally Dan got on the phone and invited him over, but Artie asked him to apologize "for calling me a leech." Dan had said, "We'll get a chance to talk about it," and Artie had refused to set a date.

———

Another month went by, and then Dan called again. "Next Tuesday's your birthday."

"I know."

"You want to come over?"

"Sure. Thanks."

If he felt glad, he didn't let on. I was elated, and thought it especially wonderful that he'd added the concept of thanks to his lexicon. I told him that it was very important he'd said it, for his sake and not just for Dan's. In retrospect I overdid it, congratulating him for that one word as if he were an astronaut come back from the moon. He winced, perhaps in annoyance with me, sensing that I did, indeed, think of him like a man returned from far away.

By chance my Tuesday session with him was scheduled just before he was to go over to Dan's. I'd expected him to be attired in his new tweed jacket and possibly the charcoal pants that he looked so good in. But no, quite the contrary! It was as if he'd gone out of his way to look threadbare. He was in his baggiest pair of pants and an old green sweater, brought from Casper, items that Dan must have seen a hundred times.

With the outfit went a hangdog look, which he hadn't shown in a while. Clearly Artie had no intention of flaunting his own recent acquisitions. He didn't want Dan to see how well he'd been doing!

I wondered why not. But after a moment's reflection I realized there could be only one answer. Artie had felt that Dan would do less for him, would stop protecting him and even stop loving him, once it came out that he could take care of himself. He had seen Dan's involvement with him as wholly contingent on his remaining in need and his being incompetent.

Artie couldn't conceive of a world in which he was capable and his brother still loved him. And for that reason he had devoted himself to failing.

The implications of this for Artie were so sweeping that I could not possibly grasp them at once. Dan was the one he'd selected as adoptive parent, but Artie's demands far exceeded that relationship. It had pervaded his life and stunted his whole development.

Artie's need to incapacitate himself had vied with any desire to succeed in every avenue of his life. He had spent a lifetime sabotaging his own growth, his coming of age, all as part of a plaintive, unconscious demand to the world to nurture him.

For the first time I truly understood why he'd done so little for himself.

And I realized too why I had felt such discomfort in his presence, and why I'd felt better when I'd gotten tough with him. I'd been weighted down by his insistence that I regard him as a child, that I exempt him as one, that I excuse him even from gratitude—from having to recognize me as a fellow mortal.

No wonder he'd been so competitive with a nine-year-old. Sylvia had the very things he had wanted most, protection and immunity, and from the very person Artie wanted them from.

He'd had no impulse to strangle her for many months, he no longer saw her as his adversary. But his greatest discovery still lay ahead of him. He would have to identify his plea for help through incompetency, and see what was wrong with it. He could strive for excellence, and show excellence, without losing love from any quarter. He could have both competency and love.

I recalled Artie's likening himself to that man he'd seen sleeping on a pile of papers in front of the church. His flash of terror, "That could be me," was an insight! I saw it now. That man was the end product of what Artie himself had sought unconsciously, even as he had struggled with the rest of his being to achieve big things. I felt like saying, "Yes, that could be you if it's what you really want. But if you think about what you're doing, it won't be."

That night the family greeted him as if there had been no break. They gave him some presents, and soon after dinner he found himself alone with his brother in the living room. Dan apologized for calling him a leech, but added, "I do feel you depend on me too much."

Artie asked him, "Why did you do all that for me if I was such a leech?"

Dan's reply suggested that he'd thought a lot about it. "Because I love you. And maybe I was guilty because mom and dad paid so much more attention to me than to you."

Artie hadn't realized that, and Dan tried to explain. "It wasn't prejudice. They loved you, but they were older when you were born. And they had less money. Maybe I was more novel to them, I don't know. I never could figure it out, but the important thing is that we're buddies again."

And that *was* the important thing.

After that he went over there regularly. Though he often fought with his brother, they were closer. He enjoyed the family much more and was utterly free of his old impulses to injure the children. One night, while sitting in Sylvia's room alone with her in front of the TV set, he scoured his thoughts for even a hint of those impulses, but he couldn't find one.

We finally got to talking about Artie's unexamined belief that his brother had deserted him. I concluded, "But, of course, he's still there, on your side, just a human being, like anyone else."

"A lot better than most," Artie corrected me.

"Wait a minute," I countered. "You weren't altogether wrong in what you said about him. He does like to show off sometimes."

"He's entitled," Artie said.

"Okay," I said. "As long as you can take it. I mean, accept having less in some ways but still being responsible for your life."

For months I kept bringing up the topic of his murderous impulses, as if tagging a shark about to resubmerge into the ocean of the unconscious. I talked repeatedly about Sylvia's role as imagined competitor, who in reality could have absolutely nothing to do with Artie's success or failure in life. One day he shut me up, saying, "I always knew that."

He began dating another woman but left so much of the relationship up to her that it became obvious that she wouldn't stay long. She would comment in dismay about his never planning an evening in advance, and about his letting her make all the decisions.

And sometimes when she didn't comment, I would. He would complain about money in front of her. He asked her for advice too much, and he didn't remember the basics of her life, including the names of her two brothers. Finally she stunned him by describing him much the way Dan had, as a "little kid."

I made capital of that relationship as long as it lasted, helping him see how he tried to pressure this woman, three years younger than he, to adopt him. Obviously she didn't want to. I could see that she was catching on to him, and that the end was near. Sure enough, soon after they'd slept together for the first time, she snapped at him for the way he criticized a waitress who'd made a mistake. She went home early and let him extinguish his hopes by dealing with her answering machine only.

Weeks after that, when Artie seemed back on his feet, we went over the behavior of his that might have ruined the relationship. He was only half surprised to see that nearly all of the acts we talked about could be construed as invitations to her to play adult to his child, to take care of him. He began to see that he made this demand of everyone and would often get angry when the other person refused to comply.

I thought he was starting to uncover a better way when he surprised me utterly by announcing that he would be going back to Casper to live.

"New York just isn't for me. I can be much happier there with what I know. And certainly I'll do better with women."

I just listened, not wanting to influence this idea by any bias of mine.

He kept saying the same thing week after week. By then Sylvia was close to twelve and Tony was almost fifteen. He would miss them all terribly. "But I'm forty. I've got to get on with my life. It's been too long getting started." He planned to work in real estate there after taking two accounting courses in New York City over the summer.

After that, though he had misgivings, he never truly swerved. There were aspects of New York Artie had come to love. He was now more capable of that emotion than he ever had been. And this was because he was developing a sense of his own individuality. Can one love others without this sense? Possibly. But surely, becoming aware of the moat of existence between ourselves and all others fosters love, as it did with Artie.

I saw him once after the summer, and then he left. Before going, he thanked me for sticking with him. No one, we agreed, would ever know about those murderous fantasies, or about how close he had come. Or had he come close? Psychometricians obviously can't measure such things, and doubtless never will, so anyone is free to speculate without fear of contradiction.

I got cards from him a few times during the next year, but not after that. Perhaps there would always remain a hint of gray in Artie, I couldn't be sure. But at least he would have his own life there in Casper, or here in New York City if he ever returned.

In retrospect I have sometimes likened Artie himself to a certain kind of suburb. I mean the suburb that remains undeveloped because of its proximity to a big city, to which its populace turns too much. Such a suburb must develop on its own, as if it were nowhere near the metropolis that offers it supplies and theaters and restaurants. Only then can it become a city in its own right, regardless of its size.

revenge

. . .

WISPS OF MEMORY SLID THROUGH my mind like fragments of film. Lydia. How she said she'd gotten the job. "I was lucky. I made three or four good moves. Financially right. Or anyhow they worked out. The comptroller, Don Simmons, liked me. He was a sweet man, not too strong. He had a bypass and left, and the next thing I knew, Dick, the company president, gave the job to me." "I guess my earliest memory of my father was getting sent to school when mother died." "You were how old?" "Eight, maybe nine. I felt happy and sad. At least I knew he wouldn't beat me anymore or keep saying I have thick legs. I think he did it for my mother. I remember her standing there and saying 'Stop,' but she never got in the middle."

Whenever Lydia Williams mentioned her father, I felt terrified for her, and more than once I marveled that she had survived. What is it in some children, what unspeakable resilience saved her? Surely, some survival trait established in our fragile ancestry over the millions of years, as the oceans rose and fell, must still be keeping us all alive. And yet she said she didn't hate him. As if she couldn't afford to, I thought.

It was a glorious April morning, and the sun washed the glass and steel towers on either side of me as I hurried up Fifth Avenue. I'd make it by nine, and she would for sure. As a rule I could walk to the door just before nine, knowing she'd be there, literally in seconds, tall, very attractive, with large deep-set blue-violet eyes. She favored silk blouses, red or gold, with big sleeves. She was great to look at, easy—but, mercifully, I didn't have erotic feelings for her, not after the first session. She was like a Greek Revival building, chaste, noble, majestic.

The light changed, and I hurried in front of the vehicles, across the Avenue of the Americas. When I'd crossed over, I thought about Mal, who'd called me for breakfast, Mal, my old friend Mal, a "sure millionaire" who never worked but bragged that he could outsmart all those Wharton graduates in pinstripe suits going to their brokerage houses every morning.

I'd turned down his request to borrow a few thousand dollars. Such a sum might not be much to him, but it mattered to me. Being old friends from the same neighborhood didn't warrant a loan he had no intention of repaying. Mal wasn't living in a dream-world, he just didn't give a damn. So what if his face dropped, if it had been a sordid breakfast? Mal's needs, Mal's possible future earnings, Mal, Mal, Mal. I could have told him I had three days to live, and he would have responded only by promising to repay the money in two and a half.

Still, I felt bad about turning him down, as if no matter how he acted or what he did, he was a kinsman, he was me, and I had broken some obligation, and as a result, I, myself, was less protected against the storm than I had been.

I thought about Lydia again, due in twenty minutes. Seeing her would be my sanctuary, helping her would be my holiness. She was sincere and clean-living and moral, and she'd made it financially, defeating Mal's thesis that cynical detachment is the formula for success. I felt proud of her.

Lydia was comptroller of a big publishing company at thirty-seven. She had said, "I'm responsible for saving and spending, you might say. I do financial analyses, and you could say I help Dick with our objectives. If it involves money, it crosses my desk. Every acquisition. Every new idea. It could be computer systems, furniture, or whether we should acquire a subsidiary, or how much we can afford to pay for a marketing director." She had said, "I know it's the kind of job you take home with you, that's for sure. But I'm agitated all the time. I can't sleep. I don't want to take pills. I don't know what to do . . ."

Then came the stories about Ben. "He blocks me at every turn. Let me give you some recent history. Last June we decided to renovate two floors, to move our editors upstairs. There just wasn't room anymore.

"I used half my staff, seeing what had to be done and pricing the move. I checked out contractors, I went over the design options, spoke to all the department heads. What did we need and who would do it? What kind of carpeting should we have? Should we keep the old furniture or get new stuff? Should we try to create new office space, knock out walls, build cubicles? That kind of thing. I checked references, met contractors and designers at night, on weekends. Finally I made my choices.

"Then Ben called Dick, my boss. Ben's *wife* wanted to use *her* contractor, some firm she had hired to renovate her parents' old house in the Hamptons. Dick told me not to go ahead with my people until I checked Ben's people out. It took our staff two more weeks, and I had to *prove* that they were no good. Which they weren't. Our job was too big for them, and it wasn't their style.

They weren't even close. Meanwhile we didn't get anything else done. He made a liar out of me to our contractor and cost us all money. And drove me crazy. It's been like that over and over."

"He has the authority?" I asked her.

"None. He's really a lawyer. The company's lawyer. And he does a lousy job there too."

"What do you mean?"

"He's gotten us into trouble more than once. He recently fouled up a case and cost us plenty. And the whole industry asked us to appeal it for their sake."

"Your boss knows he's in your way?"

"Dick knows. I told him what we lost. He sees but he doesn't see. He's the one who loses. But I look bad too. We all lose.

"Ben has broken deals more than once. '*Young lady*, do you realize that what you're suggesting is against the law?' He says that when it's not so just to upset me. He sometimes tells me to get married and retire. What do you say, without looking oversensitive, to a man who calls you 'young lady'? Now he's sick because I make more than he does. He's not above stealing my ideas either. Last year I researched a computer system, and he found out about it and recommended the exact system before I was sure."

"So he's coming at you from every angle?"

"I found out the other day that he's sleeping with one of my staff. That doesn't help either. I can't fire Amy for being stupid. And Amy's really okay. Just naive. Am I being clear?"

"What have you tried so far?"

"I'd like to try rat poison, I could write it into the budget." She smiled. "My secretary wants to put a bomb on his plane to Acapulco. But I can't do that either. It would be cost-effective, but there might be some innocent people on that plane."

"There might be," I said. "I'm still not clear where Ben gets all his power."

"Ben is about fifty. He's known Dick, the president of the company, for maybe twenty years. Their wives went to college, to Vassar, together, and they spend money together. So he's pretty tight with Dick."

"You mean you have no vote?"

"I have a vote but . . . well, maybe half a vote. I had to explain to Dick why I'd gone ahead with the office alterations just the way I did."

Listening to Lydia, I felt uneasiness, and then a sharp anger, toward Ben. I was reminded of Mal warning me that because I'd turned him down, he wasn't going to call me with a stock tip that would have made me rich. I'd told him, "I'll just have to pay the price," and he'd reminded me icily that "people who don't come through for me have a way of suffering. I'm not threatening you. It's just the way it works out." Preposterous. But I'd felt a stab of the unrest that goes with betraying a friend and forfeiting a sentry against the unseen enemy.

Better to revert to Lydia, to something constructive. Two boy-friends in her life—David, who adored her, but he didn't do it for her. Sex with him was too gentle, a favor for him; she would leave the room to masturbate while he slept, and think about Mike, who wanted what he wanted, when he wanted it. Mike, pushing her legs apart, selfishly, coarsely, deliciously, boasting and making good his boasts, but impossible to stay with for long hours and certainly not in love with her. Nor she with him. "I think I make so many decisions in a day, I like to be decided, sometimes. Doesn't that sound terrible!" But David was always in the picture, scheduling dates in advance, asking her which restaurant she preferred, calling her regularly. Mike knew about David, but David, he would have died, and so she protected him.

"Where's daddy in all this?" she asked. "You'd think I'd want gentleness and consideration. I suffer constantly with Mike; he's unpredictable in so many ways." But there was a curious similarity between Mike and her father—she never knew where she really stood with either one of them, what they liked or hated. On the other hand, David was so compulsively adoring, "he never says anything I do is wrong." Her father, though claiming he loved her, beat her and then, at the first opportunity, sent her off to boarding school. Mike was at least clear, if not ideal. "When I do my situps in the morning, and it hurts but I look good, I think of Mike, if I think of anyone."

For months we'd talked about daddy—now living with his fourth

wife in Boulder. Daddy the Marine, who beat the stuffing out of
a six-year-old girl. "Why did you think he was slapping you?" I
had asked, and she could never answer, except to say that he'd
wanted something more, he loved her but she had disappointed
him. "How?"

"I don't know."

"What comes to mind?"

"Nothing."

"Okay. Make something up."

"I wasn't pretty. I asked too many questions. Maybe he wanted
only boys. But my brother hates him too."

Her brother, two years older, ran the family store in Boulder
and would own it someday. Lydia expected nothing and, as if in
response to that inbred survival energy, had stubbornly refused
money or any aid from her father, who occasionally dangled money
offers if she'd come home for the holidays. She'd called him but
hadn't seen him in a span of eleven years and two wives. He was
in his early seventies and was coming east on his way to Europe
with wife four, Helen the Second, who "probably adores him like
all the others, because he won't have it any other way."

The previous month Ben had found out from Amy that Lydia
was lunching with an important client, whom he'd wanted to meet.
He'd pushed past her secretary and banged on the door while she
was laying out strategy to five assistants. Lydia had told him she
was busy, but ten minutes later he'd returned and opened her door
and barked at her that he was going to the lunch. "I have some
important things to discuss." She'd told him no, and he'd gone
away, but she'd been left feeling furious and with a sense that he
could invade her domain at any time.

Afterward it was Ben who did the complaining to Dick, calling
Lydia uncooperative. When Dick questioned her about the incident, Lydia had pulled punches, accounting for herself as if she'd
been in the wrong. "I was busy. I would have gotten back to him
if he'd wanted," she told Dick, "but I didn't consider him to be
appropriate at that meeting." She'd said nothing even mildly ac-
cusatory.

Her agitation had risen after that, its intensification clearly traceable to her meekness with both Ben and Dick. "I should have shoved that long-stemmed pipe down his throat and thrown him out. And I should have told Dick how rude he was, and how he humiliated me in front of my staff." While Lydia spoke to me, it crossed her mind that she might have called a meeting with Ben and Dick and gotten real tough, saying she couldn't take it anymore.

"What do you think would have happened?" I asked.

"I don't know," she said. "I imagine that Dick would take Ben's side, and maybe even tell me to go. . . . No, I know he wouldn't. But I guess I'm afraid I'd never get another job. I'd be out in the cold."

"But you told me you constantly get job offers, high-paying deals," I reminded her.

"I know it sounds silly. But I have this feeling everything would stop and I'd be ruined." It flashed through my mind that her mother had acquiesced when her father beat Lydia, and I had the terrible thought that after her mother died, that acquiescence on her mother's part was frozen into eternity. Lydia, one of the most capable people I knew, successful, strong in many respects, lived with the sense that she could be deprived of everything, on a whim, and defended against that possibility.

In actuality her only redress was to announce that no one was ever to drop in without an appointment. But that seemed tame—to her and to me.

That night she'd dreamed of being in France, among simple, hardworking people, knowing that the country was about to be invaded by shadowy troops, foot soldiers and tanks coming simultaneously from the east and west. In the dream, she knew vaguely that she was a citizen from elsewhere, but it was too late to escape. All around her the townsfolk were hurriedly wrapping up art treasures, paintings and statues, and sending them to attics and cellars of country homes.

I'd suggested that after any dream she might have, she ask herself, even before she was fully awake, what the parts of the dream reminded her of. In this instance she felt, above all, the panic of being unguarded and attacked. Ben's invasion had been an axe blow in the very slot initiated and dug deep by her father's physical beatings and insults when she was still a child.

"And the art treasures?" I asked her.

"I don't know. My sexuality, maybe. No. My creativity. My art. I didn't think of that then. But how can I possibly be creative with a maniac like that pounding at my door?"

"You certainly didn't do much in the dream to fight off the enemy or beat them back," I observed.

"No. They were overwhelming. The invasion was a foregone conclusion," she said.

I let that last statement go, but later I wished I had reminded her that, after all, it was *her* dream. She had constructed it, given strength to the relative forces, arranged the unfairness of it, stacked the odds so that all the citizens could do was hide their treasures. Arbitrary or even irrelevant as such a comment of mine might have sounded, it would have helped her consider that, even with Ben, she had truly exerted more control over the outcome than she realized. She could have been much tougher.

The note from her father that he and Helen would be staying in New York City for a few days on their way to Europe, and giving the dates, brought a torrent of memories. "He took up a lot of space," she said. I asked her what she meant. She could amplify at first only vaguely. "He was big, he walked big, I mean his arms were always out. He had a hard mouth and a square chin. I ought to show you a picture of him sometime."

I told her I'd prefer that she describe him. "Anything that comes to mind."

"He slapped me once when I wouldn't play the piano for some people. I must have been six. What a fucking bastard, now that I think about it! I wouldn't play, I don't know why. They were sitting around downstairs, and I was shy. And I ran upstairs. He came up after me and told me to just do my lesson. Then he slapped me in the face, it really hurt, and I went downstairs and played. It was terrible. I never really learned how to play, I hated it. David plays, he has a piano. I don't even like to listen. My father had a hard, cruel mouth. But when he smiled at me, it meant a lot to me. I guess that's why I didn't set the house on fire and burn him down."

"You had that thought?"

"Every day. I knew where the matches were. I even knew to use gasoline. Some kid did it, it was in the paper. There was a gas station near our house. My father knew the owner. I used to think about . . . who I would want there. But I wouldn't want to hurt my brother. My father used to really smash him."

"A great guy, your father," I said, and she gestured, as if to say, "What can you do?"

I pointed out to her that she still had fantasies of wreaking havoc on men who dominated her. She was startled and asked me what I meant, and I reminded her of those images of rat poison and the bomb on the plane for Ben, and of shoving his pipe down his throat; they were jokes, one of them originally her secretary's, but they were real at the same time. "I guess I have a lot of killer in me," she said. "I must get it from him."

Going further, I observed to her something else I'd noticed. When put down by a man, she would indulge in fantasies of the most violent kinds of revenge, but in actuality she would suffer but appease the man, becoming meek and explanatory. She was stunned but had agreed completely. "But only with Ben."

"No," I said. "Even with David you do it." I reminded her that she'd mused about his plane crashing so that she wouldn't have to tell him that she didn't want to go to bed with him anymore.

"I know," she said. "I thought about telling him it wasn't working, just last week. But it's hard."

"What comes to mind?" I asked her.

"Uh, I know this sounds funny. But no one will ever really want me again, the way David does. I'll be alone, in the cold. Sex isn't everything. Maybe I could marry him and sneak off. No, I would never do that. I don't know why I'm so afraid."

Why such deference toward the men in her life? She took elaborate precautions to cover up her time away from David, even though she was planning to leave him.

Then she remembered a Sunday when her father had promised to visit her at the Joree School but didn't get there on time. She was twelve, and she'd waited in utter panic as the other kids got calls that their parents were downstairs and rushed off. Had she done something terrible without knowing it? It was just after her first menstruation, and maybe he was furious. Maybe he didn't want her anymore. If only he'd forgive her and smack her in the face and forget it, that would be a dream come true.

Finally he got there. He looked preoccupied and went for a walk with her and then left. All was well, he was still in her life.

She'd bluffed it with the other kids when they discussed their gifts and where they'd gone with their parents. "I was always pretending. What a jerk I was." Tears slid silently over her cheeks, making her mascara run.

I had voiced the obvious. "Lydia, go easy on yourself. Even though he beat you, you needed him. You wanted him to love you. You had no mother. You *needed* him. Any relationship was better than none."

"I'm sorry I'm crying," she said to me.

"If you want to redo your makeup, feel free," I said.

She thanked me and left the room for a while.

When she came back, her mood was utterly changed. "How could anyone be so cruel! I'm going to tell him everything on Saturday. That miserable bastard! I'm glad he's still alive so I can. I'm going to read him the riot act. I'm going to nuke him right in front of wife number four."

I had nodded, like a therapist windup toy. It was her decision, not mine, and who knew where it would go?

It was only after the session that the connections all seemed to come to me, at once, like the many bridges of Königsberg. As with her father, Lydia secretly feared that *any* man in power would retaliate in the extreme. Not beat her, perhaps, but feel so betrayed and aghast that he would never forgive her. He would throw her to the winds, to fend for herself.

And as she had with her father, with good reason back then, she still felt inherently helpless, utterly unable to afford confrontation with fathers in any form. Those irrational fears of never getting another job, of never finding another boyfriend, of being unable to cope alone, of being a fraud at work, pretending to competency she didn't possess, an imposter who was fooling the world, still haunted her in their pristine simplicity.

Surely, she must feel that way with me too, to the extent that she likes me, depends on me, I thought. Who knew the degree of misgivings she'd felt about things I had said, misgivings she'd dared not voice, perhaps imagining that I too would dump her for crossing me. All this would have to come out, sooner or later, the sooner the better.

But next on her agenda was, *had* to be, that confrontation with daddy in the flesh. I once again recalled her saying, in effect, "Thank God he's still alive, the bastard."

At eight fifty-five she was standing in front of my building when I got there. She hadn't planned to ring the bell until nine sharp and was surprised to see me in the street. She waved to me, and as I reached her and said hello, I think we both felt that moment of awkwardness when therapist first meets patient in the real world, two spirits colliding for the first time in the flesh, beings reincarnated in new forms. Left unspoken was, "Oh, that's you, that's really you, standing on a real street, with a real choice of how to dress and walk in daylight."

I unlocked the street door to my office, and she followed me in. That morning we started two minutes early.

She began, "I've got a lot to tell, and it isn't all good. I failed again with my father."

"Lydia, let's not judge it. I'm very eager to hear all the details. You met him on Sunday for brunch, right?"

"Right. I didn't know how I'd get into it. But I had to tell him how terrible he was, how he'd beat me, and crushed me, and insulted me whenever he had the chance, how *overpowering* he was. But I pulled the same stuff I did with Ben. I couldn't.

"All right," she went on. "Let me start at the beginning. We met at Tavern on the Green. I'd reserved a table there. I looked fantastic. Remember, he hadn't seen me in eleven years, when I'd been much heavier. I put on my white Chanel suit with black trim, with a string of pearls and several gold chains. I mean I really looked fantastic. I wanted him to see me that way.

"I almost didn't recognize him. He was a small, little white-haired man. He and Helen were sitting in a corner, on a couch, waiting. She must be his age, seventy-four—they seemed almost frightened of the crowd, not self-assured at all. He didn't recognize me either at first. But—I made sure it was him—he had the same high brows and blunt nose and short neck, but it was like . . . like him in miniature.

"Anyway, he seemed afraid to talk to the maître d', so I spoke to him, of course; I knew him well from a few parties our office had given there, and we all sat down. My father couldn't get used to the place, he kept looking around at the chandeliers and the waiters and waitresses, and all he could say at first was, 'This restaurant is huge.'

"I ordered for them, and then he asked his famous question. It was always a question I hated, but I'd forgotten it. 'So what's new?'

"I told him I was comptroller of a big publishing house now, we have almost nine hundred employees, and I was second in command. He hadn't heard of our house. All he said was, 'Oh, I didn't know. And your health?' I asked him, 'Don't you think I look good?' He said, 'You look a little thin.' I took that as a cue.

"I said, 'You know, you really haven't followed my life very much over the years.'

" 'What do you mean?' he asked. 'Well, dad, for instance, when I came to New York City, and I was living from hand to mouth, you weren't too interested in my health then. I was working as a bookkeeper. Or when I got my B.S., all you said was, 'That's nice.' Or when I got the job at NBC. No comment from you.'

"He still didn't get the point. All he said was, 'And then you got this job.' 'No, dad. In between, I worked for the financial analyst at J. Walter Thompson. When I was living with Don, and you didn't approve of him. So you didn't want him to come home with me for Christmas. That's why I didn't see you.'

"He asked me a stupid question: 'How is Don?' I said, 'I guess he's fine, I haven't seen him in a long time. And then I came here, and now I'm comptroller. Are you proud of me?' 'Proud is a funny word,' he said.

"I couldn't make headway with him. Meanwhile, Helen was quiet. She didn't want to pad her part, she just kept looking at him with big moist eyes, which I knew she would. That's the job qualification. Oh, yes, she looked at the menu and said, almost like a criticism of New York City and me, 'Gee, things are very expensive here.' I told her, 'Don't worry. I'm paying. I mean my company is paying,' which, of course, they weren't. 'So order whatever you want, and don't think about it.'

"There were a lot of silences. They didn't talk about themselves at all. I talked, though. Not this time! I wasn't going to go under. I said, 'Dad, how come you sent me away when my mother died of cancer?' 'Oh, I thought it would be best for you.' 'Didn't you love me?' 'Of course I did.' 'Then how come you paid for my brother's college education and not mine?' He started to say something, some bullshit, 'Oh, in those days—' But I wouldn't let him. I said, 'You know, that hurts me a lot, that always hurt me.' He didn't say anything.

"Then Helen broke in. 'Your father is very devoted, he's always talking about you. I don't think you should—' Something or other, I forget her exact word, like 'censure' him. And I turned to her.

" 'Oh, really!' I said. 'Did he tell you he used to smash me in the face, that he once punched me so hard in the stomach that I couldn't breathe? And then he walked out of the room. Once a week, I mean once a week he hit me. And then he sent me away. Could either of you tell me why a grown man who had fought in the war would hit a little eight-year-old girl whose mother just died and who was crying?'

"There was silence. They hadn't bargained for that. All my father could say was, 'Did I?' And I said, 'Yes, you did.' And you know what he said? He said, 'Oh, I shouldn't have done that.' That was his whole defense for all those years. That was the best he could muster. I was flabbergasted.

"I tried again. The subject changed. We talked about New York a little, how it had changed. I guess it did. Helen told me my father had a pacemaker put in, I hadn't known that. I didn't realize he used a cane. At one point he had to go to the bathroom, and she asked him, lightly, if he wanted company on the trip. 'No,' he snapped at her, 'I don't.' He was proud. But he's tottering, he's white-haired. If I just saw him in a restaurant, I would say he was a tottering white-haired old man with little time to live.

"Then a funny thing happened. I had done some calculations of all the money he spent on me while I was away at school. Money he complained about several times. I had written out a Dreyfus check. It was fifty-seven thousand dollars. I was going to repay him, just to show him. I started to say, when he got back from the bathroom, 'Dad, I figured out what I cost you in school. I'd like to repay it. It was fifty-seven thousand dollars. I can afford it now. I make a lot of money.'

"That was my rehearsed speech. But he looked at me blankly, I think his mind is going a little. There's nothing in his eyes. Nothing. I couldn't go through with it. I just couldn't go through with it. He had no fire. No fire. So, in a way, I let him talk me out of it. He was someone else. When we parted, I kissed him goodbye, and I think he was glad. Really, it's like my real father is dead and I'm just replaying him. I wish he was young and strong again."

"Do you?" I asked. "Why?"

"Stronger. So I could really let him have it."

"Is that the only reason?" I asked.

She paused. "No, well . . . I don't like to see him this way. I helped the two of them to a cab, and they seemed confused. They're not staying at a very good hotel. I would have booked them into someplace like the Stanhope. I have a feeling I won't see him much more, if at all."

She stopped for a moment, lost in thought, before going on. "I guess I ought to admit to you how sick I am. When I called the next day to say goodbye, I had the impulse to offer them some money, no strings attached, to make the trip easier. I don't know how much he's got or feels he can spend."

"Did you?" I asked.

"No, I didn't let myself. But I have another confession to make. I wasn't going to tell you, I was too ashamed. I hired a limo to take them to the airport. They seemed so confused, with the baggage and all."

"Why is that a confession?" I asked. "Maybe, in spite of everything, you still care for him a little."

"But I should have told him off," she insisted.

"Why?" I asked.

"Well, isn't that the aim—not to get pushed around? I owed something to that little girl who was all alone, all those years, with no ally," she said.

"That's true," I admitted. "What you're saying is very powerful. She sure could have used you. I know what you mean."

Lydia drove the point home. "Remember, you told me about how the existentialists use the word 'accomplice.' As a child I guess I was an accomplice to my father's cruelty by not saying anything—"

"But you did say a lot. It's just that he didn't hear it," I countered.

"But I could have made it stronger—said it until he *had* to hear it. I betrayed myself," she said. "I wasn't fair to that little girl. In a way I abetted his cruelty."

"I understand," I insisted. "And revenge is sweet. But there's another way to look at it. Life is in front of us, not behind us. You can't drive by looking in the rear-view mirror all the time. You were helpless, and your father beat your brains out, that's true. But think of it this way. Now *he's* helpless, and you didn't want to do the same thing. In a way, until now, you were preventing yourself from forgiving his cruelty by repeating it."

"So it wasn't a total failure, then. Is that what you're saying?"

"Maybe you see it as a failure, but I don't," I said. "So what if you love him? We can forgive that. You love him, and you could have kicked his brains in. On Sunday you had all the guns. But the real enemy didn't show up. So after a few volleys you decided not to fire. You want to know something stupid, Lydia?"

"What's that?" she asked.

"I'm proud of you," I said.

During the next few days I thought about her a lot. I went back to look up H. W. Fowler's definition of "mercy," which had moved me so much when I'd first read it. "Compassion shown by one to another who is in his power and has no claim to kindness." Mercy begins where the demands of justice end. She had every right to lambaste him, it would have been only justice. Her desisting was a pure act of strength, not of weakness. Mercy, I realized, can belong only to the strong, and conversely, acts of mercy imbue the doer with strength. She had assumed a new and glorious stature.

Her father and his doting wife went off to Europe.

A few weeks later Ben crossed Lydia again. He got wind of an arrangement she was making to install a new internal telephone system in the company, with a dozen fax machines for editors and executives. Several days before she was to present it to Dick, Ben went in with a plan of his own. Lydia's staff quickly assessed it and concluded that it was inferior and more costly.

Armed with the data, she went to Dick's office and exposed the plan, as if it were an intrigue to kill the king and deplete the country. "In fact, he's cost this company a tremendous amount of money," she told Dick.

"Really! I'd like to see how," Dick had said.

"Can I give you some notes?" Lydia had asked him.

"Of course. I'd very much appreciate it."

"I'll detail everything," Lydia had promised. "You'll get it by Monday."

And the following Monday she brought in a list of recommendations Ben had made, and of his overrulings of her decisions, which had cost literally hundreds of thousands of dollars. She asserted, while Dick had his first glance at her report, that she could not go on in her role as comptroller unless Dick took a firm hand. When she left his office, Dick was having the report copied, and she was delighted.

The next time she saw Ben, he looked like a man who had donated three pints of blood at once to the enemy. He avoided her glance. When at a meeting he said something glowing about her work, she snapped, "Don't compliment me. You're not my boss. Just do your job, or *try* to do it." After that, Dick was always stern with Ben—at least in her company.

Though Lydia had considered her father to be hors de combat, she certainly didn't see Ben that way. He never troubled her again. And, interestingly, my work with Lydia helped me too. Somehow Mal came to matter less, as if in helping Lydia assert herself against intruders with no real claim I had simultaneously wriggled loose from my own imaginary chains. When I saw him again, and he made another request for money, it felt as preposterous as I knew it to be. I had finally come to understand what would have been obvious to anyone else, that I had absolutely no need of his good graces.

As for Lydia's relationship with David, she soon told him that he should consider her only a friend. He became so crestfallen, however, that he soon lost even that status. Her relationship with Mike improved—more than she or I had imagined it would. There were other men in her life, though no one who eclipsed the rest, which seemed quite all right with her, at least for the time being.

She became a different person with me too. We were close, unmistakably. But several times she told me warmly that I was smug. Once, I had observed to her that she was sexist, in the sense that she would sometimes overlook undue aggression in men but never in women, and especially not in herself. I had smiled, I thought innocently. But she told me that my smile bothered her, calling it egotistical, and I told her it probably was and apologized. I didn't always agree with her criticisms of me, but our relationship became far more robust than it had been.

Though Ben had truly been offensive, quite independent of how she saw him, the space he'd occupied in her life was a creation of her psyche, a manifestation. By resolving her own conflict, she reduced his significance to her.

Similarly, Lydia's father himself, as she described him, surely occupied much less actual space—purely geographical space—as an old man than he had in the days of his might. He had become stooped, and he walked slowly, his hands closer to his sides, and doubtless his actual physical being had shrunk. But I've always wondered to what extent Lydia's perception of him was governed by the fact that he had also diminished in her psyche. By talking about him to me, by deploring what he did, by allowing herself to see him through her own adult eyes, she had reduced him greatly, even before meeting him again in person.

Perhaps he had actually changed less than she imagined. Her shock at seeing him, her difficulty in recognizing him at first, attested to something beyond his physical decline. Even as the water drops of time had reduced him, she had done the same in her psyche. In the restaurant she'd been looking for someone bigger—bigger than he'd ever actually been. And maybe an incipient sense of this had told her to go easy: he'd been the real enemy and done great harm, but he never could again.

the ultimate voyage

. . .

THE FRENCH EXISTENTIALIST Antoine de Saint-Exupéry once wrote that "Love is not two people looking into each other's eyes, but two people looking ahead in the same direction." When Rose and Lou looked ahead, if they ever did, they saw nothing in common. And if they dared look into each other's eyes, they would certainly not see love.

Even their modes of expressing their rage were different. Rose, an attractive and very well dressed woman in her mid-sixties, spoke sharply and would utter torrents of abuse. "He's driving me crazy. He never says anything. All he does is nod. I don't know what got into me two years ago, why I ever married the jerk."

She shuffled constantly as if her energy required more discharge than she could give it. She accused her husband of giving his two terrible daughters everything and her nothing. She mimicked their suppliant tone. "They could come in here and say, 'Daddy, I need a Mercedes. I have to drive it to the shopping center.' And *you'd* give it to them. But *me*. When I go into the store, you follow me around to see if I'm really spending the whole fifty dollars you gave me for groceries."

Now she went from shrilling to bellowing. "You. You have no idea what a wife is. You're just a bastard, a cheap *bastard*." It was frightening, and yet she went on and on. "Tell the doctor, how many times did you call your two daughters this week when I was out of the house? And what did you say about me?"

Everything in my office shook with injury. Not just her volume and pitch, but the fact that she seemed *right* made her loom as unanswerable, inescapable. It was an experience of utter defeat. I certainly felt that way, and I imagined that my plants and my cats in the other room with their acute hearing did too. How could anyone retaliate?

But Lou had come equipped. He had a way of defeating her. Lou, nearing seventy, with a sensitive face covered with too many freckles from the Florida sun, this wisp of a man, impeccable in his double-breasted blue suit, fought back valiantly. He listened to her with expressionless eyes, almost as if he weren't being addressed. In the face of her vehemence his bald head tilted forward, as if he were fighting sleep. Against her mightiest blows he put up his shield of imperturbability.

She told the story of her own past life, and of his. Her first husband was hardworking but got lost in his accounting practice; he'd been good to the children, a boy and a girl. He'd died suddenly. I surmised that she now saw her first marriage as a working relationship, but not a truly intimate one. He'd left Rose a lot of money, and she lavished it on her son and daughter and her grandchildren. Both families had gone to live in other states, and Rose would visit them frequently.

Her lips curled as she began talking about Lou's life. "His relationship with his daughters is *sick*, if you ask me," she said. Looking squarely at him, she said accusingly, "They don't give a damn about you. All they want is your money. Your goddamned money." Then to me, "Doctor, he goes to the office, he's not even needed there, and he talks to them on the phone. Or he has a little lunch with them. They're not welcome in my house, not unless they talk to me like a human being."

Lou listened complacently, as if he were at a boring lecture and trying to be polite. Her every reference to him was a rebuke, and his whole aspect seemed to announce silently, "Taxation without representation." But when I turned to him and asked him to make any comments he wanted to, he just shrugged.

"And another thing," she broke in. "He's got that friend Meyer, and he just lent him ten thousand dollars, but he's always asking me how much I spend. Meyer's a bum, but he lent him ten thousand, probably with no note, nothing." Her eyes were two slits.

I turned to Lou again. "What do you think?" I asked him.

"If she says so, she's right. Rose wouldn't lie," he said, so dryly that I wasn't even sure he meant it ironically.

"Do you still work?" I asked him.

"He still goes to the factory a few times a week. I think he likes the power," she answered for him.

"Please let him talk," I cautioned her.

"He's cheap. He won't answer," she said.

At that Lou bestirred himself. "Darling, we go everywhere. To Denmark, to Japan. I'm not cheap if I'm making plans to take you to Paris and Marseilles for a week. We go everywhere, doctor—"

"Yeah, and wherever we go, you go to sleep," she retorted.

I wondered how much of that sleep was fatigue and how much a shield. "Did she say anything you disagree with?" I asked him.

When he didn't reply, I pressed. "Lou, this is your time to speak, that's what you're here for."

Again he nodded. "No, she always tells the truth."

She looked disgusted. "But maybe what I think is true isn't. Correct me if I'm wrong." This time it was a voice more of frustration than of anger.

He still didn't answer.

"He never says anything," she pleaded with me. "He's driving me crazy."

At the end of that first session, Lou asked me, "How much do I owe you, doctor?" He took out his checkbook as if this were an act so routine for him, so expected, that he was glad, even eager to pay. It was more than a way of expressing himself. It was a justification for living.

He'd obviously wanted to leave me with the idea that he dared not speak, that she would murder him if he did.

At the door Rose asked me incisively, "Well, doctor, what do you think? Is he hopeless?"

I replied, "I want to look at the relationship a lot more before I say anything." It was a tepid attempt to be optimistic and non-committal at the same time.

Naturally I wondered to myself: Why on earth did they marry? And only two years ago. It wasn't as if they had slowly grown apart over the decades.

The tenor was the same over the weeks that followed. Rose was pleasant, almost unduly warm with me, but her eyes became cobalt when she looked at her husband. He sat like a basset hound, weighed down by age and sadness, while she harangued him, but he showed no sign that she was affecting him.

Apparently her first marriage had been no picnic. Her husband had been very jealous, and they'd had violent arguments. Her sisters had told her to leave him, but she'd stayed.

According to Rose, Lou's first marriage wasn't so good either; he had given his daughters everything they asked for, but he'd never disciplined them, "which is why they're such bitches now. He has only himself to blame." That was also why, as Rose saw it, they had teamed up with their mother in treating him like a fool.

Rose told me with perverse delight that when Lou's first wife had died, she'd left each daughter fifty thousand dollars, which Lou had had no idea she'd possessed. Apparently she had saved up a fortune out of expense money he'd given her and had kept it in a secret bank account, not offering any to him even when times were hard. "And that's what he considered a marriage."

She berated him for insisting on a prenuptial agreement before marrying her, one that left her very little and his daughters everything.

"He's cheap, cheap, cheap. He's cheap as the devil with me," she said once.

Several times Rose interrupted herself, turning to Lou to ask him what he was thinking.

"Nothing, dear."

I could see that it tormented her that he wouldn't pitch in, even to contest her assertions about him. She shouted, "He doesn't say anything, and he doesn't *do* anything. All he does is go to the barber and buy clothes."

Indeed, I could easily picture him standing on a stool in front of a triptych of mirrors showing his facets while a tailor tugged at his pants or jacket and courteously questioned him, and a salesman wrote down his dimensions.

I felt sorry for Rose and for him.

At about that time I came to realize that Rose was physically very attractive. Her carping manner had at first made this hard to see. She had high cheekbones, an arched nose, and a still good figure, and she dressed beautifully. That hoarse voice was her undoing; it proclaimed a lifetime of bitterness over injustices done to her.

She was two people, one visually, another when she spoke. She might have been the quintessential silent-film actress, unable to make the jump to talkies. Yet she was likeable because she was so intense, kinetic, flowing. Even complaining life, especially in one so unsatisfied and starved for life, is infinitely more appealing than supreme, complacent, opulent resignation. As for Lou, he was still in silent films.

Rose's was a passion with no place to put it. "How much did you sneak over to your daughters this year? How much, Lou? Ten thousand? Twenty thousand? Twenty apiece? Did your older one say she was waiting for me to drop dead? Tell the doctor, Lou. Tell him."

Still no answer. He would not do battle on her high ground, but only in his own way. The more silences from him, the more unacknowledged she felt, and the hoarser her voice became. It was a slaughter, but who was doing the slaughtering? If she carried on, twisting herself out of shape, and nothing penetrated, who would die first? I recalled the famous championship fight between Sugar Ray Robinson and Joey Maxim in Madison Square Garden. Robinson won all of the first twelve rounds as Maxim hardly threw a punch. Then, with a few rounds to go, Robinson passed out from exhaustion, and the championship stayed with Maxim.

I could only surmise what had drawn them to each other. Apart from their loneliness, each saw his complementary form in the other. She chose him, perhaps, because he seemed the model of composure and quiet strength, the antidote to her inner chaos. Perhaps he could bring calm.

And he had chosen her because she expressed his outrage, and his negative feelings for others, in ways he dared not himself. For instance, I imagined that Rose's readiness to insult people who exploited Lou satisfied an unexpressed urge of his. And Lou perhaps used Rose to insulate him somewhat against his daughters when he felt powerless to stave them off. But if, indeed, each sought his complement in the other, they had surely each gotten a lot more than they bargained for.

Obviously I wasn't getting anywhere seeing them together. "Perhaps if I saw them separately . . ." I couldn't finish that sentence myself, but it seemed worth a try. I suggested it. I scheduled Lou first.

In my office his eyes focused more, and after some prodding he was willing to talk. He told me about his long years as a shirt salesman, traveling up and down the East Coast on trains and then on planes. He was well received in some places. "But if I tell you, doctor, I still remember getting spit on when a material stained and it wasn't supposed to, and having doors slammed in my face." Those were long, lonely years before he set up his own business and became solvent, then prosperous.

"And that Meyer, who Rose always curses. Meyer was a buying agent for a chain all through the South. I owed him money, a lot more than ten thousand, for many years. He never asked for it, he stuck with me, kept using my products. Without him, God knows, I wouldn't be here. I'm only glad, thank God, I can help him."

"You told Rose that story and how you feel?"

He shrugged as if to say, "What's the use?"

"What's going on between Rose and your daughters?"

"You know how women are. They were that way with their own mother too. It's nothing personal. What can you do?"

But it came out that Lou would pit his daughters against his wife—his first wife and then Rose—giving everyone money but nothing by way of love or companionship. He kept busy all the time, doing his bookkeeping even when at home, supposedly to earn money for his family. He would promise everyone too much and then tell them all that because of another one of them—in this case Rose—he couldn't give the rest of them as much as he wanted to.

I made a mental note to study this practice of his and what lay behind it, but the greater problem was emptiness—the sheer, un-adorned, vast, achromatic emptiness of Lou's life. Now that his daughters were independent, and his business could thrive without him, his days had no meaning, no direction; there was no North Star to guide him except death—and he feared that desperately.

I scheduled another hour with him, and then another. He told me how he did indeed arrange clandestine lunches with his daughters and give them money. But apart from those secret "affairs" of his, and the many phone calls that surrounded them, there seemed almost nothing of value in his life.

On a typical day at home, he would wake up at about six thirty, glance at the newspaper, get dressed, which took a long time, and then have coffee with Rose. He might pay some bills, and then go off to the barber or go shopping, usually alone. Rose would deal with repairmen, gardeners, and the like. He would drop in to the office, come home, lie down before going out to dinner with Rose, and then come home again and watch TV and go to sleep.

During such a day he would have to endure one or more harangues for being so numb. "Don't you care that your own bitch of a daughter forgot your birthday, that she didn't even thank you for those shirts you sent her son? Doesn't it bother you that the electrician charged us and the wiring is still bad?" Lou would look at her blankly, and I imagined he would have done the same had her blood been spurting into the snow, which in a sense it was.

Actually of course, Rose's shouts were the only intense voices in Lou's otherwise monotonous existence. Just as certain dogs are happier being abused by their masters than being neglected, Lou perhaps felt even consoled by Rose's attention, so little else of elevation existed for him. Only their trips (one could hardly call them vacations) constituted any kind of event, anything with a beginning, middle, and end. The many details to attend to, the decisions about where to go and the travel arrangements, the securing of their ten-room house against injury while they were gone, the packing and unpacking were the high points of his life. But those trips came only two or three times a year, and the rest of the time left plenty of nothingness.

With Rose it was the same underlying problem—the emptiness of her life. Her greatly exaggerated language and vehement tone seemed possible only for someone who felt utterly unseen and unacknowledged. Why not shout? There was no need to save dignity. Being totally asocial was the last luxury of someone convinced that "What I say doesn't matter." And yet I sensed that Rose still hoped for something out of life, possibly more than Lou did.

Like her husband, she felt like someone in a bathysphere going down for the last time. But her method was to shout and bang against the glass, knowing that outside, only the sea, dense and silent, surrounded her, but still hoping that she was wrong.

Alone in my office she kept up her fury. "He's crazy, doctor. He's crazy. All he does is go to the barber and nod off. Do you think that's a life? I ask you. . . . I can't stand the sight of him."

"Do you love him?" I asked at one point.

"How can I? Ever since he doesn't have to work, and his kids grew up, he has nothing. The man has nothing."

I said to her, "I was wondering if you felt a little the same way. You had a lot that was meaningful to you, your kids, for example. But now they're gone. I mean, your life is a lot emptier than it was."

Of course, she agreed, and we talked about that emptiness. When I asked her to tell me the high points of her life these days, she mentioned seeing her children and her grandchildren. "And sex with Lou. That's the one thing he is, a good lover. My last husband was not. I think that's why I married Lou."

And later, when she talked about her thoughts of leaving, she mentioned sex and started to say, "I'd feel lonely . . ." but stopped herself. She was reluctant to give Lou any credit. The most she would volunteer was that it could be a good life with him if he changed.

I asked her outright if he thought she loved him. She evaded the question by looking straight into my eyes and asking disarmingly, "Do you think I want too much, at my age?"

"What do you want that's too much?" I countered. "Happiness? Some adventure, some fun in life? Good times with the man you married?"

"You're not just saying that, doctor?"

It had been a dark November afternoon, but at that very moment the room brightened. We both laughed. "The spotlight's on you," I said kiddingly. "It's not what you want. It's how you're going about getting it. Or not getting it."

I had a sense that she was really thinking about what I'd said, and I was careful not to say anything more. If I kept silent, she might interpret my statement in her own way, possibly one more useful than anything I had in mind, and I wanted to give her that opportunity. The hour ended with the shutter of the camera still open, and no picture taken.

I scheduled them together the next time. Over the weekend she became very mild with him, as if she were a schoolgirl cleaning up her behavior before report card time.

In my office I directed my first question to a space midway between the two of them as they sat a few feet apart on my couch. "What's really happening in this marriage? Anyone got any ideas?"

She didn't embark on a diatribe against him, and for some reason I had sensed that she wouldn't. They waited, and I felt called upon to speak.

I looked at them attentively as I did, trying not to pontificate. "Look, you got married for a reason. You both raised kids successfully. You saw comradeship in each other. Sex. Travel. But life is short, and you're killing each other."

I asked, "Rose, did you love Lou when you married him?"

She nodded. "Yes, I did."

"And now?" I asked. "Is that all gone? I mean, if it's hopeless, you shouldn't be together." I repeated, "Life is short."

"Well, if Lou would be a man—" she started, but I broke in.

"Is it possible that you could do anything different?"

"What?" she asked me, with a hint of suppressed defiance.

"I mean, for a start, tell him that you love him," I said.

She looked over at him. He was still imperturbable, Mount Rushmore, at least on the outside. It seemed forever until she got herself to say, "He knows I love him."

"Do you, Lou?" I asked.

He nodded.

I waited, as if I hadn't seen his head move.

"Sometimes I do," he clarified.

"Would you like her to be softer?" I asked him.

Again he nodded, and this time I took his response as legal tender.

I asked them in turn if they wanted to break up the marriage, and they each said no.

"But you're not doing anything constructive either," I told them. I tried to explain that Lou's silence was as hurtful as Rose's vendettas. "Maybe if you talk more, she'll talk less."

Then we got to the nub of it. "Rose, you want Lou to give you a life and make things interesting, and Lou, you're waiting for Rose.

"So you're both waiting, and nothing's happening, and you're both getting furious."

She turned to him. "Are you furious, Lou?"

He didn't answer.

I said, "What do you think that stony silence is all about? He's punishing you."

I got them to agree to a temporary truce. Lou would try to talk more and Rose would let him, even if she hated some of the things he said. Meanwhile we would work on the real problem. They would have to create interests, put some meaning in their lives, and no one could do that for them.

They seemed optimistic. But somehow I had been cast in the role of camp counselor, there to give them a schedule and maybe even to pump them up with exuberance.

Over the next half year we searched for anything that might give meaning to their lives. "What we nourish within ourselves grows," wrote Goethe, and I led the search for seeds of anything that they could cause to sprout—interests, hobbies, an idea that could blossom into a commitment. They tried a class on horticulture; Lou invested some money in a local haberdashery and went there some afternoons. Together they joined the library, listened to some speeches on art, went to a cooking course, joined a group that met weekly and talked about exotic places to travel.

Their styles were different. She sprang at every lead but got disappointed and found fault with the other participants. If Lou didn't share her dissatisfaction, she often whirled on him. "Were you there or what?" He would react slowly to each new venture, as if he were being roused from slumber. But the result was the same. They nourished no idea enough to make it grow, and they soon tired of each activity in turn.

I knew that all this was "outside work," not the true province of the therapist—or at least not one's sole province. Obviously they individually had tendencies to grind down anything that might have meaning or value to them. I sought to show them how they sabotaged everything. I kept up my spirits, but I was failing and I knew it.

They would drive in from the country dutifully for their weekly hour, treat me with great respect, undeserved respect I thought, since I'd done nothing for them. Their very politeness and their refusal to show their discontent with me made the hours excruciating. At times I consoled myself with the observation that no one can actually inject meaning into someone else's life, but it hardly helped. A determined optimist in a losing cause cuts a sorry figure, and I was fast becoming one.

One day Rose mentioned that they'd seen people hang gliding over the Rockies, on a TV show called something like *Dangerous Adventure*. "Doctor, maybe we should try hang gliding," she said. We all laughed, but afterward I felt worse than ever. Rose saw my strategy, saw me as defeated in the case, and actually felt sorry for me.

A few weeks after that I happened to see the show myself, and pictured Rose and Lou white-water canoeing in the dangerous rapids of the Colorado River. Having no such adventure, they were lost. Rose was right, I had failed. It was as if they'd fought all the real battles, and now there remained nothing big enough to engross them.

They went back to fighting with each other, as bitterly as ever, or worse. She stormed out of a restaurant. They didn't talk to each other for days, and afterward she went off to visit her daughter for a holiday weekend without him. As they often had, they talked divorce, though I noticed that when they were apart, they chatted on the phone four or five times a day.

Soon afterward they stopped even trying to form outside interests. She once more resigned herself to insulting him viciously, and he to frustrating her by turning himself to stone. They found excuses to cancel hours with me. They liked me, but I had failed. Obviously they weren't about to go hang gliding or white-water canoeing, but it seemed that nothing less could get their attention. We stopped scheduling sessions altogether.

Two years went by, and I thought about them only on occasion. Then Rose called. "We'd like to come in and see you, if we may. A lot has happened since we saw you last, and we have a decision to make."

They came in, hand in hand, and she took his coat and hung it up. She asked me how I'd been and then said, "Lou will tell you a story." She looked over at him.

"How have you been, doctor?" he began.

"Fine," I answered.

He said, "Since I last saw you, I had a heart attack. Two vessels are blocked, one allows only fifty percent of blood through and the other less than that."

"Oh, I'm sorry to hear that," I said.

He turned to her. "Do you want to say anything, dear?"

"No, you please ask the question," she said, as if it were her husband's rightful province to ask it.

"They're suggesting a catheter procedure, but we're not sure."

"May I?" she asked him. When he nodded, she began. "Six months ago Lou collapsed in the driveway." She described the horrible helplessness of it, and the ambulance rush to the hospital.

Lou went to the bathroom. As he stood up, she said, "It's the diuretic. You don't feel dizzy or anything, do you, darling?"

"No, I'm all right."

When he was gone, she said to me, "That's another symptom they didn't tell us about." Suddenly she broke into tears. "I don't want Lou to die, doctor. I don't want Lou to die."

Then she told me an incredible story of devotion and decision over the eighteen months since the attack. Not being sure what to do, they'd gone to a dozen doctors, most of them in New York City but also two in Baltimore and one in Washington, D.C. Some had kept them waiting and seemed impersonal. Others were too radical, wanting to operate immediately. One seemed indifferent to the side effects of a drug he had given Lou. "You know, a beta blocker can interfere with the electrical stimulation of the heart," she informed me.

Lou came back into the room. She looked over at him, and I noted his tranquil gray eyes, the ever-manicured nails. I pictured him taking his usual great pains to dress for these different doctors, including me.

"Are you all right, darling?" she asked, almost flirtatiously. She described to me their strict regulation of his diet.

Then she said, "Dr. Garlock, he's board-certified. And he's not big on operating. But even he wants to put a catheter in and check the arteries, to be sure. But we're not too happy about it."

Lou added, "We read that it's not as safe as they pretend it is."

Besides visiting all those doctors, they would go to the library together, quite often, and read the most recent medical journals. "We think *Lancet* is the best," Rose informed me, in case I should have a similar need.

They had asked Dr. Garlock if he could use echocardiography; they had read that it was "less invasive." But he'd explained that it wouldn't tell him what he needed to know.

They'd also gotten in touch with all kinds of people who'd had similar or even vaguely related conditions and talked to them about their doctors and their experiences. It had been a full-time venture.

After talking to me about him, they decided to trust Dr. Garlock. They would let him give Lou a sedative and insert a catheter into his heart. There seemed little alternative. We agreed that we would stay in touch.

When they were gone, I mused about this incredible harmony they had found. Now they were thinking almost as one. I had the obvious thought that the threat of death can bring people together. Surely, for them it had done more than I ever could. But even then, I sensed that there was something else—a variable I hadn't uncovered yet—that had accounted for the enormous change in them.

They went ahead with the hospital procedure. She stayed as close as she could get to him while he was there. While still under the sedative he told her that he loved her and confided to her that he had changed his will, giving her much more than he had previously planned. She cried and said, "Don't talk like that."

When he came home, she took care of him, and they planned a vacation. After some research they decided that China still would be too much of a risk, with its poor medical care in the outlying regions and with the danger of unfamiliar microorganisms. But Russia was safe, and they asked the doctor for permission to go. He thought it would be fine, and they went and had a good time.

A few months after that they came in again. They thanked me for my concern, but, obviously, their relationship didn't require my services anymore. They expressed caring for each other, and I knew they would not be coming back.

I wondered why they had consulted me for that second round of visits. Obviously they hadn't needed my help with medical decisions; they had made themselves experts in a short time. Could it be that having found this new intimacy, they felt bad about tearing each other down in front of me and had wanted me to witness their harmony, their love?

Maybe there was even some unconscious generosity toward me, as if to say, "Doctor, you haven't failed. We have found an adventure to share."

But where had the intimacy come from? Was the threat of death in itself the unifying force? No, people accommodate themselves even to that, and though Lou was still delicate, the threat was no longer day-to-day. Human memory for outcomes that have been averted is short. As nearly any of us who drives a car will attest, after seeing a horrible traffic accident on the highway and picturing what it must have been like, we've slowed down, resolving never again to speed or be careless. But how long did it take us to resume our speed, or even hurry to make up for the lost time? An hour?

Ten minutes, more likely. After all, this was not the first fatality we'd seen. No, I couldn't imagine that Rose and Lou had simply found love of life together in his near escape, and certainly not the harmony they delighted in and were sustaining.

Then the realization struck me. Not that one near-death experience of Lou's, or even several, but their ongoing adventure was uniting them. Their studies, and visits to doctors, and their long discussions about what to do next, about who was good and who was bad, and which activities were dangerous—these life-and-death discussions took up their days, and bonded them. They had found their ultimate project at last, the great adventure they could undertake together, one that had all the needed ingredients. It offered challenge at high stakes; it required cooperation, perseverance, judgment, and loyalty; and owing to it, or, more precisely, to their joint efforts to carry it off, they were finally producing love.

This was their hang gliding mission. If only they could gauge the wind currents and calibrate their voyage at every stage, Lou would live—*they* would live, because now Rose was existing in her husband's being, so minutely was she plotting the details of his survival, along with him.

At first it seemed to me inexpressibly sad that it took a death threat to unite them, and then preposterous that they had found their adventure here. But, of course, all existence is ultimately subjective, and this was their version of adventure. They could as well have been sailing through space, clutching a delicately ribbed glider, or steering a small craft through watery rapids, or calling to each other while stalking the six-ton elephants of Nepal as they photographed them. The risks here, or at least those that Rose and Lou perceived, were every bit as great. They would sustain their love by taking these risks together, by celebrating every narrow escape, every correct judgment they had made, by their conversations late into the night about what to do next. They had at last become two people looking ahead in the same direction, looking not at death but at life.

From what I could tell of their previous marriages, neither of them had ever enjoyed such intimacy before, or shared nearly so momentous a project. Perhaps their present activities were tinged with hypochondria, and some of their suspicion of the experts was undue, but who can escape these pitfalls when the stakes get so high?

Sometime later, when I heard the quote from Horace Walpole that "The world is a comedy to those that think, a tragedy to those that feel," I thought of Rose and Lou, and I felt I understood them better.

Admittedly I've never felt fully comfortable with their solution, and doubtless never will. Like millions, they had quit on one of the most fundamental responsibilities of being human—to create purposes for themselves, goals that give shape and direction to a life. It bothered me that their finding direction came about almost as a fluke, as if circumstances outside their control had given them an assignment. I myself had failed them. I had the feeling that any relationship requiring a continuous skirmish with death for the partners to love each other and live in harmony is inherently defective.

I wondered: Suppose that Lou was suddenly cured, got a clean bill of health, would they preserve their newfound harmony, bask in the sunlight of their discovery of each other? Or would they regress to their patterned chaos, with Rose once again hurling her thunderbolts and Lou confronting her with his stony silence? My very uncertainty seemed to support my doubts over what contribution I had made.

However, the reality was that they had found purpose and love, and for that I was delighted. And it was possible, I consoled myself, that I had helped them stay together long enough to find their project. They might have turned their backs on even that possibility when it came along, but they didn't, and perhaps I had played a role in helping them see that some joint activity was necessary. Then I recalled that their best moments before Lou's physical crisis were during trips they took together. And could not this experience be viewed in that vein, as their ultimate voyage?

I never found out what happened to them, which one predeceased the other, or whether they are both still alive. If so, they would be close to ninety. But I picture them still dressing carefully, looking at their watches to be sure they will get to the next doctor on time, discussing their purpose in the car, and rejoicing in some decision, that one more hurdle has been passed and that they are still alive and together.